HIV/AIDS in China – The Economic and Social Determinants

South and East Asia may well become the epicenters of the global HIV/AIDS pandemic. More than three-quarters of a million people are now estimated to be living with HIV/AIDS in China. In 2009, AIDS had already become the leading cause of death by infectious disease. Yet, even despite China's recent economic and social progress, a number of development issues – not least the emergence of glaring inequalities – have also surfaced. The expansion of the HIV/AIDS epidemic is also an important longer term development challenge.

This book analyses China's HIV/AIDS epidemic, with particular attention to the nature and impact of current economic and social changes and how these changes may be driving the epidemic. It examines the aspects of income and gender inequality, rural–urban migration, commercial sex work, healthcare, and civil society organizations. Healthcare reforms and the role of NGOs, as well as general government policy, are considered. Overall, this book provides a full discussion of the most critical aspects of the current HIV/AIDS situation in China and its impact on Chinese society.

This book will appeal to students and scholars of Asian religion, politics, and anthropology.

Dylan Sutherland is currently Lecturer at Durham Business School, Durham University, UK. He is the co-editor of *Sustainable Reform and Development in Post-Olympic China* and author of *China's Large Enterprises and the Challenge of Late Industrialisation* (both published by Routledge).

Jennifer Y.J. Hsu is an Assistant Professor in the Department of Political Science at the University of Alberta, Edmonton, Canada. She is the co-editor of *China in an Era of Transition: Understanding Contemporary State and Society Actors*.

Routledge Contemporary China Series

HIV/AIDS in China –
The Economic and Social
Determinants

Dylan Sutherland
and
Jennifer Y.J. Hsu

Routledge
Taylor & Francis Group

LONDON AND NEW YORK

First published 2012
by Routledge
2 Park Square, Milton Park, Abingdon, Oxon OX14 4RN

Simultaneously published in the USA and Canada
by Routledge
711 Third Avenue, New York, NY 10017

*Routledge is an imprint of the Taylor & Francis Group, an informa
business*

British Library Cataloguing in Publication Data
A catalog record for this book is available from the British Library

Library of Congress Cataloguing in Publication Data
Sutherland, Dylan
HIV/AIDS in China: the economic and social determinants / Dylan Sutherland and
Jennifer Y. J. Hsu.
p. cm.—(Routledge contemporary China series ; 76)
Includes bibliographical references and index.
1. AIDS (Disease)—Economic aspects—China. 2. AIDS (Disease)—Social
aspects—China. 3. HIV infections—Economic aspects—China. 4. HIV
infections—Social aspects—China. I. Hsu, Jennifer. II. Title. III. Series: Routledge
contemporary China series ; 76.
RA643.86.C6S88 2011
614.5′9939200951—dc23
2011018399

ISBN13: 978-0-415-41875-1 (hbk)
ISBN13: 978-0-203-25386-1 (ebk)

Typeset in Times New Roman
by Book Now Ltd, London

MIX
Paper from
responsible sources
FSC
www.fsc.org   FSC® C013604

Printed and bound in Great Britain by
CPI Antony Rowe, Chippenham, Wiltshire

Contents

List of illustrations

Tables

Figure

Preface

This book is an attempt to better understand the different factors contributing to the growth of HIV/AIDS in China. The possibility of the HIV/AIDS epidemic continuing upon its exponential growth path seems incongruous given the great achievements made to date in China. China's economic growth and development over three decades of reform mean that China has achieved significant progress in nearly all areas of human development. Most economic indicators have also improved considerably. Yet, despite this phenomenal progress, a number of development issues, not least the emergence of glaring inequalities, have also surfaced. The expansion of the HIV/AIDS epidemic is also an important longer term development challenge. It is also one that economic growth alone may not help to resolve.

More than three-quarters of a million people are now estimated to be living with HIV/AIDS in China. While this means the epidemic still one of low overall national adult prevalence, there are pockets of high infection in certain subpopulations in specific regions. There is also the persistent danger of the epidemic spreading still further within the general population. Indeed, in 2009, AIDS had already become the leading cause of death by infectious disease, surpassing other diseases such as tuberculosis. The share of infections transmitted heterosexually, moreover, has been increasing quickly. This also points toward a movement of the epidemic from high-risk subpopulations to the general population at large. Most signs are that the HIV/AIDS epidemic will continue to grow quickly. As such, any further contributions that can help us better understand the forces driving this epidemic forward will be of value. We hope that this book constitutes a contribution to this debate.

This book is motivated also by our own experiences of living and working in China at different times over the past two decades. As such, we have witnessed firsthand some of the remarkable economic and social changes that have taken place and been struck by the transformation unfolding. While many of these changes have been for the better, it is clear that there are also many aspects of the current development path that raise concerns. For example, the growth of commercial sex work (CSW), now so evident throughout China, seems so at odds with the ethos and values of traditional Chinese society and declared goals of Chinese leaders. Its growth, moreover, seems also to reflect more deeply rooted problems, not least with regards to income and gender equalities, as well as law enforcement and corruption. Our negative view of local government intervention has also been reinforced by a visit to AIDS villages in rural Henan province, a region at the heart of the one of the most serious outbreaks. The visit was brief and ended in arrest and detention – which was in and of itself an interesting and insightful experience into how authorities perceive of their roles and responsibilities with regards to HIV/AIDS. It also brought home to us the extreme injustices faced by the many voiceless victims in Henan, who have little redress against the powers that be. The expansion of the HIV/AIDS epidemic in China will no doubt cause many more injustices, which also points toward the interconnections with political institutions and reforms in coping with the epidemic. It is fair to say that all aspects of society, as well as the development course China is currently steering, will have to respond to the HIV/AIDS epidemic.

Some of the insights of this book were also developed during visits to Yunnan and Sichuan. Various government agencies were visited, and those in Yunnan, in particular, presented us with a much more positive outlook. Civil society and educational organizations were also visited which allowed us to discuss the issue of HIV/AIDS with various individuals that represent all levels of society. These discussions have also informed our analysis and views of the HIV/AIDS epidemic in China and inspired us to continue to think about the problem. During this time, moreover, we have also been involved in research and teaching activities with students in the area of Development Studies. This has also led us to question how processes of development interact with epidemic diseases, such as HIV/AIDS. We have considered the nature and progress toward the United Nations Millennium Development Goals, goals which include health, education, and people's livelihoods. These goals also include progress in fighting the world's HIV/AIDS epidemics. During these studies, it has become evermore obvious to us that the emergence of disease epidemics is also intimately linked to the underlying development processes as a whole. We therefore believe that the emerging HIV/AIDS epidemic in China is not only about the choices individuals make but also about the types of social forces that act on large groups of individuals. In the final analysis, we believe that understanding China's HIV/AIDS epidemic requires a consideration of the social and economic environments in which people live and function. The focus on individual risk behavior dominant today in much of the discourse does not adequately account for the broader terrain in which disease has emerged. For example, we now believe that increasing inequalities across rural and urban areas and across the sexes are some of the more important forces fueling the epidemic, yet these are seldom mentioned in many of the official reports that discuss how individual behaviors lead to infection. While understanding the biomedical or physical properties of HIV/AIDS is important, we also believe that the focus on the individual will not be effective in choosing the policy measures that can alter widespread changes in individual behavior and susceptibility. Understanding the evolution in China's HIV/AIDS epidemic will also require understanding its ties to the broader socioeconomic environment.

This book attempts to provide insights into some of the economic and social forces contributing to the evolution of the HIV/AIDS epidemic, moving beyond biomedical explanations. While we accept that this is an emerging field and there are numerous weaknesses with our approach, we do believe, however, that by taking this alternative perspective, we can make a useful contribution to the current field and hopefully motivate others to continue research in this area.

Dylan Sutherland
and
Jennifer Hsu

Abbreviations

ADB	Asian Development Bank
CCM	Country Coordinating Mechanism
CDC	China Center for Disease Control and Prevention
CDRF	China Development Research Foundation
CMS	Cooperative Medical Scheme
CSO	Civil Society Organization
CSW	Commercial sex work/worker
FPD	Former plasma donor
GDI	Gender Development Index
HDI	Human Development Index
HDR	Human Development Report
IDU	Intravenous drug use/user
IEC	Information and education campaign
IOM	International Organization for Migration
MAP	Monitoring the AIDS Pandemic Network
MDG	Millennium Development Goal
MDR	Multidrug resistant
MOH	Ministry of Health
NMCS	New Medical Cooperative System
PLWHA	People living with HIV/AIDS
SSA	Sub-Saharan Africa
STD	Sexually transmitted disease
SW	Sex worker
TB	Tuberculosis
UNAIDS	Joint United Nations Programme on HIV/AIDS
UNDP	United Nations Development Programme
UNESCO	United Nations Education, Scientific and Cultural Organization
XDR	Extensively drug resistant

1 Understanding HIV/AIDS epidemics

Introduction

> The microbe is nothing; the terrain, everything.
>
> (Louis Pasteur, 1822–1895)

> Modern epidemiology is oriented to explaining and quantifying the bobbing of corks on the surface waters, while largely disregarding the stronger undercurrents that determine where, on average, the cluster of corks ends up along the shoreline of risk
>
> (McMichael, 1995; taken from Decosas, 2002: 4)

What is the best way to try and understand HIV/AIDS epidemics? Should we try and understand such epidemics purely as the product of individual risky behavior and individual agency? Or, instead, as a result of the broader social and economic forces acting on groups of people, so leading entire population groups into more risky types of behavior? The first type of approach, to date, has arguably been the most dominant one used by those looking to understand the world's HIV/AIDS epidemics. The second approach, on the other hand, which considers in significant detail the types of economic and social terrain in which epidemic disease flourish, has received far less attention. Looking at what has also been referred to among other things as the "biosocial," "structural," "distal," or "economic and social determinants" of disease, this approach has attempted to move beyond the subject of individual agency in its explanation of epidemic disease. Despite its neglect to date, there is now growing interest in these so-called structural determinants of disease, including those related to HIV/AIDS. The primary purpose of this book is to apply some of the ideas of this approach, with a view to further understanding China's HIV/AIDS problem from this alternative perspective. As such, this contribution to the understanding of China's HIV/AIDS epidemic takes a somewhat novel and different approach to those already made.

To explain the novel conceptual framework adopted in this book, this first chapter begins by providing a brief overview of the evolution in different approaches to understanding HIV/AIDS as an epidemic disease. First, we explain how so-called biomedical paradigms have, until recently, strongly guided understandings and conceptualizations of the HIV/AIDS epidemics. We explain why this so-called biomedical approach is now increasingly being questioned. Second, as an alternative to the predominant biomedical model, we consider and explain some of the newer, alternative ways of explaining HIV/AIDS epidemics. While embryonic and still far from perfect, these draw from the social sciences and the newly emerging discipline of social epidemiology. Third, we go on to argue that while the newer approaches to understanding HIV/AIDS epidemics are far from complete, they can provide useful alternative perspectives. This is particularly the case for a country such as China, which has undergone rapid economic and social change. These changes have profoundly affected the terrain in which epidemic disease may flourish. The speed and nature of these changes, moreover, would appear to be conducive to the further spread of HIV/AIDS.

Each of the chapters in this book goes on to identify and further investigate potential economic and social determinants of HIV/AIDS in China. This includes discussion and analysis of the impact of income and gender inequalities in China, migration, commercial sex work (CSW), public healthcare, and the role of civil society and political systems, among other things. While not exhaustive, we illustrate how further consideration of these economic and social determinants, which work predominantly at the population level, may be important drivers of the HIV/AIDS epidemic. This book also works from the basic premise that if we want to understand the fundamental causes of HIV/AIDS epidemics, we must look beyond a narrow focus of individual behavior. We must also consider the changing economic and social environment in which people live and function. By pointing to some of these deeper undercurrents and terrain in which HIV/AIDS epidemics emerge, we may also be able to create new types of policies. It is a hope that this book will also help draw attention to and discussion of these determinants.

What causes HIV/AIDS epidemics?

Our conceptualization of what causes disease and poor health has evolved in a number of long cycles, spanning the past two centuries of medical thought. Today, this conceptualization is going through another important cycle of change, particularly as regards epidemic disease. As such, before undertaking an investigation of a specific epidemic disease, such as HIV/AIDS, in a specific country such as China, it is important to understand how different approaches to understanding disease have evolved. In particular, biomedical explanations have to date largely dominated the academic understanding of HIV/AIDS. Many now argue, however, that this particular approach is proving inadequate. HIV/AIDS epidemics in many, if not most, regions continue to grow. At the same time, what is considered as a rather narrow range of "technological" solutions has also been applied to combating the epidemics. It is argued by some that traditional epidemiological accounts are "inadequate to the task of understanding public health issues as they apply to HIV/AIDS" (Barnett and Whiteside, 2006: 77). This raises the question of how biomedical views, so influential in understanding disease, have evolved. Also, why are they now considered inadequate to understanding the HIV/AIDS epidemics by some?

When thinking about HIV/AIDS, there is tendency to automatically think of it as a phenomena related to risky individual behavior – unprotected sex or intravenous drug use (IDU), for example – and in turn as a problem of individual agency.[1] Arguably, this is because of the strong influence of epidemiology and the medical sciences in our conceptualization of HIV/AIDS. A popular definition of "epidemiology" considers it as the study of why any individual becomes ill at any particular time. Despite this current day focus on the individual in our understanding of disease, there has also been recognition of the role that broader social and economic conditions play in disease generation in earlier periods of history. Rudolf Virchow, for example, a nineteenth century founder of social medicine, noted over a 100 years ago that the medical sciences were inextricably and essentially linked to the social sciences. Clearly, the way in which disease and health has been conceptualized has evolved over time. In fact, according to expert epidemiologists, it is argued that three distinct models, corresponding to different eras, are identifiable (Susser and Susser, 1996). These include the *miasmatic era*, followed by *infectious disease epidemiology*, and the highly influential paradigm known as the *germ theory*. Finally, an era of chronic disease epidemiology, accompanied by what has become known as the *black box paradigm*, is thought to have emerged (ibid.).

Miasma

According to epidemiologists, the miasmatic era may have started as early as the seventeenth century. It emerged as a result of the quantitative analysis of the social distribution of mortality that was possible with the recording for the first time of statistics that showed the kinds of people that were dying and the reasons for their deaths. The miasma model also grew out of the increasing concern for public health and the noticeable differences in health across society that was emerging. Agricultural and subsequent industrial revolutions had led to rapid changes in the way people lived. By the nineteenth century, rapid industrialization and urbanization created difficult living conditions in urban areas. These trends, incidentally, are not unlike those seen in China today. They led to high mortality rates and growing concerns about public health. The concept of miasma, therefore, emerged around this time. It was used as a framework to try and explain the newly acquired health information about the nineteenth-century city slums (in both Europe and also the United States).

A key feature of the miasmatic theory is that it did not have any specific scientific proof of causality between disease and the environment. Today, therefore, it would be considered a very simplistic model and conceptualization of disease generation. Instead, it made a rather common sense connection between high mortality rates and the accompanying poor economic and social conditions (such as water supplies, sewage and sanitation, and housing conditions). At this time, the biomechanics of organisms were not well understood. As such, miasmatic theorists went on to hypothesize that it was simply the unhealthy environmental conditions that gave off "foul emanations" or "bad air" that caused disease and high mortality (Susser and Susser, 1996: 669). As with the current day focus on social and economic determinants of health, therefore, it attributed disease and ill-health to the underlying "terrain" – both physical and social – that people inhabited. For most of the nineteenth century, this miasmatic theory was the dominant model used to explain disease. Although there was little hard science supporting the miasmatic approach, the actual policy implications of the model were straightforward and actually effective. Advocates suggested common sense policies aimed at improving the environmental factors that they believed caused disease. Thus they suggested enclosed drainage and sewage, the building of public baths as well as better housing, and rubbish collection.[2] Broader social and economic forces were also identified as having a strong bearing on health. They also recognized the two-way relationship between miasma and poverty and poverty and miasma. In this sense, the early followers of miasma adopted a broad "socially connected" approach to understanding disease (Susser and Susser, 1996). Even if their theory of disease was vague and unscientific, insofar as the exact mechanism whereby disease emerged was not really described or understood, the actual policies based on its inductive reasoning were successful.

The germ theory

Miasma, although quite effective in the public policy realm, lost appeal as an approach to understanding disease owing to revolutionary discoveries in microbiology that took place during the second half of the twentieth century. These developments led to the identification of the actual germs that caused disease. As early as 1840, Jakob Henle came to the conclusion that disease was actually caused by microorganisms, not simply the miasma found in polluted environments. Around two decades later, Louis Pasteur went on to demonstrate that living organisms were responsible for an epidemic affecting silkworms. After this, a flow of further scientific evidence emerged backing up these ideas, and far greater understanding of human diseases followed. In 1882, for example, Robert Koch established that a specific mycobacterium caused the deadly killer, tuberculosis (TB). Similar breakthroughs were also made with other diseases such as anthrax and leprosy. The growing isolation of particular organisms, now identified as the ultimate "cause" of disease, led to a growing concentration of scientists on the exact biomedical and physical understanding of disease. As time passed, the broader environmental reasons that miasmatic theory had earlier concentrated on were increasingly overlooked. These revolutionary scientific discoveries therefore led in turn to a new paradigm within medicine, known today as the *germ theory* of disease. This transition from the rather vague miasmatic understandings of disease to specific causal theories has been highly important for the way in which we conceptualize disease today. The germ theory, however, is also characterized by its "narrow laboratory perspective of a specific cause model – namely, single agents relating one to one to specific diseases" (Susser and Susser, 1996: 670). It looked to specify which particular agents were responsible for disease, establish how transmission occurred, and then to limit transmissions by vaccines, as well as isolating those infected and treat the disease. The concentration on the social dynamics of disease that the miasma theory called for, by comparison, was quickly replaced by *"a focus on control of infectious agents"* (ibid.). In the battle of competing paradigms, the supporters of the traditional philosophy of public health based around the miasma paradigm soon lost their influence in the medical hierarchy. They were also "disparaged in ways that in many places continue in the present" (ibid.). Thus the search for other causes of disease – those in the environment in particular, looking beyond the "microbe" – slowed down considerably. Today, the legacy of the germ theory for our understanding of HIV/AIDS epidemics, particularly its emphasis on the individual as host of disease, remains influential.

Interestingly, and also of importance, this revolution in the early part of the twentieth century also precipitated great changes in how the study of medicine and public health was organized. In 1916, for example, the United States undertook important reforms. Medicine concerned with the general population and that with individual health was separated. Schools of public health were split from schools of clinical medicine. This new demarcation between individual and public health, it is argued, had a further deep effect on how disease was conceptualized, reinforcing the general trend (Barnett and Whiteside, 2006: 77). Epidemiologists, as a result, were left to fill the vacuum between the fields of individual and public health. These epidemiologists became "part medical practitioners, part statisticians and part public health experts" (ibid.). It is argued that in attempting to cover such a wide field epidemiologists "were bound to fall between all possible stools" (ibid.).

The black box

By the beginning of World War II, germ theory lost some of its appeal and a third stage and new paradigm again started to emerge. By this time many infectious diseases, for example, typhoid and diphtheria, had been identified and treatments were developed. Communicable diseases no longer constituted the main threats to public health in the developed world (although this was not the case for the developing world). Scientists and policy makers, moreover, did not expect the reemergence of communicable diseases that we have seen today such as HIV/AIDS and TB. Instead, chronic diseases, including heart disease and cancer, started to become the major health concerns. Changing lifestyles and aging populations were also among the reasons driving the emergence of new types of chronic disease. Models explaining chronic disease, therefore, would again have to focus more upon the social and physical environments in which the chronic diseases were evolving. The particular paradigm adopted during the Chronic Disease era has been called the *black box paradigm* or the *risk factor paradigm*.

The modern "risk factor paradigm" composes of "studies that relate exposures to disease outcomes inform public health interventions to reduce *individual* risk for disease" (Schwartz, Susser and Susser, 1999: 19). This model, interestingly, did not dwell upon the need to understand the exact causal mechanisms (hence our lack of understanding of the "deeper undercurrents" in the modern era). Indeed, the pathogenesis of disease was not essential to the black box paradigm (in which the inner processes, the "black box" are not observable). Early studies looked at the relationships between lung cancer and heart disease and looked for associated risk factors among individuals. Based on this method, these studies established smoking and cholesterol as risk factors for these conditions. Use of increasingly larger data sets allowed for comprehensive statistical analyses leading to the identification of risk factors. These studies, moreover, related exposures to disease to outcomes to inform public health interventions to "reduce *individual* risk for disease" (Schwartz, Susser and Susser, 1999: 19). Crucially, then, there remained an emphasis on the individual, as in the earlier germ theory approach.

Reductionism has been an important part of modern scientific techniques. According to a growing number of critics, however, this has at times led to an atomization of the problem when it comes to the understanding of disease. While reductionism may benefit our comprehension of the actual physical properties of diseases, it does not necessarily help in understanding epidemic disease, which by definition involves the interaction of large numbers of people in specific social and economic environments. As noted, epidemiology as an academic discipline in general seeks to understand why any individual may contract a disease at any particular time.[3] As such it may explain why individuals become ill, but it does not explain why particular groups or sections of population are more likely to contract diseases, or even why some countries are more likely to have higher HIV/AIDS prevalence than others. When we consider HIV/AIDS epidemics as social processes, however, rather purely than the product of individuals and their actions, a different etiological question emerges: "why do some populations have much AIDS, while it is rare in others?" (Decosas, 2002: 3). This new approach has led some to believe that the present era of epidemiology is coming to an end. Instead of focusing risk factors at the individual level, we are now being urged to recognize "causal pathways at the societal level" (Susser and Susser, 1996: 668). This has led to the blossoming of new approaches to understanding health, which is enshrined in the approaches of social epidemiology and appreciation of the social determinants of health. Indeed, such is the appeal of this new approach that various organizations have been established to promote it (such as the WHO's Commission on the Social Determinants of Health) and academics are spending increasing time and effort further exploring the subject.

Alternative approaches

Dissatisfaction with the current conceptualization of HIV/AIDS and the associated policies, those that focus purely on individual agency, has led to a backlash among a variety of different groups, including academics, policy makers, and those working on the ground. Critics from among social and medical sciences, for example, argue that there are many difficulties with the current approaches. Some have argued that both context and historical perspective are missing in our understanding of the epidemics (Stillwaggon, 2006). Others have accused current approaches of suffering from "disciplinary blindness," in which alternative viewpoints are blocked and excluded from discussion (Craddock, 2004). Some echo this, pointing to the weakness of applying a "rigidly disciplined approach" to what is essentially a highly complex social phenomenon (Farmer, 1999: 15). Farmer (1999) goes further, arguing individual academic disciplines have done their best to establish their own niches in the search for greater research funding, to effectively monopolize this research area. Behind many of these criticisms, however, lies the fundamental observation that the conception of disease is driven purely by medical science, rather than "expanding into broader social science analyses required for more comprehensive understanding of an epidemic" (Barnett and Whiteside, 2006: 77). Given these problems, many now argue that there is greater need for what may be termed a "biosocial" understanding of disease, one that incorporates both the biological and social (Farmer, 1999). Of course, the rush to provide new insights into the social and economic determinants of health raises a number of fundamental questions. What, for example, does this new approach actually consists of? How can it be put into operation to yield new and improved understandings on the world's HIV/AIDS epidemics? Is it really of any scientific value?

We can get some idea of the new approaches to understanding HIV/AIDS epidemics in the growing literature that has emerged looking at how the broader social and economic conditions that may drive HIV/AIDS epidemics (see, e.g., Barnett and Whiteside, 2006; Farmer, 1999; Kalipeni *et al.*, 2004; Stillwaggon, 2006). These works have taken on titles such as the "ecology of poverty" (Stillwaggon, 2006), the "social ecology" of HIV/AIDS (Decosas, 2002), emphasizing the broader historical and socioeconomic context in which epidemic disease may emerge. In attacking what they see as the disciplinary blindness of previous work, they have also explicitly committed to an approach that they see extending "beyond epidemiology" (Kalipeni *et al.*, 2004). A variety of regions and time periods has also been studied, although an emphasis on contemporary sub-Saharan Africa has emerged. In general, as might be expected given their different conceptualization of epidemic disease, they are highly critical of current mainstream approaches to the understanding of HIV/AIDS epidemics and look to provide alternative analyses and solutions.

There are numerous approaches used in the current literature. In one comprehensive volume on southern Africa (over 400 pages), the different studies use variations on what is termed "a cultural political economy of vulnerability framework." The approach is one that reflects their understanding of AIDS "as resulting from material, symbolic, and discursive forces effectively constraining the opportunities and choices available to individuals and potentially creating conditions of vulnerability for large sectors of regional populations" (Craddock, 2004: 6). While in a broad sense this approach may be understood, it is not immediately obvious how it could be used specifically to analyze the problem or inform policy of HIV/AIDS epidemic in China. Other works, following similar broad lines, have placed the emphasis on epidemics as social processes, also driven "by history, political economy, and culture" (Schoepf, 2004: 15). While much previous research has prioritized and focused more on sexual practices and mobility, the new investigations of HIV vulnerability also have begun to uncover the roles played by specific features of societies, such as "gender, politics, poverty, colonialism, global economics, migration, and war" (Oppong and Ghosh, 2004: 323).

The broad approach of this new literature raises some interesting possibilities as well as some challenging questions. Of particular relevance to our study and this book, it raises three key questions with regards to how to apply these ideas to a particular country such as China. The first key question is related to how social scientists identify key causal factors at the social level and, further, show how these particular factors drive epidemics. To draw from the earlier analogy of Louis Pasteur, what are the strongest most important undercurrents driving the epidemics? What types of terrain do they thrive in most? If we are to expand our approach beyond the individual, we must also understand what factors place *populations* at risk. Second, if analysis at the *individual* level of organization leads to atomization of the problem, what level of analysis should we adopt? This is still far from clear. To date there are quite a wide range of different approaches used when extending their analyses beyond the individual, although national and international (comparing features of different countries) are quite common. But if we are not focusing on the individual, What level of analysis should we adopt? Should we look at the family, village, town, city, or country? This is another important question that we must answer, or at least address, if we are to develop an analysis that moves beyond a focus on the individual. Third, if history is important, which given the complex dynamics involved in epidemics is a reasonable assertion, how should we decide upon what time period to consider when analyzing any particular case?

These three issues are central in carrying out any study that looks at the economic and social determinants of China's HIV/AIDS epidemic. We now consider these issues in more detail.

Moving beyond the individual

Causes of disease can be distinct at different levels of organization. This phenomenon, some argue, can be understood through the concept of what has been referred to as "emergent group properties" (Schwartz, Susser and Susser, 1999). This idea stipulates that each level of organization has unique characteristics confined to that level. This idea has been explained using a physical example (ibid.). Water can be described at a molecular level as an arrangement of hydrogen and oxygen molecules. At a broader level, however, the liquidity of water possesses characteristics that "neither applies to nor is described by the physical assembly of molecules" (ibid.: 26). Similarly, a variety of social phenomena can be understood at both the individual level (such as suicide, alcoholism, heart disease, lung cancer, etc.) as well as at a broader social level. High levels of suicide in a society, for example, have also been related back to particular features of those societies, as well as the particular states of mind of the individuals involved. Again, studying the question at both levels may yield quite different conclusions as to what actually causes suicide within human populations.

While we may accept this idea of emergent group properties, one feature of the emerging social science literature is the varied unit it takes for analysis. There appears to be little agreement or even discussion over how we should choose our unit of analysis – if not the individual, then what? Local villages, towns, and urban areas are analyzed, for example, as well as numerous country-level studies and a variety of international comparisons (often of a statistical nature). If we are really to move "beyond epidemiology," clearly quite an important question becomes: what level of organization should we analyze? If understanding epidemic disease at the individual level is insufficient, what levels of organization or analysis should we pursue and what, if any, are the reasons for pursuing them? Some of the epidemiologists working on this new paradigm have suggested that causes of disease can be identified at all levels of organization, not only the individual. They are rather vague, however, as to what specific units of analysis we should focus on. They argue, for example, that each level may warrant investigation in its own right so that it can be investigated for its impact on health. But this clearly raises challenges and difficulties, as it may actually be hard, if not impossible, to investigate all levels. It is also unlikely that each would be equally as useful. We may find that analysis at a national level of trends in income distribution and poverty, for example, may be more useful than at the family or village level of analysis. It must be the case that certain levels of organization can explain disease emergence better than others. Unfortunately, given the current state of our understanding, embodied in the works of advanced eco-epidemiologists as well as social scientists trying to understand HIV/AIDS epidemics, it is still unclear what this might be. Indeed, it has been argued that the decision of what levels to include should be "based on the question at hand, the particular nature of the disease, and the pattern of disease rates" (ibid.). While some may consider this to be rather subjective and in some senses unsatisfactory, it appears to be the best we can do at present.

In this book, for the most part but not exclusively, the economic and social determinants of China's HIV/AIDS epidemic are investigated at a number of different broad levels. Where appropriate we use national and provincial data and general descriptions of national development and at times these are also placed in an international comparative context. Of course, as already discussed, it may be difficult to justify exactly why this level of analysis is better than others. On the other hand, as also noted, different levels of analysis may also be complementary. Pursuing one level does not exclude the possibility that others may also provide other useful insights. One further reason for adopting a national-level approach in this book is that to date no such study has been made. In fact, the annual updates published by the State Council Working Committee Office and UN Theme Group, as well as many of the independent academic studies, take more conventional biomedical approaches. They focus on high-risk populations and their behaviors and dynamics of HIV spread among these groups.

Identifying exposure variables

Even if we can decide upon the level of organization or unit of analysis, one that goes "beyond the individual," we are still faced with several more crucial questions. The question of what might cause HIV/AIDS epidemics at the population level is also very important. Again, it is unclear from current social science what exactly should be analyzed in this regard. This is because it is very difficult to identify the so-called "exposure variables" – the variables that cause epidemic diseases such as HIV/AIDS, at the level beyond the individual. These may be numerous and also complex, often interacting with one another, making them very difficult to accurately identify and then explain. Just as we know that transmission at the individual level may be increased by the interaction between certain cofactors (perhaps sexually transmitted disease [STD] infection, malnutrition, TB, and particular genetic factors), thus this may also be the case at the population level (gender and income inequality, e.g., which may in turn drive a commercial sex industry). There are evidently also innumerable variables at the social level that might be measured and tested, whereas at the individual level, by comparison, the exposure variables are more limited. This raises the basic question of how this level of complexity can actually be addressed. Statistical analyses can be of some use in this regard. They may help, for example, to discover associations between certain variables and HIV prevalence. However, establishing causation from such methods is again more complex. Perhaps, more importantly, statistical approaches are in themselves unable to actually explain which variables should be chosen in the first instance. As one study notes: "whatever we select to be examined most certainly reflects our own bias and ideology" (Decosas, 2002: 5).

Despite these problems, there are numerous cross-country studies that look to identify possible exposure variables at the population level. We will discuss some of these in more detail in the following chapters. Many experts, however, now believe that there is sufficient evidence to start talking about the social determinants of transmission dynamics: "factors that play a robust, quantifiable role in shaping the course of a local epidemic" (Nguyen and Stovel, 2004: 52). Among these, for example, one study considers poverty and social inequality, migration, state capacity, and gender relations as of key importance (ibid.). There are numerous other studies, considered later, that identify what they claim to be the social and economic determinants of HIV/AIDS epidemics.

As will become clear, this book draws from existing research to explore particular determinants that have been found to be important in other contexts to the Chinese case. Among the more important of those that we explore for the Chinese context are income and gender inequality, their interaction with CSW, mobile populations, health and healthcare, and government and the role of non-governmental organizations.

Income and gender inequalities

Despite an emerging consensus of the importance of these particular social and economic inequalities, until recently, few studies have actually examined these specific social inequalities in much detail:

> Although many who study the dynamics of infectious disease will concede that, in some sense, disease emergence is a socially produced phenomenon, few have examined the contribution of specific social inequalities. Yet such inequalities have powerfully sculpted not only the distribution of infectious diseases but also the course of health outcomes among the afflicted.
>
> (Farmer, 1999: 5)

The third and fourth chapters are dedicated to investigating income and gender inequalities and their possible relationship to the current and also the future trajectory of China's HIV/AIDS epidemic. Income and gender inequalities, according to a number of more recent large-scale statistical investigations, supported by numerous other types of study, are now considered among the more robust predictors of HIV prevalence at the national level. In general, countries with high levels of inequality in gender and income (as measured in various ways) tend also to have more severe HIV/AIDS epidemics. It is not implausible, therefore, to think that both may play an important role in shaping HIV/AIDS epidemics.

The more general link between income inequality and health, of course, is a well-researched subject in the developed world. The scale of income differences is, according to some, one of the most powerful determinants of health standards, partly thought to be because of its impact via psychosocial influences (Wilkinson, 2005). Income distribution, as well as being strongly identified by statistical investigations, is also recognized by a variety of studies using alternative methods, as central to our understanding the HIV/AIDS epidemics. In southern Africa, for example, it is often the case that countries with the greatest economic inequalities also have the worst epidemics. This relationship between income inequality and HIV/AIDS epidemics, however, while being powerful is also "nuanced" and difficult to fully understand (UNAIDS, 2006a: 84). This is because income inequality seems to capture important information about the overall development process and is itself also associated with many other things, including urbanization and migration from rural to urban areas, which may place individuals at risk. A skewed income distribution, furthermore, may also have impacts via its effect on social cohesion and sexual mixing patterns. To add to this, income inequality, when combined with other factors (such as gender inequality), may also be a very important factor in fueling the commercial sex industry. There is enough evidence now to suggest that investigation of the role of income inequality may help further our understanding of the population-level dynamics of HIV/AIDS. This may be particularly relevant in the Chinese case, moreover, owing to the rapid increase in such inequalities in recent times.

In addition to income, gender inequalities are also now thought an important determinant of the world's HIV/AIDS epidemics. For example, in sub-Saharan

Africa, women are "disproportionately affected by AIDS, compared with men – expressions of the often highly unequal social and socioeconomic status of women and men" (ibid.: 15). Most researchers place gender inequality high on their list of structural factors causing HIV/AIDS epidemics (Barnett and Whiteside, 2006; Stillwaggon, 2006; UNAIDS, 2006a). In other words, the greater the degree of gender inequalities the more serious the epidemics tend to be. A number of factors, such as lack of education, fewer and worse income earning opportunities, and weaker political rights, among other things, may place females at a disadvantageous position *vis-à-vis* men and increase female susceptibility. As well as specific case examples and local-level studies, which give real insights into just how such inequalities may lead to HIV/AIDS epidemic growth, a number of much larger national level ecologic studies, based on cross-country data sets, also show that gender inequality is related to the HIV/AIDS epidemics at the national level. Talbott (2007), using cross-country linear and multiple regressions, finds that female illiteracy levels and gender illiteracy differences (and also income inequality within countries) are also significantly positively correlated with HIV/AIDS levels. Earlier ecologic studies also make similar findings. Drain *et al.* (2004) have tested over 80 variables and found that only four, again those including gender dimensions of the epidemic, were the most significant in predicting HIV/AIDS. There is, therefore, considerable cross-country evidence suggesting that gender inequality is a strong predictor of HIV/AIDS prevalence.

Commercial sex work

How do such inequalities fuel HIV/AIDS epidemics? Much evidence suggests their link with HIV/AIDS prevalence, but what are the causal mechanisms whereby they drive the epidemic? Chapter 4, building from the previous two, shows how income and gender inequalities, among other things, may also interact to fuel the commercial sex industry. The growth of CSW is highly relevant to understanding China's HIV/AIDS epidemic. In many, if not in all of those Asian countries that have experienced serious generalized epidemics among the general population, a necessary precondition has been heterosexual transmission via CSW. The sexual mixing pattern in Asia, which has become reliant upon a class of professional sex workers, is also "a particularly efficient pattern for rapid spread of HIV." This is because commercial sex workers (CSWs) act "as a continuing reservoir of infection" (Grassly *et al.*, 2003: 2). Recent explorations of the commercial sex industry, moreover, tie its growth strongly to specific economic and social conditions: the "relationship between the growth of the sex sector and economic development cannot be ignored" (Lim, 1998: 10) – and by extension the HIV/AIDS epidemic. CSW was not the most important factor driving China's HIV/AIDS epidemics initially, instead IDU and blood and plasma donation started the epidemics (in different regions of China). The number of infections transmitted sexually, however, is growing quickly and increasing its overall share of all new infections. CSW will become, if it is not already, the most important factor in driving the future expansion of the Chinese HIV/AIDS epidemic. Indeed, the arguments presented in this book suggest some of the dynamics at work may be somewhat similar to those found in other fast growing newly industrialized Asian countries, such as Thailand. When we consider national-level population determinants, such as income and gender inequalities, the similarities are quite striking. By further exploring the reasons for the HIV/AIDS epidemics' growth, moving beyond the simple explanation of individual agency, we can obtain a fuller picture of how economic and social forces are contriving to drive its expansion.

Mobile populations

There is considerable worldwide interest in the relationship between HIV/AIDS epidemics and migration. The Partnership on HIV/AIDS and Mobile Populations, International Organization for Migration (IOM), and Regional Office for Southern Africa and the Southern African Migration Project (SAMP), for example, specifically met to consider the linkages between HIV/AIDS, population mobility, and migration in Southern Africa (IOM, 2005: 7). This gathering of researchers found that despite there being a number of important factors in the rapid spread of HIV in Africa, *"perhaps the key neglected factor in explaining the rapid spread of HIV over the last decade is population mobility"* (ibid.: 10). They concluded, however, that "we are still far from understanding just how mobility and HIV interact" (ibid.). The migrant population, as in southern Africa, is now seen as a key factor in spread of HIV in China. It is speculated that the greater geographic mobility, lower levels of education, limited HIV/AIDS knowledge combined with separation from partners and families for long periods may also make migrants more prone to high-risk behavior in China. As with southern Africa, however, the migrant population in China still remains quite poorly understood. A number of studies focusing on different aspects of the relationship between migration and HIV in China have therefore emerged. In this chapter, we further explore some of the relationships between population mobility and HIV/AIDS in China but from a slightly different perspective. The main emphasis is on province-level population movements, as opposed to what the impacts of migration are on individual behavior.

STDs, public health, and the healthcare system

An important cofactor linked to HIV/AIDS epidemics is the overall health of a given population. If overall health standards are lower, it is argued, there are reasons for believing individuals will be more susceptible to infection. Stillwaggon (2006), in an important contribution, argues that understandings of HIV epidemics have been based on a rather narrow conception of the main driving forces of epidemic disease. In particular, she argues, the contributions of poverty and poor health are at times overlooked, despite the well-known interactions of weakened populations with epidemic diseases. Stillwaggon (2006), therefore, argues that there are a number of causes of *social susceptibility* which amplify risks associated with individual behavior. Figuring with greatest prominence in her recent work are endemic diseases and their relationship with susceptibility. In the developing world (particularly sub-Saharan Africa), endemic diseases weaken the immune systems of individuals and this hugely increases susceptibility:

> An established literature in public health and a century of clinical practice demonstrate that persons with nutritional deficiencies, with parasitic diseases, whose general health is poor, who have little access to health-care services, or who are otherwise economically disadvantaged have greater susceptibility to infectious diseases, whether they are transmitted sexually or by food, water, air, or other means.
>
> (Stillwaggon, 2006: 5)

Endemic disease, therefore, is seen as an important "cofactor" in the emergence of HIV/AIDS and investigated in greater detail than the other listed cofactors. Such diseases weaken the immune system, increase white blood cell (CD4) count. Lower nutritional intake also increases the chance of coinfection. Stillwaggon (2006: 12), therefore, argues among other things that: "[S]topping AIDS requires attacking the underlying causes ... Behaviour change is important, but the downward spiral can only be stopped if there is substantial change in the health profile of sub-Saharan Africa and other poor regions."

China's healthcare system has undergone major change with important implications for the general well-being of China's population and the spread of a number of important diseases that are important co-factors in HIV/AIDS transmission. Chapter 6, therefore, investigates how healthcare delivery has changed in China since the beginning of economic reforms and considers the implications for meeting the challenges of the HIV epidemic. Of most obvious concern is the explosion of sexually transmitted infections (unlikely to be solely related to cultural change), many of which remain untreated owing to the increasing cost of buying drugs. Chapter 6, thus, focuses on reforms in China's healthcare system with special emphasis on STDs and what these can teach us about the Chinese HIV/AIDS epidemic.

Government and civil society

The relationship between political organization and HIV/AIDS epidemics is increasingly highlighted. The 2006 UNAIDS Epidemic Update for the first time included inputs from civil society. More recent updates published by China's State Council Working Committee on HIV/AIDS have also emphasized the importance they attach to the civil society and governmental responses. The way in which people may empower and organize themselves to respond to the HIV challenge plays a central part in determining how an epidemic may unfold. A weak government and lack of civil society participation are likely to hamper responses to HIV/AIDS epidemics. What is happening in China today and how is the political response evolving?

Civil society organizations (CSOs) have played and continue to play a key role as advocates in promoting positive social change. Chapter 7 looks at what role China's civil society has played and may play in the future struggle against the rapidly growing epidemic. The role of civil society is especially important given the weak role of the state in a number of crucial areas, particularly health-care. Unlike some other nations that have mounted quite effective responses (e.g., Thailand), China has not yet shown the necessary political leadership or will to deal with the huge problem it faces. Observers believe that this is where CSOs should come in, to bridge that gap by offering to work with local governments. Suspicion and misunderstanding on the part of the local governments, however, is itself another hurdle.

There is substantial room for CSOs to offer their expertise in areas such as health education. There are over 50 nationally registered Chinese CSOs targeting HIV/AIDS and perhaps hundreds of thousands more unregistered organizations, focusing on a wide range of issues from basic health to environmental issues. This chapter looks at whether these CSOs can contribute to curbing the HIV/AIDS epidemic and the role they will play in future responses.

What time period?

We first have highlighted how it is important to identify key causal factors at the social level and consider how these particular factors drive epidemics. Second, if analysis at the individual level of organization leads to atomization of the problem, we have also argued that alternative levels of analysis may be required. Finally, we noted that a historical perspective is important, which raises an important question to which we now return: what length of historical context should be used and how should we decide upon it? While all social science-related studies currently incorporate the temporal element, it is unclear what rules are being used. Ideally, at all levels accessible to research, consideration should be given to the "dynamic processes linking antecedent events and development with later outcomes" (Schwartz, Susser and Susser, 1999: 25). While the intuition behind this approach is clear, its actual application remains subjective.

In this study of China, we focus primarily on the reform period, particularly on what we consider to be the major periods of social and economic change covering the period in which the HIV/AIDS epidemic has rapidly emerged. Of course, China's preceding history is also important in understanding the current trajectory of the HIV/AIDS epidemics. To give an instructive example, because of the near eradication of STDs by the 1970s, natural immunity to STDs, such as syphilis, was reportedly very low by the 1980s. This meant that when the disease was reintroduced into the population, it spreads very rapidly.

Broadly speaking, the growth of China's HIV/AIDS epidemic has been divided into three phases. Three phases of the epidemic can be seen as mirroring China's economic transition. The first phase disproportionately affected plasma donors. Between mid-1980s–1990s, poor farmers in the central provinces, most notably Henan, were paid for selling their blood. Donors were not tested for blood-borne diseases or HIV. The plasma was separated and the remaining blood samples were pooled and transfused back into the donors to prevent anemia. Repeated donations for cash and such practices escalated the possibility of donors contracting blood-borne diseases and HIV. The practice was formally banned in 1996. The government estimates that there are some 35,000 HIV-positive cases in Henan, although figures could be much higher. The second phase is related to the spread of HIV among intravenous drug users (IDUs). The spread of drug use through shared needles has predominantly centered around China's southern provinces, those bordering Laos, Myanmar, and Thailand. While the southern province of Yunnan registered China's first domestic case of HIV/AIDS among IDUs, the rate of both drug use and HIV/AIDS has increased significantly since China's economic reforms and the opening of its borders for trade with neighboring countries. Between 1989–2006, 3.2 million blood samples were tested in Yunnan and 48,951 HIV-1 cases were detected, with 3,935 AIDS patients and 1,768 resultant deaths (Lu *et al.*, 2008: 609). In 2003, the government estimated that IDUs accounted for approximately 44 percent of HIV cases (quoted in Thompson, 2005: 7). Sexual transmission of HIV/AIDS is the third phase of China's epidemic. The rate of sexual transmission of HIV is on the rise. The prevalence to infection is still relatively low at 0.04–0.07 percent in 2007, but this rate masks the 8 percent increase since 2006 (Lu *et al.*, 2008: 690). Moreover, 38 percent of cases were due to heterosexual contact, more than triple the 11 percent in 2005 (ibid.). It is this third phase and its relationship to economic and social determinants that we are most interested in. It is also, going forward, important to further appreciate the likely factors that will drive the epidemic. It is on these factors, as well as evidence of how they have driven the current epidemic, that we most closely focus.

Conclusion

Biomedical approaches have expanded our understanding of HIV/AIDS as a disease. In particular, the actual nature of the retrovirus itself and how it works is now quite well understood. This understanding has followed from the rigorous scientific method that evolved to produce the germ theory of disease. Despite this understanding of the physical properties of the virus and its transmission mechanisms, however, it is increasingly being argued that complementary approaches, anchored predominantly in the social sciences, may also contribute in important ways, ways that may create fuller understandings of what causes HIV/AIDS *epidemics*. As Louis Pasteur, a nineteenth-century father of modern medicine is said to have once remarked: "the microbe is nothing; the terrain, everything." This may be interpreted as referring to the broad array of circumstances that may contribute to disease emergence, including physical, social, and political environments. Over 100 years later, the understanding of health of societies, and the social and economic forces that give rise to good or bad health, is attracting ever greater attention once again.

By overlooking the broader environmental influences on health outcomes, many argue that it is actually quite difficult to explain exactly why today's global health crises have developed. This is because even though the actual organisms responsible for disease and the main risk factors are now quite well understood, infectious diseases have still not been well controlled in certain cases. The HIV and TB epidemics are notable examples. The number of infections worldwide has continued to rise, despite considerable efforts to eradicate them. Even after the discovery of cheap and effective methods of treatment, TB remains one of the world's leading causes of preventable illness. As one recent paper notes: "There is growing recognition that the conquest of this disease cannot be achieved by medical advances alone … bio-medical research must be complemented by work from within the social and historical sciences" (Gandy and Zumla, 2002: 386). In the final consideration of the black box approach, based on analysis of mass data at the individual level, it is not effective at predicting which *social* interventions are likely to lead to large-scale changes in individual behavior and susceptibility. This leaves a situation in which "we know which social behaviors need to change, but we know little about how to change them" (Susser and Susser, 1996: 670). Such a view is strongly echoed elsewhere, such as in the popular works of Paul Farmer:

> Models of disease emergence need to be dynamic, systemic, and critical. They need to be critical of facile claims of causality, particularly those that scant the *pathogenic roles of social inequalities*. Critical perspectives on emerging infections must ask how *large-scale social forces* come to have their effects on unequally positioned individuals in increasingly interconnected populations; a critical epistemology needs to ask what features of disease emergence are obscured by dominant analytic frameworks.
>
> (1999: 5; emphasis added)

There are, of course, still numerous problems with new approaches to understanding HIV/AIDS at levels that extend beyond the individual. This is partly because to date, in most analytic approaches, individuals have been the preferred unit of interest and analysis. Using this approach, as a school of epidemiologists has recently commented, specific questions about the particular "macro-level social and physical environments or micro-level mediators and antecedents are difficult (although not impossible) to frame" (Schwartz, Susser and Susser, 1999: 24). A problem with the emerging literature moving beyond the individual is that it is "still in its infancy and has not yet developed a clear theoretical framework" (Decosas, 2002: 3). To this end we agree, with the evolving field of social epidemiology, that reductionism is an "essential research tool" but not "an organizing philosophy" (Schwartz, Susser and Susser, 1999: 25).

The following chapters attempt to apply some of the ideas found in the biosocial approach to understanding disease emergence. This book investigates what it considers to be some of the key underlying forces driving the epidemic at the population level. As such, it does not claim to be a complete and definitive account of China's epidemic. Instead, it looks to identify and explain some of the more important economic and social forces that are central to the epidemic. It is about some of the "stronger undercurrents" driving HIV/AIDS epidemics and the "terrain" in which HIV/AIDS epidemics flourish, as well as how inequalities may "manifest themselves in biosocial forms" (Farmer, 1999). Indeed, a basic underlying premise of this book is that while certain aspects of the crisis are biological, explanations should not be restricted to the biomedical sciences alone.

There is one final point to make regarding China's emerging HIV/AIDS and what we can learn about it from the study of economic and social determinants. In East Asia the HIV/AIDS epidemic has been expanding faster than anywhere else in the world (UNAIDS, 2008). Contrasting with many of the sub-Saharan African epidemics, many parts of Asia have seen their epidemics expand under conditions of speedy economic growth. This is unusual, as for the most part the HIV/AIDS epidemics are more commonly regarded as "diseases of poverty." The fast growing epidemics of Southeast, East, and South Asia, by contrast, have occurred during periods of speedy economic growth and great social transformation. Unlike in many of the other areas of human development (education, health, and the environment), however, which tend to improve with economic development, the HIV/AIDS epidemics appear to show no obvious relationship with economic growth. Indeed, there is some evidence that the rapid but often unbalanced development processes in East Asia may themselves exacerbate the aforementioned structural factors, or terrain, in which HIV/AIDS epidemics flourish. This includes such things as income inequality, migration patterns, and gender differences. In other words, economic growth may not be a panacea for HIV/AIDS epidemics. The overwhelming emphasis of the Chinese leadership, to date, has been primarily on achieving economic growth as a cure for most of its ills. But if China's leaders want to tackle the emerging HIV/AIDS epidemics head-on, they may also have to pay more attention to the type of economic growth and social and economic transformation taking place.

2 Economic and social determinants of HIV/AIDS

Introduction

Many studies and reports, such as those produced by UNAIDS or the Monitoring AIDS Pandemic Network (MAP, 2005), provide detailed descriptions and analysis of the *individual* risk factors associated with HIV/AIDS. These publications include discussion on the behavior and action of certain high-risk population groups, such as the frequency of condom use, changes in HIV prevalence among intravenous drug users (IDUs) and homosexual population groups. It is common that incidence and prevalence rates among these important risk groups, as well as some of their behavioral patterns, are monitored in detail. This general approach to understanding HIV/AIDS, as discussed, focuses much upon the risk factors that we can say with certainty cause HIV infection and transmission in individuals. The broader socioeconomic factors and trends that have also been identified as placing populations at risk, such as gender inequality, poverty, and income distribution, levels of education and political representation, are generally not given nearly as much attention. This is partly because it is harder, if not impossible, to directly relate these broader human development trends (and their interaction) to overall HIV/AIDS prevalence. Despite these difficulties, as discussed in the previous chapter, many now believe that there are strong connections and the particular ''terrain'' and ''undercurrents'' within society are also vital in understanding epidemics. In keeping with this interest on the population-level determinants of HIV/AIDS epidemics, this chapter considers more broadly the type of development pattern that China has embarked upon, making comparisons with other countries. It frames the Chinese HIV/AIDS epidemic in a wider social and economic context by looking at a range of human development indicators.

First, we briefly describe the comparative approach used in this chapter for investigating the underlying ''terrain'' in China with the purpose of providing a broad outline of the socioeconomic conditions, rather than just the biomedical facts and details of individual behavior patterns with the aim to move beyond the focus on the individual. Second, we examine the differences in current progress toward the Millennium Development Goals (MDGs), looking at China and other regions. The purpose is to present a clearer background to China's emerging HIV/AIDS epidemic by considering the speed of economic growth, income distribution, poverty, education, gender, health, and the environment. An international comparative context using different aspects of economic and human development, as captured by human development indicators, is therefore presented. Third, we discuss the implications of these findings. Other Asian countries may share similarities with China in terms of the underlying development process and its relationship to the HIV/AIDS epidemic. Comparisons are also made with some of the sub-Saharan African (SSA) countries experiencing generalized outbreaks. The conclusion notes that fast but unbalanced development, which contrasts with the stagnation seen in SSA during much of the 1990s, may also unleash powerful national forces conducive to the spread of HIV/AIDS. These must be better understood if the real nature, which extends beyond the current focus on high-risk populations, of China's HIV/AIDS epidemic is to be understood.

What approach?

For the purposes of sketching the broader context of the Chinese HIV/AIDS epidemic, national data are concentrated on for the most part in this chapter. The creation of the MDGs means that there is now a considerable amount of data monitoring human development progress, including China. Interestingly, some of these human and social indicators of development are also now included in recent UNAIDS Epidemic Updates (UNAIDS, 2007). The explicit recognition of these reports is that HIV/AIDS epidemics are closely related to a country's overall economic, social, and human development levels and progress:

> To get us to the point where future generations are free from AIDS will require that every aspect of the response be sustained over the longer term – leadership commitment, activism, financial resources, innovation in developing new medicines and preventive technologies, *and, not least, real action to tackle the fundamental drivers of this pandemic, particularly gender inequality, poverty and discrimination.*
>
> (Peter Piot, UNAIDS, 2006a; emphasis added)

Despite making this point, it is also of note that the amount of data and level of analysis undertaken by UNAIDS in its annual updates, even of a simple comparative nature, is minimal. The human development indicators reported at the national level, for example, include the human development index (HDI), human poverty index, and an estimate of people living under US$2 per day, as well as per capita income. Estimated population and population growth, government health expenditure per capita, and life expectancy at birth are also included. Despite incorporating this data, few comparisons are made between countries over time, and there is no analysis of how different poverty levels or inequalities may contribute to the different epidemics. Thus, in the final analysis, although a step in the right direction appears to be being made (in acknowledging the broader social and economic forces shaping epidemics), little useful analysis is actually undertaken.

This, of course, contrasts strikingly with the very extensive discussion of individual risk factors, where there are many comparisons of general HIV prevalence levels and prevalence within specific groups and between countries. Such comparisons are used to gauge the extent to which the epidemic has progressed. Of course, the ways in which social and economic development may interact to increase population susceptibility, or how this leads to different outcomes in prevalence, are complex. So it is perhaps not so surprising that while the idea is introduced, comparatively little is made of it. Ultimately then, while the ideas we have referred to in the first chapter are acknowledged, in the final analysis they are largely ignored. As one recent study that summarizes literature on the East Asian epidemics notes, capturing the spirit of this very point:

> While the basic behavioural parameters (e.g. rates of condom usage, rates of needle sharing and the number of men visiting sex workers) are clear, what is less obvious is *why* these behaviours persist in spite of high levels of awareness of HIV and how it is transmitted. According to one key informant, much research (as well as interventions) is constrained by a focus on "risk groups" imported from epidemiological models. Hence, there is not much rigorous research on vulnerability to HIV/AIDS. *Such research could include investigation of the interaction between HIV vulnerability and socio-cultural factors such as poverty, environmental degradation, gender (including transgenders), urbanization and destruction of traditional cultures.*
> (UNESCO, 2005: 20–1; emphasis added)

In this chapter, we look to include further comparative analysis away from the area of "risk groups" specifically, moving into the domain of broader socioeconomic factors.

A biomedical approach

Before doing so, however, it is useful to also briefly consider a biomedical perspective, so as to illustrate the differences between the two approaches. The conventional biomedical view of what causes HIV/AIDS epidemics sees, among other things, HIV-infected drug injectors helping to build up a "critical mass" of infections in sexual networks, from where HIV spreads across to wider society (MAP, 2005). Introduction of HIV into networks of injecting drug users can result in the rapid spread of HIV where multiple use of nonsterile needles is common. Many injecting drug users are also engaged in sex work or are clients of sex workers. This provides transmission pathways from the high-prevalence intravenous drug use (IDU) groups into lower prevalence commercial sex work (CSW) groups, from where transmission to the general population may more easily take place.[1] In addition to IDU populations, homosexual population groups may also be important in kick-starting a generalized epidemic, as well as individuals infected through blood donation or transfusion.[2] Thus, the conceptualization of HIV/AIDS epidemics using this biomedical approach focuses the attention on high-risk groups and the extent to which bridging between high- and low-risk populations may take place. According to the biomedical viewpoint, at the heart of most of Asia's epidemics "*lies the interplay between injecting drug use and unprotected sex, much of it commercial*" (UNAIDS/WHO, 2005a: 31).

Table 2.1 as such illustrates some of the indicators commonly considered in the biomedical approach. It provides a snapshot comparison of HIV prevalence within certain key population groups nationally, including IDUs and CSW [but not men who have sex with men (MSM), for which there is less information] for a number of East and Southeast Asian countries at the turn of the millennium.[3] This includes Cambodia, Myanmar, Thailand, China, Indonesia, Malaysia, Vietnam, Lao PDR, Mongolia, and the Philippines. The biomedical approach also classifies HIV/AIDS epidemics into "generalized," "concentrated," and "low-level" epidemics. Generalized epidemics are those in which HIV is close to saturation in populations that practice high-risk behaviors with prevalence also greater than 1 percent among the general population (usually as measured by antenatal clinic attendees). Within the sample considered here, generalized epidemics exist in Thailand, Cambodia, and Burma. Concentrated epidemics, in contrast, have HIV prevalence above 5 percent in one or more subpopulations undertaking high-risk behavior. Prevalence among the general population, however, is less than 1 percent. Low-level countries are those in which HIV prevalence is less than 5 percent in all known high-risk subpopulations (World Bank, 2004a). Among the sample considered in Table 2.1, concentrated epidemics exist in five countries and low-level epidemics in three.[4] China, currently, has high-prevalence pockets among high-risk groups and is experiencing a concentrated epidemic.

As well as briefly considering the more commonly described areas (IDU, CSW, and general population prevalence), this chapter briefly looks at income growth and distribution, trends in employment, poverty levels, gender inequalities, public health expenditures, education levels, and demographic patterns. It does so to further sketch-out, in a comparative context, the specific economic and social terrain in which China's HIV/AIDS epidemic is emerging. For some of these indicators, such as gender and income inequalities, as later chapters show in more detail, there is strong evidence of linkages to HIV/AIDS prevalence at the national and international level. This broad comparative perspective is therefore built upon with deeper analysis of specific areas (such as income and gender inequalities) in the following chapters. These explore specific population-level determinants, their interrelationships, and how they may work to contribute toward population-level susceptibility.

A number of different countries and indicators are also used to provide comparative insights into the background development process. As well as looking at aggregate-level data for some Southeast and East Asian nations, comparisons are also made with SSA.[5] The SSA countries are selected from different low and medium human development countries with adult HIV/AIDS prevalence levels

Table 2.1 Features of Asian HIV/AIDS epidemics at the turn of the millennium

Country	Population, (adults aged, 15–49, million)	Population living with HIV	Prevalence (adult population aged 15–49)	Estimated cases of tuberculosis	Rate per 100,000	IDU prevalence	Estimated number of IDUs	CSW prevalence	Estimated number of CSWs	STD, male prevalence	Women, prevalence antenatal care clinics
Generalized epidemics											
Cambodia	13.4	170,000	2.7	78,564	585	–	–	26.3–31	12,290	8.5	2.7
Myanmar	48.3	400,000	–	78,473	162	37.1–63	150,000–250,000	26.0–50.0	–	12.1–13	2.0–3.5
Thailand	63.6	670,000	1.8	85,870	135	39.6–50	100,000–250,000	6.7–10.5	200,000	2.5	1.6
Concentrated epidemics											
China	1,284.0	850,000	0.1	1,447,948	113	0.0–80	3.5 million	0.0–10.3	> 3 million	0–1.3	0
Indonesia	214.8	120,000	0.1	581,847	271	19–48	150,000	2.0–27	200,000–270,000		0
Malaysia	22.6	42,000	0.4	27,119	120	16.8	200,000	2.0–6.3	50,000	4.2	
Papua New Guinea	4.9	17,000	0.7	11,602	236	–	–	16	–	7	0.2
Vietnam	79.0	130,000	0.3	141,353	179	26.8–30.4	69,000	4.2–6.0	–	2–3.2	0.4
Low-level epidemics											
Lao PDR	5.4	1,400	<0.1	8,512	158	2	Low	1	–	–	–
Mongolia	2.5	<100	<0.1	4,969	194	1	–	–	–	0	–
Philippines	77.0	9,400	<0.1	228,931	297	1	10,000	0.3	–	0	–

Sources: World Bank (2004b: 11, 18, 65–70); UNDP (2003).

Note: Data in the table are from UNAIDS (2002); UNDP's *Thailand Human Development Report*, various years.

of over 5 percent and that have reasonably complete data. This sample includes South Africa (prevalence 21.5 percent), Botswana (37.3 percent), Kenya (6.7 percent), Lesotho (28.9 percent), and Malawi (14.2 percent) (UNDP, 2005: 248).[6] Incorporating some SSA countries provides an alternative perspective in thinking about where the Chinese and East Asian epidemics stand, not only in terms of overall prevalence among risk groups but also the possible roles of different economic and social determinants.

A broader perspective: comparative human development

As this chapter compares SSA, East and Southeast Asian, and Chinese economic and social indicators, with a view to framing China's HIV/AIDS epidemic, it is relevant to first appreciate the greater overall disparity in development progress between Asia and SSA of the past several decades. The creation of the MDGs in 2000 means comprehensive and accessible information on the comparative human development performances of different world regions.

In terms of human development, there is a significant difference in performance across regions and time periods. In many parts of Africa during the 1990s, for example, little progress and even setbacks were suffered. A brief comparison of the evidence between East Asia and SSA reveals striking differences in human development outcomes. Poverty fell dramatically in East Asia, driven in large part, by China. The proportion of people living on less than US$1 per day fell from 33 to 14.1 percent between 1990–2002 (UNDP, 2006: 4). By any standards, this was a remarkable achievement. SSA, in comparison, saw no progress in poverty reduction with 44 percent of the population or approximately 140 million people remained living in poverty during this period (ibid.). In terms of other indicators, such as food and nutrition, similarly poor performances were recorded. Since the early 1970s food production in all developing countries roughly tripled, exceeding population growth and prices also fell considerably (UNDP, 2003: 87). Between 1980–1995, per capita food production increased 27 percent in Asia and 12 percent in South America leading to a decrease in the undernourished. In SSA, however, food production actually fell 8 percent (ibid.). Concomitantly, one-third of Africa's population remained undernourished, and the number actually increased over the 1990s. In East Asia, by contrast, chronic hunger fell from 16 to 12 percent between 1990–2002 (UNDP, 2006: 5).

Similar contrasts between SSA and East Asia can be seen in other human development indicators, such as education and gender. Less than 60 percent of children in SSA are enrolled in primary education (UNDP, 2003: 86). By contrast, in most other regions, including East Asia, enrollment rates exceeded 90 percent. In East Asia, they increased from 94 to 98 percent between 1990–2003 (UNDP, 2006: 6). However, in SSA, approximately 42 percent of girls and 38 percent of boys of primary school age did not attend school in the 1996–2004 period, whereas in East Asia the rate remained at 1 percent (ibid.: 7). Large differences in both enrollments and attendance in primary education, therefore, existed between these regions. Moreover, in the area of health, SSA displayed a similar record. The under-5 mortality rate, for example, fell from 185 to 168 per 1,000 live births between 1990–2004. In comparison, East Asia's rate fell from 48 to 31 (ibid.: 10). Closely interrelated to overall health, large differences in basic environmental services also existed. The proportion of population using improved sanitation between 1990–2004 rose from 32 to 37 percent in SSA, whereas in East Asia it rose from 24 to 45 percent (UNDP, 2007: 23). Overall, SSA's performance in achieving the MDGs has lagged well behind East Asia and it is on course to meet none. In contrast, East Asia's overall progress has been significantly better. In conjunction with the overall performance in HDI, China has adopted its own concept of improving human development which is expressed in the need to build a *xiaokang*, or well-off, society.

China's progress in a global perspective

The first of the ambitious MDGs is to "eradicate extreme poverty and hunger." The goal is not actual eradication, but instead a large reduction in poverty and hunger. Associated with this goal are two explicit targets. First, to halve, between 1990–2015, the proportion of people whose income is less than US$1 per day. The second target is to halve, between 1990–2015, the proportion of people who suffer from hunger. According to the United Nations Development Programme (UNDP), these goals are quite achievable, even if the contrast in progress between regions is stark. In terms of both poverty and hunger reduction, the first of the MDGs, China has done very well. China has also contributed significantly to the overall aggregate global progress of the goals. While there is considerable debate and also controversy over how exactly to measure poverty (particularly across nations), and hence also poverty reduction, according to estimates used by the UNDP's (2003) *Human Development Report* (HDR), China lifted 150 million people out of poverty in a single decade between 1990–1999. According to the World Bank, consumption surveys indicate the proportion of people in China living on less than US$1 per day fell from 33 percent in 1990 to 16 percent in 2000 (quoted in UNDP, 2003: 73). The halving of poverty rates in only a decade suggests a significant achievement of the MDGs.

The Chinese performance, unsurprisingly, has done much to keep the world on track to meet the first MDG. In fact, according to the UNDP, almost 30 percent of the world's population lived with less than US$1 per day in 1990. This proportion fell to 23 percent in 1999 including China's contribution (a fall in absolute numbers from an estimated 1.3 billion to 0.92 billion) (UNDP, 2003: 41). This meant that the *global* target, of reducing by half the proportion of people whose income is less than US$1 per day by 2015, was roughly on target. If China were excluded from this calculation, however, world poverty would only have fallen from 28.5 percent to 25.0 percent of the world's population in this time period (leaving still close to a billion people in absolute poverty, with about 2.8 billion living on under US$2 per day). As a result, the target would not be achieved (ibid.). In terms of absolute numbers, moreover, the number of people living in world poverty would have actually increased from 917 to 945 million.

China's contribution to poverty reduction, therefore, has been vital to meeting the overall global poverty reduction target.

China is also well on target to halve the proportion of people who suffer from hunger in the 1990–2015 period specified by the MDGs (hunger is defined, following the UNDP, as consuming fewer than 1,960 calories a day). The number of people living below minimum dietary requirement in China fell from 17 percent in 1990 to 11 percent in 2000 (UN Country Team China, 2004: 11). The prevalence of underweight children (less than 5 years in age) fell even faster, from 21 percent to just 10 percent (ibid.). Despite these achievements, it should be remembered that China still has a large number of poor and malnourished with 120 million still living in hunger at the beginning of new millennium (UNDP, 2003: 87). In spite of the success, China is not on track to meet the development goals for HIV/AIDS, including gender equality and public health-related indicators (UN Country Team China, 2004: 1).

In summary, China's progress in human development has been impressive in many respects. Growing disparities between rich and poor, however, are now an area of increasing concern.

Income growth and distribution

Economic growth, income levels, and distribution and employment may tell us a lot about the nature of overall development in a country and therefore the terrain in which epidemic disease may emerge. It is worth briefly noting how China's historical growth path compares with other countries.

The financial crisis of 1997–1998 had a negative impact on East and Southeast Asian development. Over a decade later, however, the region has become far wealthier, with considerably fewer living in poverty. It also has a larger global role than ever before, supported by sustained strong growth in China. Real per capita incomes now significantly exceed precrisis levels and the poverty rate, measured at US$2 a day level, has fallen from 50 percent of the population to 29 percent in 2007 (World Bank, 2007: 25). When Vietnam reaches middle-income status, which is projected for 2010 (defined as annual per capita income of US$900), more than nine out of ten East Asians will live in a middle-income economy (ibid.). In China, the real per capita income growth averaged 8 percent over the past decade. By comparison, incomes are lower in many of the SSA countries experiencing generalized epidemics, although not all.

Annual growth rates in the Asian countries sampled have been impressive, despite the setbacks of the East Asian financial crisis. China, Thailand, and Vietnam grew at over 5 percent in the 1975–2003 period. Few SSA countries have matched this performance, with the exception of perhaps Botswana (although growth here has been very unequally shared). It is important to stress, however, that although growth may bring improvements in many areas of human development, it does not necessarily check the spread of HIV/AIDS. Indeed, it might plausibly be argued, given some countries in Southeast and East Asia are now experiencing the most rapidly growing epidemics in the world, that growth may also create forces favorable to the promotion of HIV/AIDS epidemics due to factors such as increased migration, drug use, growth of commercial sex sectors owing to rising income, and gender inequalities. Clearly, the relationship between a society's susceptibility to HIV/AIDS epidemics and economic development is complex, but it cannot be taken for granted that economic growth will reduce the chances of an epidemic from developing. Thus while it is true that poverty may also create favorable conditions for epidemic growth resulting from such factors as low levels of education, overall healthcare provision, and malnutrition, strong economic growth may create others.

Inequalities in income, in particular, have been considered important drivers of HIV/AIDS epidemics. It has been noted that some of the wealthiest SSA countries, including South Africa and Botswana, have among the most serious HIV epidemics (UNAIDS, 2006a: 84). Incomes in our sample range from around US$2,000 to $10,000 in the Asian and SSA countries (see Table 2.2), with both Botswana and South Africa sharing high per capita incomes, albeit with extremely high levels of inequality. It is too simple, therefore, to argue HIV is a "disease of poverty." There appears to be a more complex relationship between per capita wealth and the epidemic. The relationship between inequality, poverty, and HIV/AIDS epidemics, it has been cautioned, while being "powerful" is also "nuanced" (ibid.).

In terms of the overall general pattern of growth and income distribution, it is noteworthy to mention that China appears to share some similarities with Thailand. From a biomedical perspective, Thailand has experienced a more generalized epidemic which spread to the general population via CSW. Its epidemic is more advanced than China but from the perspective of the underlying economic conditions, similarities appear. Thailand is currently wealthier on a per capita basis than China. Its per capita gross domestic product (GDP) was US$7,595 (China's was US$5,003, as estimated in 2003). More importantly, however, the annual average growth rates of China and Thailand over several decades have been similar. From 1975 to 2003, growth rates averaged 8 and 5 percent, respectively, the highest rates in the sample of countries we are looking at. In conjunction with economic growth, extensive socioeconomic changes also took place in both countries, such as rural–urban migration, rapid industrialization, attraction of foreign investment, and also a growing export orientation. Both experienced an approximate doubling in the exports of goods and services as a share of GDP (Thailand from 34 to 64 percent and China from 18 to 34 percent), reflecting the growing openness of these economies. However, both economies have seen growing inequalities emerge. The share of the income of upper and lower quintiles was approximately the same by the turn of the millennium, at approximately 5 percent for the lower group and 50 percent for the upper. Both had Gini coefficients of around 44, suggesting similarly high levels of income inequality.

While many countries have experienced income growth in recent decades, there is an increasing trend toward unequal growth. In particular, evidence

Table 2.2 Income, inequality, and economic growth

Country	GDP per capita (ppp US$) in 2003	Annual growth rate		Share of income of poorest 20% of population	Share of income of richest 20% of population	Gini coefficient	Population beneath US$1 per day (1990–2003)	Population beneath US$2 per day (1990–2003)	Exports, goods, and services	
		1975–2003	1990–2003						% GDP 1990	% GDP 2003
Generalized epidemics										
Cambodia	2,078	–	4	6.9	47.6	40.4	34.1	77.7	6	62
Myanmar		1.8	5.7	–	–	–	–	–	3	–
Thailand	7,595	5.1	2.8	6.1	50	43.2	<2	32.5	34	66
Concentrated epidemics										
China	5,003	8.2	8.5	4.7	50	44.7	16.6	46.7	18	34
Indonesia	3,361	4.1	2	8.4	43.3	34.3	7.5	52.4	25	31
Malaysia	9,512	3.9	3.4	4.4	54.3	49.2	<2	9.3		
Vietnam	2,490	5	5.9	7.5	45.5	34.8	–	–	36	60
Low-level epidemics										
Lao PDR	1,759	3.3	3.7	7.6	45	–	26.3	73.2	11	25
Mongolia	1,850	–2	–2.5	5.6	51.2	30.3	27	75	24	68
Philippines	4,321	0.3	1.2	5.4	52.3	46.1	14.6	46.4	28	48
South Africa	10,346	–0.6	0.1	3.5	62	57.8	10.7	34.1	24	28
Botswana	8,714	5.1	2.7	2.2	70	63	23.5	50.1	55	44
Lesotho	2,561	3.1	2.3	1.5	66	63	36.4	56.1	17	41
Kenya	1,037	0.2	–0.6	6	49	42.5	22.8	58.3	26	25
Malawi	605	0.2	0.9	4.9	56	50	41.7	76.1	24	27
Uganda	1,457	2.6	3.9	5.9	47	43	–	–	7	12

Source: UNDP (2005).

suggests that the least well-off sections of the population are not benefiting as much as they might from growth. Income inequalities are particularly extreme in some SSA regions. While per capita incomes may be high in countries like Botswana and South Africa, the number living in poverty is also large owing to uneven income distributions. In Botswana, the poorest 20 percent of the population share about 2 percent of national income, compared with 70 percent for the wealthiest 20 percent of the population. Similarly in Lesotho and South Africa, equally large disparities exist. In comparison, East and Southeast Asia's share of the income for the poorest 20 percent of the population ranges between 5–10 percent of national income and the wealthiest 20 percent ranges between around 45–50 percent. It should be noted, however, that income inequality is an increasing problem in East and Southeast Asia and which we return to later.

Employment opportunities have also in part been driven by a development pattern based upon foreign direct investment and the emergence of large export-processing industries in East and Southeast Asia. Such policies, some argue, have further exacerbated unequal development, leading to lack of employment opportunities or the creation of very-low-paid basic employment. Emerging East Asian economies have continued to become more exposed to international trade over the last decade, with merchandise exports increasing from 34 percent of GDP in 1995 to 42 percent in 2005 (World Bank, 2007: 28). Trade to GDP ratios rose in all of the major economies of the region. East Asia's overall share of world exports also continued to rise, from 15.5 percent in 1995 to 17.9 percent in 2005. The increase in East Asia's world trade share, however, came from China (including Hong Kong), which rose from 4.5 to 7.7 percent of world trade (ibid.). In the 1980s, Asian countries created 337 million jobs but by the 1990s this had decreased to 176 million. With a growing population, insufficient jobs have been created. Between 1993–2003, unemployment increased from 3.9 to 6.3 percent in Southeast Asia. The situation is often more serious in the most trade-intensive countries. China and Singapore, for example, have seen substantial increase in unemployment rates. It is important to note, moreover, that a large share of unemployment has fallen on young people: "in 2004, while those aged 15–24 made up one-fifth of Asia–Pacific's labor force, they constituted nearly half of the unemployed. Women too have lost out: in most countries their unemployment rates are higher than men's" (UNDP, 2006: 4). Why is the region experiencing "jobless growth?" Although manufacturing output increased by 180 percent, employment has increased by only 3 percent (ibid.). As countries move higher up the value chain, they look to become producers of more sophisticated capital intensive products. This, in turn, leads to the phenomena of jobless growth (ibid.: 9).

East and Southeast Asia has experienced dramatic change during the last several decades. Increasing economic growth has also led to growing income inequalities. Among the examples discussed, Thailand, a country that has experienced a generalized HIV epidemic, appears to share similarities with China in terms of overall structural economic change. The lessons from this example may be of particular relevance to China given the underlying economic terrain appears comparable.

Gender inequality

Gender inequalities have been considered important population-level drivers of HIV/AIDS epidemics. Indeed, an increasing number of females, particularly young females, are also being infected with HIV/AIDS. The global feminization of the HIV/AIDS epidemic is a marked and disturbing trend (UNAIDS, 2006a). WHO/UNAIDS estimate that for every adult woman living with HIV in the Asia–Pacific region, there are four men living with the virus (MAP, 2005: 8). This ratio, however, has been changing quickly. Between 1990–2005, the number of female adults aged 15 and over with HIV/AIDS increased from 15 to 28 percent in the Asia–Pacific region. Globally, the proportion of women living with HIV/AIDS has also increased steadily, from 41 percent in 1997 to 50 percent by the end of 2002. In SSA, where the epidemics are far more advanced, 59 percent of all infections were in females, particularly among younger groups (UNDP, 2007: 18). Women in SSA are particularly vulnerable:

> Women and girls make up almost 57% of all people infected with HIV in sub-Saharan Africa, where a striking 76% of young people (aged 15–24 years) living with HIV are female. In most other regions, women and girls represent an increasing proportion of people living with HIV, compared with a few years ago
>
> (UNAIDS, 2004: 4)

Similarly in China, female prevalence has also risen quickly, as the epidemic moves out from IDU and MSM populations. Heterosexual transmission (particularly via CSW) is taking over from IDU and plasma-driven infections in China. It is generally argued that there are a number of reasons why females are more susceptible, determined by a variety of social, cultural, economic, and physiological factors.

Despite the third MDG "to eliminate gender disparity in primary and secondary education, preferably by 2005, and in all levels of education no later than 2015," progress toward gender equality has been slow. According to UNDP, there were 680 million children of primary school age in all developing countries in 2003 of which 115 million did not attend school and three-fifths of these nonattendees were girls (UNDP, 2003: 86). Some progress, nevertheless, has been made in gender equality in education. Between 1990–2001, the ratio of literate 15- to 24-year-olds female to male in countries with a low HDI increased from 70 to 81 women per 100 men. In countries with medium human development (those more similar to China), this ratio increased far more slowly (from 91 to 93). The gender ratio in primary education also made limited progress, rising from 86 to 92 girls per 100 boys in all developing countries between 1990 and 1999–2000. According to the UNDP, at current rates "gender equality in education will not be achieved until 2025 – 20 years after the target set by the Millennium Development Goals" (ibid.). Among young women (15- to 24-year-olds) in developing countries, literacy stands at just 60 percent compared to 80 percent for young men (ibid.). There are about 900 million illiterate adults of which, two-thirds are women (ibid.: 94). Against this background of educational attainments, or lack of, it is perhaps not so surprising that infections are growing rapidly among young women.[7]

Table 2.3 provides a summary of relevant indicators of gender inequality (including education, income generation, and political representation) for different East and Southeast Asian nations, as well as a sample of SSA countries with high HIV/AIDS prevalence (the SSA countries listed below have prevalence ranging from 6.7 percent in Kenya up to 37 percent in Botswana). In terms of gender inequalities in education, many of the East and Southeast Asian countries sampled here show female literacy at 85 percent, with exceptions being Laos and Cambodia. In general, they far surpassed the least developed countries, which had average female literacy of only 44.6 and 70 percent for men (UNDP, 2005). This was also greater than in SSA, where female adult literacy averaged 53 percent for women and 76 percent for men.[8] Developing countries as a whole had an average female adult literacy of around 70 and 84 percent for men.[9] Nonetheless, net primary and secondary enrollment of women in the Southeast Asian nations with generalized epidemics was very low, in some instances lower than the SSA-sampled countries.

Male adult literacy in general exceeded female literacy by several percentage points in the Asian countries, but with variations. For most of the current "concentrated" epidemics (such as Malaysia, Vietnam, and China), female literacy was around 90 percent that of male. By contrast with the sample of SSA countries, female adult literacy was on the whole higher (around 85 percent) but the relative gender inequality with men was also greater as measured by the "female rate as percentage of male." Surprisingly, in some of SSA countries sampled in Table 2.3, female literacy was even higher than male literacy (this was also reflected in higher relative primary and secondary enrollment of females). What this indicates is that while the East and Southeast Asian countries may have, in general, higher levels of literacy (particularly when also taking account of income levels, which were actually higher in South Africa and Botswana than in some of the Asian countries examined), relative education inequalities between the sexes are not necessarily worse in SSA. Thailand, for example (per capita income of US$7,595, an HDI of 0.78, and ranking of 73), had net primary enrollment of women of 84 percent but Lesotho's was 89 percent (per capita income US$2,561, the HDI was 0.49, and ranking 149). Data for Thailand's net secondary enrollment are not provided, but the other examples suggest that the ratios of women to men were relatively greater in the SSA countries. This implies that while overall provision of education may be greater in many of the East and Southeast Asian examples, the position of women when compared to men may be worse.

This surprising fact is also reflected by the difference in the ranks between the human development and gender development indexes (GDIs). The GDI is composite measure of female empowerment incorporating differences between male and females in aspects of education, life expectancy, and income. It is therefore a broader measure of female empowerment and quality of life compared against

Table 2.3 HIV and gender in education

Country	GDI	GDI rank	HDI	HDI rank	HDI rank minus GDI rank	Female adult literacy	Male adult literacy	Female adult literacy rate as % male women	Net primary enrollment women	Net primary women to men ratio	Net secondary enrollment women	Net secondary women to men ratio	Ratio of female to male earned income	Year first woman elected/appointed to parliament	Women in government ministerial level (%)	Seats in parliament held by women in 1990 (%)	Seats in parliament held by women in 2005 (%)	Convention on the elimination of all forms of discrimination against women
Generalized epidemics																		
Cambodia	0.57	99	0.57	130	31	64.1	76	76	91	0.95	19	0.64	0.76	1976	11.5	18	27	Yes
Myanmar	–	–	0.58	129		86.2	92	92	85	1.01	34	0.94	–	1947	–	3	–	Yes
Thailand	0.77	57	0.78	73	16	90.5	95	95	84	0.97	–	–	0.61	1948	7.7		10.6	Yes
Concentrated epidemics																		
China	0.75	64	0.76	85	21	86.5	91	91	90	0.9	85	0.85	0.66	1954	6.3	21	20	Yes
Indonesia	0.69	87	0.7	110	23	83.4	90	90	92	0.98	54	0.99	0.52	1950	10.8	12	11	Yes
Malaysia	0.79	50	0.8	61	11	85.4	93	93	93	1	74	1.11	0.47	1959	9.1	5	9.10	Yes
Vietnam	0.7	83	0.7	108	25	86.9	93	93	92	0.94	–	–	0.68					Yes
Low-level epidemics																		
Lao PDR	0.54	102	0.55	133	31	60.9	79	79	82	0.93	32	0.83	0.65	1958	0.0	6	22	Yes
Mongolia	0.68	90	0.68	114	24	97.5	100		80	1.03	83	1.16	0.66	1951	5.9	25	6.7	
Philippines	0.76	63	0.76	84	21	92.7	100		95	1.02	65	1.19	0.59	1941	25.0	9	15	
Sub-Saharan Africa																		
South Africa	0.65	92	0.66	120	28	81	84	96	89	1.01	68	1.09	0.45	1994	41.0	3	32.8	Yes
Botswana	0.56	100	0.57	131	31	81.5	76.1	107	83	1.04	57	1.15	0.61	1979	26.7	5	11	Yes
Lesotho	0.49	114	0.5	149	35	90	74	123	89	1.07	27	1.53	0.39	1965	27.8	0	11.7	Yes
Kenya	0.472	117	0.47	154	37	70	77	90	66	1	24	0.98	0.93	1969	10.3	1	7.1	Yes
Malawi	0.4	129	0.3	165	36	54	75	72	68	0.98	21	0.83	0.68	1964	14.3	10	14	Yes

Sources: UNDP (2005: 309); also based on previous tables.

Note: Data for incomes based on 2003 estimates (UNDP, 2005: 302).

men. If we again compare our sample, it is evident that greater gender inequality appears to exist in the East and Southeast Asia for their given level of human development. We can estimate such disparities by subtracting the GDI from the HDI. The difference, in keeping with the findings for education enrollment, appears to be greater in many of the SSA countries sampled. Differences in the ranks appear mostly in the 30s as opposed to 20s for the observed East and Southeast Asian countries. The HDI rank minus GDI rank, for example, was 16 for Thailand, 21 for China, and 25 for Vietnam. In Lesotho, it was 35, South Africa 28, and Kenya 37. Again, this points toward larger relative gender differences between men and women within the Asian sample for their given level of development.

What about the political representation of women? While this is difficult to measure accurately, particularly the more informal aspects, some indicators also suggest a relative underperformance in this regard for some of the East and Southeast Asian countries. Indeed, for some SSA, the indicators suggest healthy female political representation when compared to the Asian sample. While women may have been included much later in the formal political processes in SSA (as measured, for example, by the year the first woman was elected/ appointed to parliament is generally later), the actual number of women in government at ministerial level compares favorably, as do the number of seats held in parliament to developed nations such as Norway, the United Kingdom, and the United States.[10]

What about relative earnings of women to men? In all of the countries observed, women earn less than men, but the ratios are perhaps not as great as might be expected, given that even the most developed countries also had significant discrepancies (in the most developed countries, this stood at around 70 percent). The main point to emerge from this comparison is that no obvious discernible trends can be distinguished across the samples, other than to note that in many cases the wage gap is large.

China's progress in gender quality

While China has done well with regard to the universal primary schooling, progress toward the gender equality in education (MDG 3) has been less encouraging. Unfortunately, HDRs do not provide good data on education enrollment. The UN China office, however, does provide a recent evaluation of progress toward the MDGs. According to this report, it may well be offtrack to meet MDG 3. This is reflected in both primary enrollment rates and also secondary education. According to the Ministry of Education data, girls to boys ratio in primary education stood at 90 girls to 100 boys in 2002, an increase from 86 to 100 in 1990. While some progress has been made, it will be insufficient to meet the MDG target of complete equality by 2015. The girl to boy ratio is even more pronounced in secondary education as many females are withdrawn after primary school, with only 85 girls per 100 boys (UN Country Team China, 2004: 16). This suggests that China has lower relative female to male enrollment in both primary and secondary education than South Africa, Botswana, Lesotho, and Kenya, and is only roughly comparable to Malawi in secondary enrollment. Progress in absolute levels of education provision should be acknowledged in China. In light of this comparative analysis, however, it is evident that serious education gender inequalities exist. Moreover, a country of China's size and diversity masks pockets of underdevelopment. In terms of illiteracy, China's low human development regions fared particularly badly. The average low human development high HIV prevalence regions, for example, had 20 percent illiteracy among females and 9 percent for males. The female illiteracy rate falls to 12 percent in medium-HDI regions and 10 percent in developed regions. The male illiteracy rate falls from 9 to 2.5 as we move from low to high human development regions, illustrating how averages mask wide disparities (UNDP/ CDRF, 2005).

This brief investigation of gender inequalities shows that while the East and Southeast Asia exhibit diversity in the extent of their HIV/AIDS epidemics and the underlying levels of development, with HDI ranging from 0.5 to 0.7, a general feature to emerge is the greater relative gender inequalities that appear to exist in these countries. China is no exception in this regard.

Health and environment

Public health, including factors such as endemic disease, malnourishment, sanitation, and water supply, is an important factor shaping the course of an HIV epidemic. In the developing world and particularly in SSA, it is argued that endemic diseases, related to poor general public health infrastructure, weaken the immune systems of individuals and increases susceptibility (Stillwaggon, 2006). This line of reasoning argues that epidemiological, clinical, and laboratory evidence show that HIV infection is influenced by the same factors that promote transmission of other infectious diseases. A number of such diseases are considered by some to play a prominent role as cofactors in the spread of HIV, including malaria; leishmaniasis (visceral and cutaneous); worm infections (heminthic and filarial); schistosomiasis (Bihharzia); tuberculosis (TB; the most lethal and widespread infectious disease in history), and sexually transmitted diseases (STDs). Such diseases may weaken the immune systems of infected individuals and thus increase susceptibility. At the same time, higher levels of disease increase the white blood cell (CD4) count, and this may also increase susceptibility. Relatedly, lower nutritional intake may also increase the chance of coinfection, as do poor sanitary conditions and potable water supplies. Moving "beyond epidemiology" Stillwaggon (2006: 12), therefore argues that among other things, "stopping AIDS requires attacking the underlying causes ... Behaviour change is important, but the downward spiral can only be stopped if there is substantial change in the health profile of sub-Saharan Africa and other poor regions." What then is the overall health profile of China and how does this look in a comparative perspective?

Progress at a global level toward the health indicators, as shown in the MDGs, is not on track. For example, reducing under-5 mortality rate by two-thirds between 1990–2015 is believed to be the one MDG that is furthest off target at the global level (UNDP, 2003: 97). The reason for high mortality of children, it should be noted, is closely tied to factors such as a poor environment (sanitation and water) as well as inadequate healthcare provision (immunization):

> Every day more than 30,000 of the world's children die from preventable causes – dehydration, hunger, disease … *Every year more than 500,000 women die in pregnancy and childbirth – one every minute of the day.* A pregnant woman is 100 times more likely to die in pregnancy and childbirth in Sub Saharan Africa than in a high-income OECD country.
>
> (Ibid.; emphasis added)

Again, it is in SSA where mortality is highest followed by South Asia. South Asia has been making some progress. Child mortality fell from 12.6 percent to around 10 percent during the 1990s. In SSA, however, 17 percent of children do not reach age five: "At current rates the region will not achieve the Goal for child mortality for almost 150 years" (ibid.). Associated with this goal is the target to reduce maternal mortality ratio by three-quarters for the same period. As we see in the above UNDP statistics, 500,000 women die during pregnancy or childbirth. "A key issue for addressing this goal is improving public health services: skilled birth attendants, emergency obstetric services and greater reproductive healthcare services" (ibid.: 99).

In comparison, China's progress to these MDGs has been good. China's history illustrates how even simple health interventions may be effective. Yet, the growing introduction of fees and the privatization of health services are increasingly preventing many of the poorer sections of the population from participating in improved healthcare. Increasing medical fees (usually levied on medicines) has become a major social issue. Nonetheless, despite unequal access to healthcare, it is still reported that during the 1990s infant mortality dropped from 50 to 30 per 1,000 live births, while under-5 mortality dropped from 61 in 1991 to 36 by 2001 (UN Country Team China, 2004: 19). In order to meet the MDG by 2015, the under-5 rate must be lowered to 20. This will bring China into the ranks of middle-income countries, such as Malaysia. The maternal mortality ratio is also reported to be on track, having dropped from 89 per 100,000 live births in 1990 to 50 in 2001. Part of the reason for a fall in the maternal death rate may be associated with the strict family planning laws. The proportion of births attended by skilled health workers in hospital, however, is also reported to have increased from 51 percent in 1990 to 76 percent in 2001 (ibid.: 22). Again, however, large regional differences exist and there is concern that the underfunding of public health services has led to a decline in the rural health infrastructure. The 1998 National Health Survey, moreover, revealed that 63 percent of cases referred to hospital "did not attend due to financial reasons" (ibid.: 24). National health accounts data show that government expenditure has dropped from 25 percent of total health expenditure in 1990 to 15 percent in 1999. Major and urgent effort is required to improve access to hospital services in rural areas, especially for the poor.

Progress toward targets set in some of the MDGs has been made in China. However, the question remains as to those indicators that have an impact on the emerging HIV/AIDS epidemic, including TB, public health expenditures, and environmental conditions. Table 2.4 provides data on a number of these for our sample. First, if we consider public health expenditure, it is of interest to note that public expenditure in the East and Southeast Asian sample appears low, even when compared to SSA. China is recorded as spending 2 percent of its GDP on public health in 2002. By comparison, all SSA countries considered in the sample had higher shares, ranging from 3 to 5 percent. Countries with high human development indicators typically have public expenditure in the 6–8 percent range. Low public health expenditures in the sample, as might be expected, were compensated for in some part by relatively larger private expenditures. On average it appears, private expenditures relative to public expenditures were greater in the non-SSA countries. However, observing the entire sample, per capita expenditures were still rather low (ranging from US$150 to $350 in the "concentrated" epidemics), with expenditures in some of the more severely affected countries being very low (under US$50 per capita). China's per capita expenditure stood at US$261. This again, however, concealed large regional disparities. By comparison, high human development countries spent on average closer to ten times this amount, nearer to US$3,000 per capita. From this, we can infer that public health provision in the East and Southeast Asian countries has not been a priority area of public spending, rather private provision appears more important. This may have implications for the treatment of many diseases, particularly with resistant strains emerging in these regions owing to incomplete treatment regimes. China, for example, has a serious problem with drug-resistant strains of TB.

TB, owing to the weakening of the immune system that HIV causes, may take hold in HIV-stricken countries. TB is one of the world's biggest killers as a contagious disease, notwithstanding the relatively low cost for the cure. It remains a worldwide pandemic, growing at around 1 percent a year and killing 5,000 people each day. TB patients have approximately a 5 percent chance of developing secondary TB during their lives. HIV-infected persons have an 8 percent chance *annually* of developing TB, rising to a total of 50 percent during the remainder of their shortened life span (Dolin, Raviglione and Kochi, 1994). A third of the world's population (nearly two billion people) carries quiescent TB infection with devastating consequences for the immune system. More recent concerns surround the advent of multidrug resistant (MDR) and extensively drug resistant (XDR) TB, these now pose a major threat for countries such as China where the quasi privatization of healthcare services creates fertile conditions for drug resistance to emerge. A third of the world's cases of MDR TB are in China according to the WHO, despite having only 15 percent of the global burden of TB. The 2000 national TB prevalence survey revealed that one in ten patients had MDR TB.

Table 2.4 Public health indicators

Country	HDI rank	% GDP in 2002		Per capita health expenditure	1-year-olds immunized against TB	Malaria cases (per 100,000 people) in 2000	Tuberculosis cases per 100,000 in 2003	Population undernourished		Population with access to improved sanitation		Population with access to improved water source	
		Public health expenditure	Private health expenditure					1990/1992 (%)	2000/2002 (%)	1990	2002	1990	2002
Generalized epidemics													
Cambodia	130	2.1	9.9	192	76	476	742	43	33	–	16	–	34
Myanmar	129	0.4	1.8	30	79	224	183	10	6	21	73	48	80
Thailand	73	3.1	1.3	321	99	130	203	28	20	80	90	81	85
Concentrated epidemics													
China	85	2	3.8	261	93	1	245	16	11	23	44	70	77
Indonesia	110	1.2	2	110	82	920	674	9	6	46	52	71	78
Malaysia	61	2	1.8	349	99	57	135	3	2	96	–	–	95
Vietnam	108	1.5	3.7	148	98	95	238	31	19	22	41	72	73
Low-level epidemics													
Lao PDR	133	1.5	1.4	49	65	759	327	29	22	–	24	–	43
Mongolia	114	4.6	2	128	98	–	237	34	28	–	59	62	62
Philippines	84	1.1	1.8	153	91	15	458	26	22	54	73	87	85
South Africa	120	3.5	5.2	689	97	143	341	–	–	63	67	83	87
Botswana	131	3.7	2.3	387	99	48,704	342	23	32	38	41	93	95
Lesotho	149	5.3	0.9	119	83	0	390	17	12	37	37	–	76
Kenya	154	2.2	2.7	70	87	545	821	44	33	42	48	45	62
Malawi	165	4	5.8	48	91	25,948	469	50	33	36	46	41	67

Source: UNDP (2005: 238, 239, 242, 243, 248, 249).

Each year, around 400 million people in China are infected with TB and 1.45 million people develop active TB, among which 650,000 are highly infectious with approximately 130,000 deaths (Xinhua, September 18, 2004). Again, there are large differences between regions, reflecting general development patterns and access to healthcare. The vast majority of infections have been in rural areas, showing a similarity with early HIV infections: "More than eighty percent of China's TB patients are living in rural areas, especially in the poor areas" (ibid.). Many cannot afford proper medical treatment. In contrast, the prevalence of TB was lowest in the three municipalities of Beijing, Shanghai, and Tianjin in 2000 (China Tuberculosis Control Collaboration, 2004: 420). Generally, prevalence increases across the urban–rural gradient: from the municipalities, through provincial and county capitals, to rural areas (ibid.). Prevalence also differed significantly between the male and female populations and increased with age (ibid.).

Table 2.4 shows that TB immunization was relatively high for many of the countries considered, although in some of the high HIV prevalence Southeast Asian nations, such as Cambodia and Myanmar, immunization levels were lower than SSA. China's immunization rate stood at 93 percent, roughly equivalent to that of Malawi, but lower than South Africa and Botswana. In terms of total TB cases found, as discussed, the SSA countries had much higher rates of secondary infection, in part owing to the more advanced HIV epidemics. China's TB problem is particularly related to the advent of drug-resistant strains. As HIV moves further into the general population and national adult prevalence rises, it is possible that the TB problem will also worsen.

Nutrition, sanitation, and water

Overall levels of health are likely to be affected by nutrition, sanitation, and water supplies. How does China perform in these areas when compared to other countries? As might be expected, within most of the sample countries, undernourishment has decreased in recent years. However, absolute level of undernourishment remains higher in the SSA countries. Undernourishment in the Asian sample, such as the generalized epidemic of Cambodia, is close to levels found in Malawi and Kenya. In other Asian countries, however, they remain, in general, lower, reflecting the better economic performance of this region. For developing countries as a whole, the share of the population undernourished fell from 19 to 16 percent on average (UNDP, 2005). As seen in Table 2.4, China has outperformed the developing country average.

Regarding sanitation, the Asian countries in general have seen greater improvements than the SSA countries. China, for example, has experienced an almost doubling of its population share with access to improved sanitation, compared with an improvement of only several percentage points in Malawi and Botswana, and ten or so in Kenya. Nonetheless, some Asian countries, including China, still have quite low levels of sanitation even in comparison to their African counterparts. For example, China reports 44 percent of its population in 2002 with access to improved sanitation (sitting below the developing country average of 48 percent), compared with 46 and 48 percent for Malawi and Kenya, respectively.

China's performance in access to improved water supplies is even less impressive, with only 77 percent of the population with access, a similar level to Lesotho. Again China is below the developing country average, where access to improved water supplies increased from 70 to 79 percent between 1990–2002. In the area of public provision such as sanitation and water supply, China has underperformed despite its overall progress in economic development. Such underperformance is attributable in part to fiscal decentralization which has led to, among other things, reduction in many areas of public services.

It is hard to conclude, on aggregate, that China has a better track record in some of the public health-related areas considered here when compared with the SSA sample. Indeed, public health expenditure remains comparatively low in China. Moreover, given the disparities in the overall speed of economic growth, we might also expect to see larger improvements in measures of undernourishment, sanitation, and water supply in China. On the other hand, the presence of endemic malaria appears to stand out in SSA, as do higher overall rates of TB. This captures, however, the reality of the Chinese economic development, namely that it has been accompanied by a comparative reduction of state involvement across a number of areas, including those related to public health.

Education

The overall level of education may be an important social determinant of HIV/AIDS epidemics. A better-educated population may not only acquire specific information regarding HIV transmission, it is also more likely to find employment and develop patterns of behavior which are less likely to place them in high-risk situations. The overall level of education in a society may also be an important determinant of its susceptibility to HIV/AIDS.

In this section, we consider China's education levels with other countries. Previously we have discussed gender aspects of educational attainment, here we briefly summarize overall education progress by looking at the second MDG, that is to ensure by 2015 both male and female will be able to complete a full course of primary schooling. The success of the late industrializing nations in East Asia, such as South Korea and Japan, has been attributable in part to favorable primary education policies. Education systems in general, as with healthcare, are weak in the developing world, where roughly one-quarter of adults can neither read nor write.

Fortunately, recent global development experience shows some progress in the universal education goal. According to the UNDP, every region saw increases in primary enrollment:

> In East Asia and the Pacific, Central and Eastern Europe and the Commonwealth of Independent States (CIS) and Latin America and the Caribbean

more than 90 percent of children are enrolled in primary school. In South Asia 79 percent are enrolled, and in the Arab States 77 percent. In Sub-Saharan Africa net primary enrolments increased by 3 percentage points in the 1990s, yet less than 60 percent of children are enrolled.

(UNDP, 2003: 92)

Again, SSA registers one of the poorest performances with the lowest enrollment rates. Nonetheless, such a measure may bear little relation to final graduation figures or the quality of education. Many children may drop out of school once enrolled, particularly girls. One estimate suggests about half of all children who start primary school in the developing world finish it. In SSA, only one-third finish primary education (ibid.: 86).

According to a recent survey of China's progress toward the MDGs, the country is well ahead of target in improving its net primary enrollment rate. By 2002, approximately 99 percent of children were enrolled in primary school, up from 96 percent in 1990 (UN Country Team China, 2004: 11). China, therefore, is quickly moving to universal primary education. In India, by comparison, 40 million children were still not in primary school by the turn of the millennium, about one-third the world's total primary school absentees (UNDP, 2003: 88). There is still, of course, room for improvement in China's education system. In China, public spending on education is only 2.3 percent of GDP (health spending is 2.1 percent) which actually compares less favorably with India (ibid.: 73). The government is also committed toward a compulsory 9 years of primary education. Increasingly it is the poorest regions, often those with ethnic minorities (and in some cases the highest HIV infection rates), that are being targeted as laggards. Currently, education funding is largely the responsibility of the local governments which holds back progress in education delivery. These mechanisms are in need of reform as the poorest regions often have inadequate funds to improve their education systems. There is also a very serious problem in the provision of education services to the children of migrant families. The migrant population, as later chapters show, plays a significant part in the HIV/AIDS epidemic. The implications of a growing migrant underclass receiving inadequate education may be significant for the future spread of HIV/AIDS in China.

Demography

HIV/AIDS may have an impact on demography but also at the same time the demographic structure may play an important part in shaping an epidemic. It is important to consider the share of young people in the population (those that are sexually active) as the majority of both female sex workers and drug injectors are under the age of 25 in the Asia region, and significant proportions of men who buy sex and who have multiple male partners are also adolescents or young adults (MAP, 2005: 8). Groups with more high-risk behaviors tend to be concentrated among the youth. More generally, the demographic profile may also

Table 2.5 Demographic trends

Country	Share (%) of urban population in total in 1975	Urban population		Share of population under 15		Total population (billion)	
		2003	2015	2003	2015	Today	2015
Generalized epidemics							
Cambodia	10.3	18.6	26.1	38.3	34.1	13.5	17.1
Myanmar	23.9	29.5	37.6	30.8	23.6	49.5	55
Thailand	23.8	32	36.7	24.5	21.2	63.1	69.1
Concentrated epidemics							
China	17.4	38.6	49.5	22.7	18.5	1,300	1,393
Indonesia	19.3	45.5	57.8	29	25	217	246
Malaysia	37.3	63.8	71	33	27	24	30
Vietnam	18.9	25.8	32.4	31.1	25	82	95
Low-level epidemics							
Lao PDR	11.1	20.7	27.4	41.7	37.1	5.7	7.3
Mongolia	48.7	56.8	59.5	32.2	26.3	2.6	3
Philippines	35.6	61	69	36.1	30	80	97
South Africa	48	56.9	62.7	32.9	30.2	46.9	47.9
Botswana	12.8	51.6	57.5	38.2	34.7	1.8	1.7
Lesotho	10.8	18	21	39.3	36.6	1.8	1.7
Kenya	12.9	39.3	51.8	43.1	42.6	32.7	44.2
Malawi	7.7	16.3	22.2	47.1	44.9	12.3	16

Source: UNDP (2005).

provide insights into possible impacts of an HIV epidemic. In the Chinese case, the one-child policy has worrying implications for excess mortality resulting from an HIV/AIDS epidemic as future populations will have very high dependency ratios, with the old dependent on a relatively small younger age population. Indeed, China's demographic profile is almost unique owing to the one-child policy, and this may also lead to future problems.

We note from our sample that the share of the urban population is expanding rapidly (see Table 2.5). This is true for all countries considered, but China is undergoing the most rapid urbanization process when compared to other nations. Certainly, in terms of the overall scale of rural–urban migration, it is unsurpassed. In 1975, 17 percent of the population lived in urban areas. According to UN statistics, this will increase to almost 50 percent by 2015. In numbers alone, around 300 million will have moved from rural to urban areas, indicating major changes in the way people live. On the one hand, some believe growing urbanization may create a more fertile environment for HIV transmission, as greater opportunities for sexual mixing arise. On the other hand, urbanization may provide environments for better targeting among high-risk groups with more effective measures and healthcare. Therefore, the net result, for urbanization, may be unclear.

When looking at the age structure of the population, many developing countries have significant bulges in the most sexually active age groups. The under-15 age group in high human development countries stood in the range of 15–20 percent in 2003 and is predicted to fall several percentage points by 2015. Low human development countries, by contrast, typically have very young populations, often with over 40 percent of their populations being under 15 in 2003. The total fertility rate in these countries (births per women) is also typically very high over five, compared with nearer to two in developed countries. In China, births per woman dropped precipitously from 4.9 to 1.7 between 1970–1975 and 2000–2005 due to the one-child policy.

Conclusion

East Asia and the Pacific region are the world's most highly populated area. Within Asia, China's emerging epidemic is considered to be "the next big challenge on the horizon" (World Bank, 2004b: 5). Further understanding the dynamics of the HIV/AIDS epidemic in this region, including China's, is therefore important. However, many studies on the East Asian epidemics to date, such as the annual UNAIDS updates, focus overwhelmingly on the stark biomedical facts. This is understandable in some ways, as it still remains difficult to draw concrete causal links between epidemics and other socioeconomic conditions. Owing to the way in which we generally conceptualize HIV/AIDS epidemics, as a disease of the individual, it is far easier to make the links between high-risk populations (such as IDU and CSW) and high national prevalence. The development of an epidemic is usually seen as the product of numerous individual actions. This approach stems from the biomedical paradigm, which frames disease emergence at an individual level. Epidemics, however, also reflect the type of development process that a country is undergoing. In trying to present a comparative description of the economic and social terrain of China's HIV/AIDS epidemic, this chapter has introduced a number of important economic and human development indicators to provide further insights into the type of terrain in which the epidemic is emerging.

To this end, first we considered income growth and distribution, outward orientation of the economy, and employment (Table 2.2). It is important to emphasize that many of the East and Southeast Asian economies have grown very quickly in recent decades. Uneven growth, however, has also been a problem, particularly in more recent times. China is no exception in this regard and has experienced very rapid growth in inequality. When looking at these dimensions, we found that China and Thailand appeared to share some similarities. While China's real income is still lower than Thailand's, it is catching up quickly. Both of them have experienced very rapid average annual income growth, over extended periods. They are among the fastest growing countries in the sample. Both have also developed export-processing industries and outward orientation. They have been more open recipients of globalization processes, using foreign direct investment. Considerable shares of total income, however, are concentrated in quite small segments of the population, exacerbating inequality. Both countries have seen large-scale migration, often from poorer regions with higher HIV prevalence.

Second, we also looked at dimensions of gender inequality an international comparative perspective, including those related to levels of education, political rights, and income and wealth. Inequalities in education and political rights are widely considered to be the important determinants of national HIV/AIDS epidemics. While absolute levels of education may be higher in East Asia than in SSA, relative inequalities in education (when females are compared against males) still appear greater. Thus access to education for females when compared to males appears quite low in many of the East and Southeast Asian countries. This is an important finding if we consider that inequalities, as well as absolute levels of education, are related to the dynamics of HIV epidemics. In addition, it seems that progress toward gender equality in China has been more limited when compared with some of the other internationally recognized development goals embodied in the MDGs. Inequalities between males and females with regard to education and income also appear particularly relevant to the Chinese epidemic. Previous focus has tended to be on absolute rather than relative progress. The larger relative differences found in East Asia compared to many other countries have, to some extent, so far been overlooked. As a recent HDR notes, however: "Unless women's capabilities are improved and gender equality increased, the other Millennium Development Goals will not be achieved. Strengthening women's agency and voice is essential" (UNDP, 2003: 86). While China has done remarkably well in achieving such rapid human development, a critical outstanding issue, and one central to the HIV/AIDS epidemic, relates to the increasing gaps between the sexes. This is in fact one of the few goals, including HIV and the environment (goals six and eight of the MDGs), in which China specifically lags behind the official targets. It is also an area in which the government, in its concept of "scientific development," appears to have overlooked. As the United Nations has rightly pointed out, "the plight of women and children in the face of AIDS underlines the need for realistic strategies that address the interplay between inequality – particularly gender inequality – and HIV" (UNAIDS, 2004: 4). Later chapters will consider in greater detail how these inequalities directly relate to the booming commercial sex industry that has become central to the dynamics of HIV transmission in China today.

Third, this chapter considered public health indicators, with an emphasis on public health expenditure. From a financing perspective, China's public expenditures as a share of national income are lower than those found in SSA countries. The burden of care is increasingly being pushed onto individuals and families, leading to a number of resurgent public health crises. The rapid growth of STDs (considered in more detail in later chapters) as well as TB, diseases that interact in important ways with the HIV/AIDS epidemics, indicates the challenges that China's healthcare system faces.

Finally, is it worth noting that China's HIV/AIDS problem is in some respects incongruous when viewed against the backdrop of remarkable progress and achievements in most areas of human development. The Chinese HDI has risen from 0.533 in 1980 to 0.772 in 2007 (UNDP, 2009). China shows significantly better scores in all areas of human development than a comparatively large developing country such as India. For example, China spent US$144 per capita on health compared to India's US$21 in 2006, or China's adult literacy rate stood at 93.3 percent, well above India's 66 percent in 2007 (ibid.). By 2002, no Chinese province remained classified as a "low human development" region (0.5 being the UN cutoff). All provinces are now considered to be in the medium or high human development groups. But a large range exists, from about 0.9 in Shanghai to 0.6 in Tibet (UN Country Team China, 2004: 3). This compared favorably with other developed countries, placing Shanghai alongside countries such as Italy, Israel, Greece, and Singapore. Tibet's HDI, by comparison, placed it alongside countries such as Namibia, India, Botswana, Vanuatu, and Cambodia (UNDP, 2004b: 139).

Do aspects of the development process itself, however, actually contribute toward the expansion of the HIV/AIDS epidemic in China's case? With economic and social development, various pressures emerge that appear to facilitate the epidemics' expansion, including large-scale rural to urban migration, the feminization of migration, privatization and reduction in health provision to marginalized groups, and increased income inequality, among other things. What this shows is that HIV/AIDS epidemics can also take root and expand in some of the most successful developing regions. While progress toward many of the MDGs may be boosted by strong economic performance and rapid development, the economic and social changes such development brings may itself also promote HIV/AIDS epidemics.

3 Inequality and HIV/AIDS epidemics

Introduction

> Although many who study the dynamics of infectious disease will concede that, in some sense, disease emergence is a socially produced phenomenon, few have examined the contribution of specific social inequalities. Yet such inequalities have powerfully sculpted not only the distribution of infectious diseases but also the course of health outcomes among the afflicted.
>
> (Farmer, 1999: 5)

This chapter further looks at whether a better understanding of certain social inequalities, particularly income and, to a lesser extent, gender inequalities, may help explain China's rapidly growing and evolving HIV/AIDS epidemic. The second chapter framed China's HIV/AIDS epidemic within the development process it is experiencing. This was done so as to provide background beyond that given in many biomedical descriptions of HIV/AIDS epidemics. As noted, these focus mainly on prevalence and incidence rates among different population groups. Moving now to a more specific area, we look to shed more light, in this and future chapters, on how certain inequalities may play a role in the evolving HIV/AIDS epidemic in China. We believe such inequalities are particularly important. This insight builds from a range of studies, spanning a variety of disciplines and using different methods, which argue that social and economic inequalities have a strong impact on population health (Farmer, 1999; Gandy and Zumla, 2002; Wilkinson, 2005). Income inequality, moreover, has been found to have a particularly strong association with health, in both the developed and developing world (Pei and Rodriguez, 2006: 1069; Wilkinson and Pickett, 2006). Additionally, it is of importance to note that a growing body of quite recent research also finds a very strong empirical association between HIV/AIDS prevalence and income inequality (Holtgrave and Crosby, 2003; Drain et al., 2004; Nepal, 2007; Talbott, 2007).[1] Other studies, using different methods, also make very similar arguments (Barnett and Whiteside, 2006; Craddock, 2004; Schoepf, 2004).

Given that a strong international association has been established between income inequality and HIV/AIDS, this raises the question of whether China has a similar type of relationships and whether the unprecedented increases in income inequality in China been important in driving China's HIV/AIDS epidemic. This chapter, as well as building on the work of a number of so-called ecologic studies, also looks to empirically investigate the relationship between income and gender inequality and HIV/AIDS prevalence in China. By focusing on inequalities, this chapter also introduces themes that are returned to in subsequent chapters. The development of commercial sex work (CSW) is arguably closely interwoven with the nature of China's uneven development process, as are the processes of migration.

The chapter is organized as follows. First, the trends in income inequality are reviewed and the evidence on the link between income inequality, health, and HIV/AIDS explored. Second, working toward a method for investigating China's HIV/AIDS/inequality relationship, the evidence and methodology from "ecologic" studies on income inequalities and HIV/AIDS prevalence is explained. Much evidence, at the population level, now suggests a strong association between the two. We then consider some of the causal mechanisms linking inequality to HIV/AIDS epidemics. Third, a method for further exploring this relationship in China is devised. A regional breakdown of HIV/AIDS infections is also analyzed in comparison to a variety of human development indicators with a view to better understand the HIV/AIDS inequality relationship in China. Following this description, some empirical tests are carried out, building on established methods, to see if any similar patterns can be found in China. As it happens, income inequality, as measured by rural/urban differences, is by far the most robust and strongest predictor of HIV/AIDS prevalence in China's regions. These findings are somewhat similar to others already established in cross-national ecologic studies. The conclusion discusses the relevance of the income inequality and HIV/AIDS relationship in China.

Inequality: the relationship with health

Before considering in more detail the evidence on the relationship between HIV/AIDS and income inequality, it is worth briefly noting that global trends in income distribution are worrisome. The World Bank's World Development Report for 2006 marked a milestone in the focus of the its research. For the first time, issues of equity were mainstreamed. The Asian Development Bank (ADB) followed suit and produced a similar report in 2007, focusing on Asian inequality. Numerous other academic articles in the disciplines of economics and international development have also focused on this subject (Wade, 2004). Their conclusions, on the whole, are quite negative: "there is a growing sense that the impression of stable, unchanging income inequality may well be misleading" (World Bank, 2006: 45). While it is difficult to obtain data and measuring inequality across time and countries, data for 73 countries in the past two decades showed that 53 countries, encompassing 80 percent of the world's population, saw increases in domestic inequality. Only 4 percent have experienced decreases (UNDP, 2005: 55).

While Asia's developing economies continue to grow at some of the fastest rates in the world, the concern today is the poor are being bypassed by growth (ADB, 2007: 87). As the World Bank note:

> In general, the recent evidence in East Asia suggests that inequality has risen faster in the second round of high growth Asian economies – such as China and Vietnam – than had been observed in the first round – Hong Kong (China), Republic of Korea, Malaysia, Singapore, and Taiwan (China).
>
> (2006: 45)

Indeed, relative inequality between the early 1990s to the early 2000s increased in many Asian countries. Gini coefficients[2] for both incomes and expenditures increased in 15 out of 21 ADB member countries. Very large increases took place in Bangladesh, Cambodia, China, Lao PDR, Nepal, and Sri Lanka. At an aggregate level in Asia, the share of income of the poorest 25 percent of the population fell from 7.3 percent in 1990 to 4.5 percent in 2004. By contrast, in sub-Saharan Africa, the share of income of the bottom 25 percent remained the same at 3.4 percent (ADB, 2007).

Inequality in China

In China's case, the Gini coefficient has risen precipitously. In 1981, China was an egalitarian society. The Gini coefficient was 28.8 according to the World Bank (1997: 7). Its level of inequality was similar to that of Finland, the Netherlands, Poland, and Romania. By 1996, China's income inequality had risen to average levels by international standards. In 1995, it was 38.8, "lower than in most Latin American, African, and East Asian countries and similar to that in the United States, but higher than in most transition economies in Eastern Europe and many high-income countries in Western Europe" (World Bank, 1997: 7). The increase in China's Gini coefficient during the 1990s was by far the largest of all countries for which comparable data were available: "such a large change is unusual" (ibid.: 3). Indeed, there is general agreement today that China's income distribution "has become much more unequal" (Naughton, 2007: 209). By 2004, it had reached around 47, approaching figures typically associated with Latin America (ADB, 2007: 87). As well as having the highest Gini coefficient in Asia, spending by the wealthiest 20 percent in China compared to the bottom quintile is increasing fastest than any other Asian country (ADB, 2007).

The exact reasons for growing inequality remain controversial and cannot be discussed at length here. Nonetheless, China's rural/urban income gap historically has been particularly large by international standards. Internationally, urban incomes are rarely more than twice rural incomes. Indeed, in most countries, rural incomes are at least two-thirds or more of urban incomes. In China, however, rural incomes were only 40 percent of urban incomes in 1995, down from a peak of 59 percent in 1983. These figures, moreover, did not take into account differential increases in cost of living (World Bank, 1997: 15). Only limited international comparative data on urban/rural income inequality exist. The International Labor Organization only publishes the ratio between per capita income from nonfarm occupations and income from farming. Although this ratio is not entirely identical to urban/rural income inequality, it is close. In the 1990s, among eight countries whose ratio exceeded 2:1 were Kenya (2.86:1), Botswana (3.02:1), South Africa (3.14:1), Zimbabwe (3.57:1), and Malawi (4.33:1, 1990) – all with serious generalized HIV/AIDS epidemics (UNDP/CDRF, 2005: 27). There may be a special relationship between HIV/AIDS and rural/urban income differences. This is examined in later sections.

Income inequality and HIV/AIDS

Growing inequality is of direct relevance to these countries' overall health and also the trajectory of their HIV/AIDS epidemics, as will be shown. One of the most interesting and remarkable insights of modern public health and social epidemiology is the discovery of the association between population health and income inequality. It has been observed that the international relationship between per capita income and life expectancy grows progressively weaker across countries as they get richer and "disappears altogether among the wealthiest countries" (Wilkinson and Pickett, 2006: 1774). In wealthy nations, income inequalities become far better at explaining health. It is argued in these countries that the social gradient in health within countries is primarily a gradient in relative income, or social status, rather than a reflection of absolute material living standards. Even in poorer countries, such as China, there is evidence that income inequality affects individual health even after controlling for other individual factors such as income. Pei and Rodriguez (2006) test the relationship between self-reported health and income inequality (using the Gini coefficient) from data of nine provinces in 1991, 1993, and 1997. Their results show an increased risk of about 10–15 percent on average for fair or poor health for people living in provinces with greater income inequalities compared with provinces with modest income inequalities. Furthermore, the effect of income inequality on health intensified from 1991 to 1997 as inequalities grew. Having established such links, the following section will consider evidence of a relationship between HIV/AIDS and income inequality and other social and economic indicators with a view to better understanding the inequality/HIV/AIDS relationship in China.

Income distribution and changes in income distribution have been identified by a number of different researchers using different methods as being of great importance in understanding HIV/AIDS epidemics (see Barnett and Whiteside, 2006; Farmer, 1999; as well as a range of "ecologic" studies such as Drain *et al.*, 2004; Halperin and Bailey, 1999; Talbott, 2007). Indeed, a brief consideration of cross sectional evidence on adult HIV/AIDS prevalence and the Gini coefficient vividly illustrates this phenomenon. Figure 3.1 is a sample of 57 countries, including China, and all other countries with human development indexes (HDIs) lower than China's with available data. A statistically significant

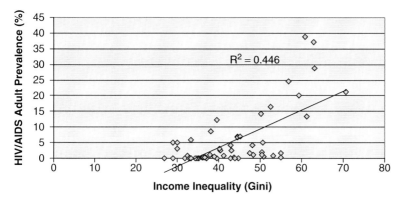

Figure 3.1 HIV prevalence and income distribution.

Source: Based on data reported in the UNDP *Human Development Report*, 2005.

relationship exists between the HIV/AIDS prevalence and income inequality in this sample, a finding that is repeated in numerous other studies.

To explore the relationship between HIV/AIDS and inequality, an understanding of recent research in this area is useful. "Ecologic" studies arguably provide some of the most important evidence for the relationship between income inequality and HIV/AIDS epidemics. Their purpose, in large part, is to better understand the influence of societal characteristics on HIV transmission. By doing so, it is argued that insights on population-level interventions may be found. Recent studies also provide insights into methods of analysis that could be used to investigate the relationship of HIV/AIDS with inequality and other economic and sociocultural factors in China. The ecologic literature is reviewed below before applying some of the methods to China's province level data in the next section.

Ecologic studies provide statistical analyses of the interrelationships between HIV/AIDS and a variety of explanatory variables, often using large international data sets. Such studies, although not all, often begin by looking for statistical associations between the dependent variable (HIV prevalence) and a range of possible explanatory variables. From initial bivariate analysis, multivariate models are specified. Such studies, while having limitations, have proved quite powerful. Drain *et al.* (2004), for example, identified male circumcision as being associated with lower HIV prevalence from an ecologic study. Subsequent clinical trials in Uganda and Kenya confirmed that male circumcision does indeed appear to reduce the chances of HIV infection. Ecologic analyses are therefore useful, as they help point toward the economic and social determinants of HIV/AIDS epidemics within population groups (as opposed to the individual). Evidence of specific associations and even causality between different variables, when confirmed by a number of studies, provides help in thinking about the economic and social determinants of HIV/AIDS epidemics. Indeed, such ecologic studies now find, quite consistently, that a small number of variables are associated with adult HIV prevalence, both at national and even at the subnational level.

Table 3.1 summarizes some of the findings of relevant studies. Over (1998), in an early study, looks at urban population groups, and examines the influence of 13 variables for 72 countries. The age of the epidemic, gross national product (GNP) per capita, and Gini index were most strongly correlated with HIV prevalence (after adjusting for other variables). Over also found a significant relationship with education differences between sexes. Drain *et al.* (2004), in a widely cited research, undertake regression analyses for 122 developing countries using 81 different socioeconomic and developmental variables. Only four variables that had enough data gathered to make meaningful comparisons were significant in predicting HIV/AIDS levels in both linear and multiple regressions. These variables included the Gini coefficient, the percentage of a country's population who are of the Muslim faith, and the percentage of a country's young adult (age 15–24 years) and women who are illiterate. Other variables that were found to be significantly correlated with HIV/AIDS prevalence levels were either measuring a result of high HIV prevalence, such as life expectancy, or represented sexual behavior variables for which limited data were available (Talbott, 2007: 2).

Talbott (2007), using a different specification but building upon insights of earlier studies (by incorporating income and gender inequality and education), refutes some of the findings made by Drain *et al.* (2004), questioning their method, in particular the weighting of countries by population. Talbott instead carries out cross-country linear and multiple regressions using newly gathered data from UNAIDS but this time with unweighted populations, also including the number of female commercial sex workers (CSWs) as a percentage of the female adult population as an explanatory variable and using a different sample (including both developed and developing countries). Talbott argues that the previous findings of Drain *et al.* (2004) should be treated with care, as:

> In effect, they make data from China 400 times more weighted in their analysis than that from small population Botswana, an error that leads to many false conclusions. There is no reason to think that China's reported data is any more accurate than Botswana's and in trying to uncover possible government and social action that could correlate with HIV it makes no sense to weight one country's experiences or attempts more highly than another. More populous countries do not necessarily conduct more or better testing of their CSW populations.
>
> (2007: 2)

Talbott's work, it should be noted, even when incorporating CSW, does actually confirm some of the findings of earlier studies. In particular, it finds that female illiteracy levels, gender illiteracy differences, and income inequality within countries are significantly and positively correlated with HIV/AIDS prevalence. CSW, moreover, is robustly positively correlated with countrywide HIV/AIDS prevalence levels. When CSW is incorporated in the model, the

Table 3.1 Summary of some ecological studies on HIV/AIDS, including explanatory variables included and samples used

Study	Sample	Year	Country sample	Data source	Income inequality (significant – yes/no)	Gender inequality (significant – yes/no)	Some other explanatory variables investigated (significant – yes/no)
Drain et al. (2004)	122 Countries	2000	Low HDI	UNAIDS, UNDP	Yes	Yes	Examine 81 different socioeconomic/development variables
Talbott (2007)	77 Countries		Both low and high	UNAIDS, UNDP	Yes (Gini)	Yes (significant)	Muslim faith, female/male illiteracy difference
Nepal (2007)	Developed and developing countries	2000	Both low and high	UNAIDS, UNDP	Yes (Gini)	Yes (significant)	Governance (Yes)
Over (1998)	72 Countries	1997	Developing countries	US Census Bureau	Yes (Gini)		13 Variables
Holtgrave and Crosby (2003)	The United States	1999	The United States	Federal surveillance documents	Yes (richest/poorest deciles)	Not tested	Social capital, poverty
Moran and Jordaan (2007)	Russian regions	2002	Russia		No	Not tested	Per capita wealth, population mobility income inequality, drug use, healthcare, age of epidemic
This study	30 Chinese provinces	2005	China – low and medium HDI	UNAIDS, China Ministry of Health, China Development Research Foundation/UNDP	Yes (significant)	Yes (significant)	Education, rural/urban income gap, female illiteracy

Sources: Over (1998); Holtgrave and Crosby (2003); Drain et al. (2004); Moran and Jordaan (2007); Nepal (2007); Talbott (2007).

finding, at least at the population level, that the Muslim faith/circumcision reduces HIV prevalence is rejected. It is argued that the Muslim faith reduces HIV prevalence via its influence in reducing the size of the commercial sex industry.

Nepal (2007) undertakes further cross-country regression analysis, building on previous studies but looking at both adult HIV prevalence as well as the percentage of women among adults living with HIV/AIDS, thus specifically addressing the feminization of HIV/AIDS. Nepal includes both the developed and developing countries in the sample. The estimates on HIV/AIDS prevalence provided by UNAIDS are the "best ever" (Nepal, 2007: 5). Nepal finds in preliminary analysis a significant correlation with wealth, economic equity, gender equity, and good governance. Further multivariate linear regression analysis, when accounting for collinearity among explanatory variables, identified economic and gender equity in particular as the two most important factors linked with the HIV/AIDS epidemic. Thus gender equity, when measured using the gender-related development index, emerged as a "consistently significant" determinant of the overall epidemic and the female epidemic as well (ibid.: 1). Thus it is argued that good governance and wealth, while being important, are not key factors, instead economic and gender equity were found to be much more important factors in determining the overall level of feminization of the HIV/AIDS pandemic: "gender equity appears to be a consistently significant correlate of both the HIV/AIDS pandemic and its female face" (ibid.: 4). In terms of policy, promoting equity, and particularly gender equity, should be a primary concern.

Two national-level ecologic studies, looking at the national determinants of HIV/AIDS epidemics, also provide some insights into the economic and social determinants of HIV/AIDS epidemics. Holtgrave and Crosby (2003) investigated the relationship between social capital[3] and HIV/AIDS and other sexually transmitted infections in the United States. They complement other work that has related social capital to a number of important public health variables. As poverty and income inequality are closely related to, and thought to be, important factors explaining the observed strength of social capital and health outcomes, they also consider poverty and inequality. They obtain state-level data and examine the relationship between poverty, income inequality, and social capital and four sexually transmitted diseases (Holtgrave and Crosby, 2003: 62). They find that social capital was the only significant predictor for gonorrhea and syphilis. The variance explained by social capital for these two, moreover, was quite large (45 and 34.9 percent, respectively). For AIDS case rates, however, both social capital and income inequality were significantly correlated. The greater the social capital the lower the AIDS case rate, and the more income inequality the higher the AIDS case rate (ibid.: 63).

Finally, Moran and Jordaan (2007) look at Russia and identify four main factors influencing HIV prevalence in Russian regions. These factors all consist of elements that represent the processes of economic and social development. They find urbanization, mobility, crime, and income growth are important factors. They do not, unfortunately, explicitly test for inequalities, which is unusual given the strong associations found in previous studies. The strong statistical relationships they do uncover, however, still note the strong impact of social and economic development patterns on the trajectory of the epidemic. They argue that economic and social forces cannot be ignored in constructing policy.

Ecologic studies on HIV/AIDS prevalence are increasing in number. They point toward a number of explanatory variables that could be used to further investigate population-level HIV/AIDS prevalence. Income and gender inequality, however, do emerge consistently throughout many of these studies as strong predictors of HIV/AIDS prevalence [covering different time periods and samples (Table 3.1)]. These studies, moreover, also suggest several possible methods that could be used. Finally, for the most part, international cross sections are used. Based on the insights of these studies, we now consider the relationship between HIV/AIDS, inequality, and gender in China, at the national and subnational level, in more detail.

How and why does income inequality cause HIV/AIDS epidemics?

Inferring causality in ecologic studies remains problematic owing to the inherent difficulties of such estimation procedures. Holtgrave and Crosby (2003) note that their analysis does not allow them to infer definitive causal associations. Moran and Jordaan (2007) acknowledge that their variables are measured at a high level of aggregation and represent diverse processes within regions. Urbanization, for example, is likely to represent the composite effect of many factors (ibid.: 8). Within the vast literature on the health/inequality relationship in developed countries, moreover, much debate exists as to what exactly income inequality really reflects (Wilkinson and Pickett, 2006). Thus, even though a relationship between certain variables may be established, the exact nature and mechanisms of causal processes still remain rather vague. By highlighting certain aspects of causal mechanisms in which recent research has brought to the fore, we may begin to establish modes of HIV/AIDS transmission, moving beyond the risky behavior of individuals.

It is clear that income inequality itself is closely associated with numerous other factors that may individually, or working together, predispose populations to high risk. Changes in income distribution, for example, may occur as a result of the overall development process. As Kuznets (1955) hypothesized, an inverted U-shape relationship may exist between inequality and income. Growing inequality occurs in early stages of growth because differences between rural and urban areas become more pronounced as industrialization occurs. It is only as the new urban migrant classes become assimilated to the working and middle classes and start to participate politically, that income distributions again become more even. Inequality, therefore, in this interpretation, is also intimately related to the entire development process – industrialization, urbanization, large-scale migration, evolving state–society relationships, governance, social and political change, and so on. As we will see in Chapter 5, an understanding of the rural/urban migration, and the creation of a class of disenfranchised migrant workers predisposed to high-risk behavior, is integral to this development process and also central to understanding HIV/AIDS in China. Over 100 million migrants, with limited access to healthcare, lower levels of education and salaries, habitual insecurity, and psychosocial stress, are now part of the social landscape in China. Moreover, the feminization of migration (Gaetano and Jacka, 2004) has contributed to a boom in the commercial sex industry driven by extremely favorable demand. Other factors contributing to the expansion of the commercial sex industry include the growth of urban male middle class, and on the supply side conditions include intensification of gender inequalities in health and education, lack of poverty reduction in rural areas, weak legal systems, and deeply corrupt local governments (Pan, 1999).

While migration is a part of the larger picture of HIV/AIDS transmission across the general population, others point to the relationship between income inequality and poverty. Other things being equal, higher income inequality is likely to exacerbate poverty. For any given amount of growth, poverty reduction will be reduced in unequal societies. Some argue that "AIDS has been exacerbated by deepening poverty experienced by the majority of African countries over the past 20 years" (Craddock, 2004: 5). Poverty may in turn be related to poor health, untreated sexually transmitted diseases, lower levels of nutritional intake, and in turn greater susceptibility (Stillwaggon, 2006). Poverty reduction has been dramatic in China but highly uneven. From 1981 to 2001, the number of people living in poverty fell from 53 to 8 percent – a massive reduction (Ravallion and Chen, 2004: 16). About half of the entire decline, however, took place in the first few years of the 1980s. Poverty reduction stalled in the late 1980s and early 1990s recovered in the mid-1990s but then stagnated again later in the decade (ibid.). Other household data surveys find that

> after initially rising, the absolute living standards of the poor declined considerably from 1995 to 1999, so that they approach income levels of 1987. Moreover, as much as half of all households were not unambiguously better off in 1999 than in 1987: *the rising tide did not lift all boats.*
>
> (Benjamin, Brandt and Giles, 2005: 771)

Others argue that a skewed income distribution may impact on the HIV/AIDS epidemic via its effect on social capital and cohesion. Barnett and Whiteside (2006: 92) note that: "The existence of a risk environment reflects the breakdown of social order and cohesion." Closely related to social cohesion are issues of sexual mixing patterns:

> There appears to be some relationship between the degree of order in a society and the variability of patterns of sexual mixing groups. In times of rapid change and even more in times of political uncertainty or disruption, these mixing patterns, are more likely to become dissassortive.
>
> (Quoted in Barnett and Whiteside, 2006: 88)

In periods of fast economic change, where livelihoods are uncertain either because of growth or decline in people's livelihood strategies may facilitate rapid change of sexual partners within and between diverse groups (ibid.: 92).

Finally, even if we establish the reasons why income inequality may cause HIV/AIDS epidemics, it must be recognized that different types and patterns of inequality exist, and these are not fully captured in a metric such as the Gini coefficient. The relationship between poverty and inequality is "powerful but nuanced":

> In the most affected countries (prevalence over 20% – all in southern Africa), the richest 10% of the population have revenues that are almost 70 times those of the poorest 10% of the population. This compares with much lower disparities or ratios of between 20 and 27 in countries with lower prevalence. On average, one-third of the population in the most-affected countries with high income disparity lives on less than US$1 per day – a large proportion, given their relatively high gross domestic product.
>
> (UNAIDS, 2006a: 84)

In this analysis, countries most affected by HIV/AIDS are not necessarily the poorest, rather countries with especially large gaps between the very poorest and richest.

Applying an ecologic approach

To further explore the relationship between HIV/AIDS prevalence and economic and social development variables, a number of candidates present themselves (Table 3.1). To recap, the Gini coefficient, the percentage of a country's young adult population who are Muslims, the percentage of country's young adult and women who are illiterate, the difference between the young female and male illiteracy rates, and the size of CSW are among just some of the variables that have been found to be significant predictors in explaining HIV/AIDS prevalence at the population level (see Table 3.1). Talbott (2007: 4), for example, finds that approximately 45 percent of the variance in HIV could be explained in his model. Examination of the studies presented in Table 3.1, however, suggests that two variables appear to emerge most consistently as being strongly associated with HIV/AIDS prevalence. These are related to income and gender inequality.

This section briefly explores and tests this empirical relationship for China, using a comparative as well as ecologic approach. First, we identify high-prevalence provinces (with greater than 1 percent of China's total HIV/AIDS infections) and these are scrutinized for possible relationships between human development indicators and HIV/AIDS prevalence (Table 3.2). This is the high-prevalence sample. Second, the sample is expanded (to include 30 as opposed to 15 of China's provinces, excluding the outlier of Tibet), and multivariate regression analysis is used to explore possible statistical relationships for the full sample. The more parsimonious model of Nepal (2007) is used to test both the full and reduced sample. Following Drain *et al.* (2004) and Holtgrave and Crosby (2003), a variety of different bivariate associations between HIV/AIDS prevalence and social and economic development indicators are also examined. Some

Table 3.2 Human development and HIV/AIDS infections in China

Region	Share of total cumulative HIV infections in China end of 2005 (%)	Total HDI	HDI rank	Population	Urban per capita GDP	Rural per capita GDP	Urban/ rural	Poverty (% beneath poverty line)	Illiteracy rate	Male illiteracy (%)	Female illiteracy (%)	Illiterate females/ males	Primary school enrollments	High school enrollments	University and college
China		0.75						3.2	10.9	6.1	15.9	2.6	98.7	55.4	28.6
Shanghai	1.1	0.91	1	17.11	49,946	22,353	2.2	0.7	5.88	2.14	9.6	4.5	99.6	91.5	57.4
Beijing	1.8	0.88	2	14.56	37,031	14,942	2.5		4.61	1.96	7.41	3.8	99.6	87.6	68.3
Tianjin		0.85	3	10.11	31,437	13,919	2.3	6.7	6.36	2.97	9.62	3.2	99.6	79.3	51.9
Guangdong	8.3	0.81	6	79.54	24,683	8,084	3.1	0.7	7.55	3.06	12	3.9	99.4	47.8	25.9
Total high HDI	11.2	0.81	Averages	121.32	35,774.3	14,824.5	2.5		6.1	2.5	9.7	3.9	99.6	76.6	50.9
Xinjiang	8.3	0.76	14	19.34	18,221	5,350	3.4	6.1	6.94	5.32	8.62	1.6	96.2	49.8	18.2
Hubei	2.0	0.76	15	60.02	14,732	5,164	2.9	5.6	11.83	5.77	17.99	3.1	99.2	58.5	37.9
Shanxi	1.0	0.75	16	33.14	13,214	4,337	3.0	7.1	5.79	3.34	8.32	2.5	99.3	71.4	26.3
Hunan	1.9	0.75	17	66.63	14,279	4,713	3.0	3.6	8.47	4.51	12.67	2.8	98.2	60.6	32.2
Chongqing	1.3	0.75	18	31.3	14,024	3,837	3.7	4.0	8.4	4.42	12.4	2.8	95.4	59.3	39.5
Total medium HDI	14.5		Averages	210.43	14,894.0	4,680.2	3.2		8.3	4.7	12.0	2.6	97.7	59.9	30.8
Henan	21.4	0.74	19	96.67	15,774	5,092	3.1	8.3	9.21	5.13	13.37	2.6	99.2	43.2	14.1
Guangxi	12.2	0.73	22	48.57	12,581	3,385	3.7	3.0	8.85	4.28	13.72	3.2	98.1	41.8	14.6
Sichuan	4.5	0.73	24	87	12,859	4,072	3.2	4.7	11.73	7.06	16.42	2.3	95.8	55	32.1
Anhui	2.7	0.73	25	64.1	12,792	4,015	3.2	2.9	13.67	7.76	19.72	2.5	99.3	59	21.3
Yunnan	26.0	0.66	29	43.76	14,012	3,111	4.5	3.7	21.5	13.84	29.81	2.2	98	35.8	13.3
Guizhou	2.1	0.64	30	38.7	8,573	2,042	4.2	5.0	19.68	11.97	27.72	2.3	97	39.5	15.3
Total low HDI	67.3		Averages	378.8	12,765.2	3,619.5	3.6		15.1	9.0	21.5	2.5	97.9	45.7	18.5

Source: China Human Development Report, 2005.

alternative models are also specified and tested to examine the robustness of income inequality.

Data and sources

Province-level data on HIV/AIDS prevalence have been estimated by China's Ministry of Health (based on data collected from sentinel surveillance sites by local and central disease control centers) and is reported by China UNAIDS as well as the Ministry of Health. In recent years, as more surveillance sites representing lower risk populations have been included, downward revisions have been made. This analysis uses the more recent estimates, as reported by Lu *et al.* (2006). These estimates are given in terms of total infections estimated within certain bounds. They are, therefore, not specific. From these bounds, mid points are taken and province-wide prevalence is estimated using population figures from the *China Statistical Yearbook*. The results are also cross-checked against earlier estimates of adult prevalence to check for consistency of results. Earlier estimates are expressed in prevalence per 10,000 people (see Qian, Vermund and Wang, 2005).

All other human, economic, and social development variables are taken from the *China Human Development Report 2005*. As no Gini coefficients are available at the provincial level, income inequality is calculated using urban/rural income. Income inequality and distribution can, of course, be captured in numerous ways. Although the Gini coefficient is a common method of estimating inequality (calculated from the Lorenz curve), this single aggregate figure can capture a wide variety of different income distributions. Two identical Gini coefficients, for example, may hide very different income distributions. Using the rural/urban income gap may highlight one important element of Chinese inequality, as it has been suggested that rural/urban differences are central to understanding Chinese inequality (World Bank, 1997). As noted, large rural/urban income gaps have been found in some of the highest prevalence countries of Africa. On the other hand, some recent studies also show that intraregional inequalities are of more importance to Chinese inequality than previously recognized (Benjamin, Brandt and Giles, 2005). Thus using rural/urban differences may not fully capture the nature of income inequality in China. Measurements of female illiteracy and the male/female illiteracy differences are also constructed. Poverty rates, various measures of educational attainment (university, high school, and primary enrollment), the extent of industrialization, unemployment, rural and urban HDIs, per capita gross domestic product (GDP), and medical care are other variables that are also investigated.

Data description and analysis

Table 3.2 provides summary details of some human development indicators for provinces that are recorded as having over 1 percent of national total of HIV infections as reported by China UNAIDS for the end of 2005. This table provides information on 15 of the 30 most affected provinces in China. It is worth briefly examining the regional HIV/AIDS situation to gain an overview and insight into the possible relationships between HIV/AIDS prevalence and human and social development indicators.

First, it is evident that, in general, the regions with lower levels of human development, even when accounting for their larger populations, have relatively more infections than other regions. Thus Henan, Jiangxi, Guangxi, Sichuan, Anhui, Yunnan, and Guizhou, which for the purposes of this table are recorded as low-HDI provinces (less than 0.75), had 67 percent of all recorded HIV infections in China by the end of 2005. Yunnan, Henan, and Guangxi had the most infections in these provinces. In the provinces with a medium-HDI score (for the purpose of this exercise with indicators ranging from 0.75 to 0.8, including Xinjiang, Hubei, Shanxi, Hunan, and Chongqing), the cumulative number of infections reached 14.5 percent of China's total population. For the provinces with higher HDI scores (Shanghai, Beijing, Tianjin, and Guangdong), the share of the national total HIV infections stood at 11.2 percent.

Second, it is evident that there are wide disparities within provinces between rural and urban areas and that these disparities vary between high- and low-HDI regions. In the low-HDI regions, for example, the average urban per capita income was 12,765 RMB but only 3,619 RMB in rural areas, thus 3.6 times less than the urban level. In the medium human development regions, urban per capita incomes were slightly higher (14,894 RMB) as were rural (4,680 RMB). The difference between rural and urban was now close to the national average (at 3.2 times). In the high human development regions, incomes were significantly higher (urban per capita incomes 35,774 RMB and rural 14,824 RMB) and the relative income difference between rural and urban areas is also less (urban incomes were 2.5 times those of rural).

Third, it is noticeable that in terms of illiteracy, the low human development regions fared particularly badly. The average for the region saw 20 percent illiteracy among females and 9 percent for males. The female illiteracy rate falls to 12 percent in medium-HDI regions and almost 10 percent in developed regions. The male illiteracy rate falls from 9 to 4.7 to 2.5 as we move from low to high human development regions. Interestingly, however, the ratio of male to female illiterates deteriorates as we make this move. Nevertheless, other studies suggest that female illiteracy is of great significance for the understanding of HIV epidemics. The low levels of literacy more generally reflect gender discrimination and the lack of empowerment females may experience in these regions.

A comparison of China's regional HIV prevalence and human development indicators reveals some insights into the inequality/HIV relationship. It would appear, among other things, that regions with greater income inequality and lower female literacy have higher rates of infection. Does this apparent relationship hold when undertaking a more formal statistical analysis?

Multivariate regression analysis

Following Nepal (2007), we first look to estimate a simple model that includes only our measure of inequality and female education as measured by the female

Table 3.3 Provincial HIV/AIDS prevalence regressed on income inequality and female illiteracy

HIV prevalence	Coefficient	Standard error	t	P > t
Rural/urban gap	8.76	3.16	2.77	0.01
Female illiteracy	− 0.29	0.26	− 1.11	0.28

Note: 30 observations, $F(2, 27) = 3.97$, probability $> F = 0.03$, adjusted R^2 0.17.

illiteracy rate (Table 3.3). We use the full sample. This model has the advantage of parsimony, which is important given our relatively small sample, as well as strong intuitive appeal and sound theoretical backing. It has the disadvantage, however, of a degree of collinearity among the explanatory variables.

Table 3.3, however, shows that although the estimation is statistically significant ($F = 3.97$) and that income inequality is significant at the 5 percent level, the overall fit is by no means as close as the international cross section presented earlier (Figure 3.1). Having this said, it is not far from that found for the United States (partial R^2 approaching 0.1 for income inequality). Female education, on the other hand, is insignificant and has a coefficient contrary to that found in previous studies. As noted, however, care in interpreting the coefficients on these variables is needed given the quite strong correlation between the rural/urban income difference and female illiteracy (with an adjusted R^2 of 0.29 and significance at the 1 percent level). The rural/urban gap, as noted, is highly related to female illiteracy – the greater the disparity between rural and urban regions the higher the female illiteracy rate. This will inflate the variances of our estimators and make them unreliable (although the overall regression findings will not be affected).

In a second estimation, we use the restricted sample, as reported in Table 3.2. It may be more sensible to only consider provinces in which the virus constitutes at least 1 percent of China's total infections. HIV/AIDS epidemics are still very much in their infancy in many provinces. Attempting to ascertain the impact of economic and social determinants in these provinces may, therefore, have limited meaning. On the other hand, in regions in which the epidemic is more established, we may be better able to gauge the influence of social and economic factors. Using this sample, similar results are found, although the degree of association between the two explanatory variables becomes even higher (R^2 over 0.5).

While the coefficient on this variable on female illiteracy is insignificant, it is also worth noting some interesting properties of the observations on female illiteracy. It is noticeable that even in high-HDI regions (Table 3.2), high levels of female illiteracy, and particularly relative levels of illiteracy (female illiteracy/male illiteracy), exist. This interesting result may reflect the particular method of data collection, or alternatively may actually be an accurate representation of relatively high levels of female illiteracy in developed regions of China. In any case, the relative gender imbalances in education, as reflected in illiteracy rates, are of interest.

Following the procedures of previous ecologic studies such as, Drain *et al.* (2004), we test the robustness of the income inequality variable to a number of different specifications drawing from over 15 other explanatory variables using our full and restricted sample. Our income inequality explanatory variable holds up strongly and is particularly robust to the inclusion of new variables. These results suggest income inequality, as measured by the rural/urban income difference, is a good predictor of HIV/AIDS prevalence in China.

More on gender

As we have noted in the previous chapter, the global HIV/AIDS epidemic is becoming increasingly feminized. Consequently, the feminization of the epidemic in China also cannot be ignored. Globally, progress toward gender equality in education has been slow, and this has important implications of the global HIV epidemic. According to the UN China office's recent evaluation of progress toward the Millennium Development Goals (MDGs), China may well be offtrack to meet the gender equality goal. This is reflected in both primary enrollment rates and also secondary education. According to the Ministry of Education, girl to boy ratio in primary education stood at 90 girls to 100 boys in 2002. This was up from 86 to 100 in 1990. While some progress has therefore been made, it will still not be enough to meet the 2015 MDG target of complete equality by 2015. Moreover, it goes without saying that these disparities are more pronounced in the less-developed regions of the country from which the migrant population is drawn. The level of education for both boys and girls is particularly pertinent to the spread of HIV/AIDS "because it serves as a vehicle for transforming attitudes and beliefs and entrenched social norms that perpetuate discrimination and inequality" (UNESCAP, 2005: 13). The gender difference in education and thus its relationship with HIV/AIDS is already becoming clearer within China. Li *et al.* (2004) surveyed 1,081 university students in Beijing and Nanjing of their knowledge of HIV/AIDS and found that men were more knowledgeable than women when it comes to modes of HIV transmission and treatment. Furthermore, Li *et al.* (2004: 351) also showed that there was a positive trend between years of education and knowledge of HIV. As more female university students are experiencing their sexual debut before reaching university in conjunction with unsafe sexual practices, with one study citing that less than 35 percent of both male and female students rarely or never used a condom (Ma *et al.*, 2006: 240), the gender imbalance of China's HIV/AIDS epidemic is clearly on the horizon as it spreads from subpopulation groups to the general population. Female literacy, enrollments in both primary and secondary schools, and the quality of education are vital components in preventing the spread of HIV/AIDS. However, as the epidemic becomes more generalized, the studies cited here indicate that women within the general population are more susceptible to infection due to their relative lack of education and knowledge in comparison to men. When we compare income between men and women, the vulnerability of women to HIV is further reinforced.

The linkages between gender, wage, and HIV/AIDS involve several dimensions within the Chinese context, such as migration. The issue of migration will be addressed more comprehensively in Chapter 5. Nonetheless, it would suffice to observe at this point that female to male wages are lower in China than in most European countries, as would be expected. Gender wage gaps are also smaller in South Korea (0.56), Hong Kong (0.64), Singapore (0.72), and Sri Lanka (0.75) (Maurer-Fazio, Rawski and Zhang, 1999: 67). When economic sector is controlled for, however, this wage gap does shrink. Yet, women who work in a similar sector earned 0.86 of men in 1988 but 0.75 in 1994 (ibid.). The decline in the wage gap, moreover, is statistically significant, implying that even within the same economic sectors, women's wages were falling over this period. This would suggest that the growing wage gap cannot be explained entirely by the entrance of female migrants to low-paying economic sectors. Situating the gender income inequality and the rural/urban income gap within the perspective of China's internal migration where hundreds of thousands of rural women entering the sex industry each year, with approximately 3 million sex workers in 2002 (quoted in Kaufman and Jing, 2002: 2339), substantial number of women are at risk of HIV/AIDS. To further understand China's HIV/AIDS epidemic and thus the formulation of appropriate policy measures necessitate an approach that stretches beyond an analysis of risky behavior on the part of the individual. The aspect of gender and HIV/AIDS clearly demonstrates the interlinking of social and economic factors in the transmission of HIV/AIDS.

Conclusions

If we are to concede, along with Farmer (1999) and numerous others, that disease emergence is a socially produced phenomenon, this raises the question of which specific social inequalities contribute toward the development of HIV/AIDS epidemics. This chapter looks to identify whether inequalities are also associated with more severe HIV/AIDS outbreaks in China. While income inequality has been found to be important in a number of studies, others also find that gender inequality has a strong association with HIV prevalence (Nepal, 2007; Talbott, 2007). Our results here provide some support that a similar relationship can be found in China.

Despite these interesting results, it is also important to note the limitations of ecologic studies. Attempting to infer causality from such studies, in particular, is not straightforward. Such analyses also look at population groups as a whole. They therefore do not inform us specifically about individual risk factors or causal associations. HIV prevalence in a population group, moreover, reflects the cumulated effects of risky behaviors and exposure to the virus over a number of years. Care is required in making inferences based on static cross sections about epidemic dynamics. There are also obvious issues in use of data for some of the variables used in these studies. While some data may be inaccurate, it is also true that measures of several key potential influences on the HIV/AIDS epidemic, including drug use and sexual networks, are far from complete or missing entirely. This limits what can and cannot be tested for. Finally, in this case, our sample size is limited to 30 provinces in China, which makes it rather a small sample. Smaller units of analysis warrant further investigation, not only to increase sample size but also to investigate whether income inequalities within smaller units have similar impacts. Studies on health in the developed world find the health/inequality relationship starts to breakdown when smaller units are used.

It is worth also stressing that a number of studies do not find a close association between absolute levels of income and HIV/AIDS prevalence (ibid.). We also find that there is no such association in the Chinese example looked at here. This is important for two reasons. First, all regions of China, both wealthy and poor, given similar levels of inequalities, may be equally vulnerable to HIV/AIDS. Second, growth, which has been seen by policy leaders as a panacea for so many of China's ills, may not provide any solution to the rapidly expanding HIV/AIDS epidemic. Indeed, it is quite possible that growth, when uneven, as has been the case in China, provides the perfect economic and social environment for a disease such as HIV/AIDS to thrive. Thus alternative policies, at least at the structural level of the broader economy, may be required.

In this chapter, we have summarized some of the literature on the relationship between income inequality and health and also considered some empirical evidence for China. In the next chapter, we go on to look in more detail at some of the causal mechanisms associated with an unbalanced economic development process and the emergence of an HIV/AIDS epidemic.

4   Commercial sex work

Introduction

Commercial sex work (CSW) is central to understanding both the Chinese and Asian HIV/AIDS epidemics. In the case of China, the commercial sex industry is becoming a significant mode of transmission of HIV/AIDS to the general population. In general, these have been kick-started by intravenous drug use (IDU) populations with subsequent widespread heterosexual transmission necessary for full-blown generalized epidemics to take place. In Asian countries that have experienced large-scale epidemics among the general population, heterosexual transmission via CSW has been a necessary precondition. This is partly because the sexual mixing pattern in Asia, reliant upon a class of professional sex workers, is also an efficient pattern for rapid spread of HIV as commercial sex workers (CSWs) act as a continuing reservoir of infection (Grassly *et al.*, 2003).[1] Given the far greater absolute numbers that engage in risky sexual activity, it is now predicted that heterosexual transmission will become the dominant mode of transmission in China (Wu, Rou and Cui, 2004: 10). Indeed, evidence increasingly suggests that the epidemic is already spreading swiftly from high-risk groups to the general population via sexual transmission (Zhang, 2004: 1156). According to the sentinel surveillance data available, between 1997–2002 the proportion of reported HIV cases attributed to sexual transmission doubled from 5.5 to 10.9 percent of the total number of cases according to one official estimate (Han *et al.*, 2010: ii47). Corresponding to the movement out of the predominantly male-IDU population, the infection rate of women has increased, as noted in Chapter 2. The proportion of female HIV cases rose from 15 percent in 1998 to nearly 40 percent in 2004 (State Council Aids Working Committee Office and the UN Theme Group on HIV/AIDS, 2004: 4).[2] More recent estimates suggest that about 44 percent of individuals with HIV were infected through sexual transmission (Gill, Huang and Lu, 2007: 4). Among new cases in 2005, about 50 percent were via sexual transmission, the other half being infected through IDU. In areas of Yunnan, Henan, and Xinjiang, HIV prevalence exceeds 1 percent among pregnant women and those receiving premarital HIV testing (ibid.: vi). Prevalence among Chinese sex workers has risen from only 0.02 percent in 1996 to 0.93 percent in 2004 (ibid.). Recent estimates suggest 127,000 sex workers (SWs) and their clients are living with HIV/AIDS, that is, 20 percent of the total number of infections. Partners of HIV-positive individuals and the general public make up 17 percent of the total number of estimated cases (MOH/ UNAIDS/WHO, 2005: 4).

Understanding the forces in society that promote CSW and with this the sexual transmission of disease is important to the comprehension of HIV/AIDS epidemics. This chapter explores the social and economic factors related to the underlying development process that drive the expansion of the sex industry. The first section will summarize the relatively little knowledge we have on the size and growth of CSW in China. Most evidence points to the extremely rapid development of the sex industry there. Second, historical experiences of the development of CSW in some other nations are examined, including examples from Southeast Asia. Third, building from the insights taken from the Southeast Asian experiences, several possible drivers behind CSW growth in China are explored. The conclusion points to the entrenched nature of some of these forces driving CSW in China.

CSW in China

Given the centrality of heterosexual transmission to generalized epidemics, the starting point of any study on the present and future evolution of HIV/AIDS in China is recognition of the explosive growth in the sex sector. During the Communist era, prostitution was largely eradicated as well as the epidemics of sexually transmitted diseases (STDs) that existed in pre-Communist China. This was, at the time, rightly seen as a major achievement of the newly created state. Indirect measures, such as the creation of new employment opportunities, reducing income inequalities, are likely to have been as influential as indirect intervention measures, such as closing down of brothels. As such the dramatic re-emergence in scale and sophistication of prostitution today is one of the more marked changes in Chinese society. Despite an inherent conservative approach to sexual matters in Chinese society, there appears increasing acceptance of prostitution. It has become much discussed feature of social change in China today. It is also one that holds a deep symbolism as regards the course of socialist economic development, in so far as the emergence and tolerance of CSW appears deeply antithetical to the Party's driving ideology.

As in many East Asian nations, the commercial sex sector has become increasingly large, but also complex. While the sex sector is "not recognised as an economic sector in official statistics, development plans or government budgets," most experts on the subject believe that it has become a significant economic sector in Southeast Asia (Lim, 1998: 1). Owing to its informal nature, it is difficult to know with any certainty the size of the commercial sex sectors in different nations. Based on the best available estimates of detailed country studies in Southeast Asia (Indonesia, Malaysia, the Philippines, and Thailand), it is estimated that the commercial sex industry accounted for between 2–14 percent of GDP in the 1990s (ibid.: 7). Because it is essentially an informal sector activity, typified by the ease of entry and exit, low capital costs of start-up and absence of taxation, no official economic information is gathered on the sector. Furthermore, the constant turnover of individuals taking part in the sex industry means estimates at any given point of time will underestimate the true numbers that have participated in the sex sector. Surveys in Thailand, for example, suggest that the median length of employment is about 18 months to 2 years.

How big is China's sex sector? Some surveys of female migrants found that no respondents had taken part in the sex industry, reflecting the stigma attached with such work (Gaetano and Jacka, 2004). Most women are reluctant to admit participation in the sex industry. Nonetheless, it is estimated for a number of different East Asian countries between 0.25–1.5 percent of the total female population are reportedly engaged in prostitution[3] (MAP, 2004: 37). Of the numerous estimates for SWs in China, some suggest a very significant number. Indeed, it is now widely recognized that most cities are riddled with a range of outlets for CSW. These outlets include karaoke bars, massage parlors, hotels, saunas, and beauty salons.[4] The sex sector, and accompanying entertainment industry, is undoubtedly large in China. Its growth and increasing sophistication, as with the economy as a whole, have also been rapid. Changes in consumer demand, the evolution of new technology (mobile phones, the internet, pagers), as well as changes in law-enforcement policies, are among some of the factors contributing to its development.

One estimate by Chinese police puts the number at around 4 million SWs (Gill, Chang and Palmer, 2002).[5] According to the Public Security Bureau, in 1982, there were only 12,281 arrests related to CSW. This number has risen dramatically over time. The number of arrests of SWs increased to 250,000 by 1992 and 246,000 by 1993 (Pan, 1999: 5). The number of SWs and their clients arrested in the late 1990s was around 700,000 (Zhang and Ma, 2002: 804).[6] There is, however, also uncertainty as to what the actual arrest rate is in any given year. It is a costly and time-consuming process to detain SWs, which discourages police forces. The only scientific estimate of the police arrest rate (undertaken in only one city, however) suggests it may stand in the region of only 2.5–5 percent (Pan, 1999). This suggests that during any given year in the region of 1 in 40 to 1 in 20 SWs will be arrested. On this basis, and if it is assumed that 250,000 prostitutes are arrested, the actual number of females engaging in prostitution may stand at something more like 5–10 million people. This estimate would place the share of population engaged in prostitution close to the Thai level.[7] Such a number, if in any way close to being accurate, would imply that quite a significant share of the female migrant population is engaged in CSW.[8] Other evidence of the growth of prostitution in China can be found in the spiraling cases of STDs.

The linkages between China's explosive growth in STDs infection and HIV/ AIDS will be detailed in Chapter 6. Nevertheless, a brief outline of the rise of STDs is in order to provide a sense of the size of the problem. National estimates, given the hidden and undercover nature of the sex sector, are inevitably likely to be inaccurate. Local observation, however, at the city level and below, gives a broad indication of its gargantuan scale. In a study of Dalian, a coastal city of 5 million people, it was estimated that the migrant population stood at 300,000 and an estimated 80 percent of all migrant women were reported to work in the sex industry. According to the authorities, there were 4,000 nightclubs, saunas, and KTV bars. The city has been referred to as one "gigantic sauna salon or KTV bar" (Zheng, 2004: 84). Dalian, of course, is no exception. Dongguan, located in China's southern Guangdong province, has estimated that 300,000 people were involved in CSW. They serve, among others, Hong Kong business-men who regularly travel to the mainland. Similar areas on the coast of Fujian province cater to Taiwanese businessmen who "frequent nightclubs, beauty par-lors, massage parlors, and karaoke bars that also provide sexual services" (Gill, Chang and Palmer, 2002: 4). Numerous examples and substantial evidence tes-tify to the size and growth of China's sex industry which influences the spread and transmission of HIV. Before further investigating the reasons for its develop-ment in China, it is useful to consider the experiences of other nations.

Comparative perspectives on CSW in China

The examples of Southeast Asia and even the now developed countries in earlier periods are useful in identifying the underlying factors driving CSW. It is largely forgotten, for example, during the mid-nineteenth century, Victorian Britain was a center of prostitution. The growth of prostitution in Britain, as with developing countries today, was associated with profound economic and social changes related to rapid industrialization and urbanization, as well as the increasing movement of young migrant females to work in new industries. Prostitution in Victorian Britain became so large a problem because of its association with untreatable diseases, that by the late 1840s it had become labeled as "the great social evil." The issue worked its way into literature and politics. With its increasing scale and the often fatal STDs associated with it, CSW became a major social concern. By the 1850s, a significant share of outpatients in London's main hospitals suffered from STDs (mainly syphilis but also gonor-rhea). To deal with this social problem, several controversial acts known as the Contagious Diseases Acts (1864) were passed by the government. These acts allowed women to be forcibly examined and detained if they suffered from any STD (ostensibly to protect their sexual partners, often soldiers and sailors), as well as the creation of specialized asylums for treatment.

It is of interest that the historical records of now developed countries show that at certain points during their development, CSW became more widespread and a major social issue. This suggests that economic development may itself bring cer-tain social and economic changes that in turn favor the development of CSW.

Southeast Asia

While the examples of now developed nations are instructive, in so far as they point toward the role of fundamental economic and social conditions propelling

CSW, the more contemporary examples of CSW in Southeast Asia may be more relevant to a study of China. These nations are closer geographically and culturally, have generally grown at faster rates than the now developed world, and have themselves also suffered serious HIV/AIDS epidemics related to CSW (Thailand and Cambodia in particular). They are also nations that have attracted research attention in this area. The rapid speed of economic development in Southeast Asia has also been unbalanced at times. Looking back, in Chapter 2, we discussed the rise of inequality in the Southeast Asia region, including Thailand's, where average annual growth in gross domestic product (GDP) of over 5 percent took place between 1975–2003, but it was accompanied by a rise in inequality. China's average annual growth of 8 percent has also seen increasing income inequalities and they have arguably been greater than that in the first round of late-industrializing East Asian nations.

Thailand as with China has experienced rapid but uneven economic development and a massive growth in its sex industry. It had a Gini coefficient of 43.2 in 2005 with China not too far off at 44.7 (UNDP, 2005). The income share of Thailand's richest 20 percent of the population stood at around 50 percent (China's was also 50 percent) and the poorest 20 percent held 6.1 percent of national income (as compared with China's 4.7 percent). It is a country now notorious for its sex industry as well as a severe HIV/AIDS epidemic related in large part to it. The sex industry, as in most nations, has existed for centuries, but for Thailand it is only since the 1960s and significant economic growth that the sex industry has grown quickly. The sector continued to grow throughout the 1970s, and 1980s, driven by continued economic and structural changes in the Thai economy. Today, it is in its own right a significant economic sector in Thailand. The number of CSWs, according to the Thai Ministry of Public Health, increased from 41,522 to 75,376 between 1979–1992 (Boochalaksi and Guest, 1998: 139). Other estimates for Thailand in 1993 placed the number at 200,000–300,000 prostitutes (with up to 100,000 working abroad). The sex industry has grown in the 1990s and despite a downturn after the economic recession the numbers were, according to one study, "still much higher than they were a decade ago" (Lim, 1998: 7). Indeed, such is its scale that much of the Thai population is "directly touched by prostitution" (Boochalaksi and Guest, 1998: 162). A survey between 1998–2003 recorded a 50 percent increase in the total number of sex service establishments. The number rose from 8,000 in 1998 to more than 12,200 in 2003. The growth was entirely due to the huge increase in indirect sex service establishments (UNDP, 2004a: 52).

Why has the sex industry grown so quickly in Thailand? Experts believe that the particular patterns and structure of economic development in Thailand over the last 30 years have been favorable to the growth of the sex industry (Boochalaksi and Guest, 1998: 133). Thailand has experienced rapid but uneven growth, with the southern regions (closer to the capital Bangkok) faring better than the northern rural areas. While industrialization has proceeded in urban areas, agriculture did not develop as quickly. As a result, large rural–urban differences emerged. Poverty, as in China, has become increasingly concentrated in these rural areas. In Thailand, poverty rates in the 1980s were five times greater in rural than in urban areas, as compared to only three in the 1970s (ibid.: 134). With rapid but uneven economic development, the pressures for rural–urban migration also increased. At the same time, more and more females started to migrate from rural areas. Both push and pull factors led to the feminization of migration. Economic policies led to increased opportunities for women in export-oriented industries (such as textiles). With urban opportunities increasing, employment prospects for females in rural areas reduced because of the rising productivity in agriculture (ibid.: 130). Changes in inheritance laws, allowing men to inherit land, also encouraged female migration. Thus both push and pull factors caused growing migration of females during the course of development. The pool of female migrants in urban areas thus created a large potential supply of females to the sex sector. Given the high-potential earnings, a certain share of these migrants is attracted to the sector. The relative wealth of Thai sex workers is reflected in above average remittances, which on average are about three times the average monthly wage of rural areas (ibid.: 162). As in many developing countries, young migrant females make up the majority of those working in the sex sector.

A common misperception is that sex tourism has been important to the growth of the Thai sex sector. This misperception arose as US investment and the location of armed forces meant foreign demand played a role in the early development of the industry. Areas such as Pattaya grew via demand from US servicemen taking breaks from the Vietnam War. Foreigners today, however, still constitute only a small proportion of customers in the commercial sex market (ibid.: 135). This is an important observation, as it implies internal economic change, in particular domestic demand growth for CSW and the comparatively favorable supply of females were most likely the main factors driving the commercial sex industry in Thailand. It is now generally argued that rapid economic growth created a combination of "propitious development and social and cultural factors" (ibid.: 139).

Thailand's case also illustrates how quickly HIV/AIDS can spread within the sex sector. The first sentinel surveillance survey of female CSWs in June 1989 revealed HIV prevalence of 1–5 percent in Bangkok and 12 provinces. A second survey 6 months later recorded prevalence as high as 13 percent and showed a severe epidemic was underway among SWs in areas of northern Thailand. HIV prevalence of 43 percent was being found among brothel-based sex workers in Chiang Mai (UNDP, 2004a: 9). In 1989, the median-HIV prevalence among brothel-based sex workers was 3 percent in all provinces surveyed. Only a year later, it had climbed to 9.3 percent and by June 1991, national HIV prevalence among SWs had passed the 15 percent mark (ibid.). Thus, it is possible for infections to grow rapidly in the commercial sex sector and for it to subsequently drive a heterosexual epidemic, given the right conditions.

In Indonesia, a country with an emerging HIV crisis, as in Thailand, economic transformation since the 1970s has been rapid. It grew on average at 4 percent between 1975–2003 and the primary sector decreased from 70 percent of total output to less than 50 percent (Hull, Sulistyaningsih and Jones, 1998: 29). As in the Thai case, the displacement from agriculture led to many women moving to cities for employment in "manufacturing, clerical work, sales, hotels and restaurants, and domestic service" (ibid.: 33). As development proceeded so too did migration among women, further increasing competition among the relatively less educated and employable females, thus leading to the growth of informal sector employment, including prostitution. And while poverty reduction has been impressive, many millions still live in poverty, creating a comparatively large potential pool of labor from which it can draw. Again, according to experts, it is the combination of poverty and inequality, linked with migration, that has promoted the sex industry: "It may be that wide income differentials, as well as poverty *per se*, make for prostitution, providing both customers from the better-off groups and potential prostitutes from the lower-income groups" (ibid.: 35). As in Thailand, it seems the process of economic development has contributed toward the growth of prostitution. Increased demand, moreover, is driven mainly from the urban centers. In an attempt to manage the growing industry, government authorities legalized and controlled some brothels (known as "recreation centers") with the purpose of legally taxing the establishments: "these facilities became instant revenue earners for the economically strapped city" (ibid.).

Malaysia also experienced phenomenal economic growth between 1970–1990. Economic growth and the development pattern associated with such rapid growth are also believed to have been responsible for the development of its sex sector. It is argued that the pace and nature of socioeconomic development have influenced both the supply of workers and the demand for the services of the sex sector. Once again, particular emphasis has been placed on growing income inequality: "it has not been growing poverty but the substantial income differentials that account for the expansion of the sex industry" (Nagaraj and Yahya, 1998: 72). As with China, the growth pattern is one of increasing rural–urban differentials as late industrialization has set in and changes in the employment pattern move away from agriculture toward urbanized manufacturing and service sectors (ibid.: 73). Furthermore, the demand for sex services is increasingly seen as a "part of the recreation associated with a modern urban lifestyle" (ibid.: 72). Creation of employment opportunities, particularly in export processing zones, has also led to greater migration of females.

It may be tempting to attribute the growth in a country's sex industry and resulting HIV epidemics to changes in moral values or to a "hypersexualized" population with unusual sexual tastes. The examples of Thailand, Indonesia, and Malaysia demonstrate that the factors relating to individual sexual preferences are unlikely to be the fundamental reasons for growth in a commercial sex sector. What these countries show is that a set of important underlying parameters, related in a large part to the stage of development process a country is at, and the speed at which it is changing, all contribute strongly to the sex sector's growth. Fundamental changes that occur in the supply of labor (particularly female rural–urban migrants) as well as demand-side conditions are central to the sex industry's growth. This is not, however, to say that sociocultural factors, such as the idea of how men and women should behave and ideas concerning obligations of daughters, do not also play a role, simply that other preconditions are likely to be needed for its rapid development.

What emerges from the discussion of the Southeast Asian examples is that certain fundamental forces related to the overall development process drive the growth of the sex sector and thus have significant influences on how HIV/AIDS epidemics may evolve and unfold. According to one expert, the "nature and pace of development in these countries has influenced both the supply of workers to, and the demand for, the services of the sex sector" (Lim, 1998: 11). From a policy point of view what this means is that "sanctions or other measures targeted at individual prostitutes will not be effective unless the economic and social bases of prostitution can be dismantled" (ibid.: 13).

The economic and social foundations of CSW in China

In the context of the examples discussed, it is evident that the supply of female migrants to the sex sector as well as demand-side conditions related to urban income growth are important factors involved in driving its growth. The following sections therefore consider aspects of female migration in more detail, including also discussion of demand-side considerations, in an attempt to explore and explain the growth of China's sex sector. Deep inequalities that have emerged over the course of economic reforms are also factors central to understanding CSW growth in China.

The feminization of migration

The Southeast Asian examples illustrate that widespread and large-scale female migration is one important, even necessary condition, for the sex sector to develop. It is the female migrants who make up a significant share of SWs. The following considers in more detail the characteristics of female migrants *vis-à-vis* the commercial sex industry. There are three key factors to note. First, the female off-farm labor force has grown dramatically. Females are increasingly participating in migration. Females are increasingly participating in migration and it is an important aspect of China's current development pattern. Second, and of equal significance for the purpose of this study, the increasing feminization of migration is being led by young women – particularly teenagers and those in their early twenties. Third, the increased participation of females in the migrant labor force has at the same time been accompanied by a reduction in the relative wages of the female population when compared with the male population. This is caused in part by the particular economic sectors that young female migrants are drawn to and employed in, which are in general lower paying. The implications of growing gender wage imbalances are important, as they create further incentives to move from these very low-wage-paying sectors of the economy to alternative, more lucrative work. These three trends combined, which are not dissimilar to those witnessed in other countries in other periods, have clear implications for the growth of the commercial sex sector. Young female migrants are an important component of the workforce in China's burgeoning sex sector.

The number of rural–urban migrants has grown significantly. In 2000, there were around 130 million migrants in China (UNDP/CDRF, 2005: 40). While most migrants are male, more and more females, as in the other Asian examples discussed, are migrating. Although details are sketchy, it is now estimated that between one-half and one-third of all migrants are female. As one village leader in Anhui observes: "It used to be unmarried men who migrated. But now unmarried women migrate also. People's opinions are changing, and nobody blames them anymore" (quoted in Lou *et al.*, 2004: 213).[9] According to the 1990 China Population Census, migrant women account for 46 percent of intraprovincial migrants and 42 percent of interprovincial migrants in China. Data from the 2000 Chinese census showed that 52 percent of migrants were women (Liang and Chen, 2004). This trend in China is by no means unique. There is much evidence to suggest that Asia as a whole has experienced a feminization of migration in recent decades. Sex ratios of rural to urban migrants, for example, show that it is in Asian countries in which the greatest feminization of migration flows has occurred. There were 116.8 males for every 100 female rural–urban migrants in the 1960s, but this declined to 111 in the 1970s and 96.6 in the 1980s (Hugo, 2003). Both Africa and Latin America during this period experienced fairly constant sex ratios among migrants. One explanation for the increasing feminization of the Asian workforce is related to the types of industry that have emerged in these regions, particularly textiles and assembly-type processes in which female labor is preferred.

While the evidence concerning female migration is not as complete as we would like, some studies (often based upon household surveys) give further indication as to the patterns of female migration. A variety of sources examining the participation of females in the Chinese migrant labor force confirms the rapid increase in their participation (Lohmar, Rozelle and Zhao, 2001; Rozelle *et al.*, 1999; Zhang, De Brauw and Rozelle, 2004). Zhang, De Brauw and Rozelle (2004) in their study separate male and female migration patterns by age groups from 1990 to 2000 in a random sample of 60 villages from six rural provinces and found that the proportion of the rural labor force that obtained some off-farm employment increased from 16 percent in 1981 to 48 percent by 2000. This was consistent with previous findings of other national studies of rural off-farm employment, indicating its reliability. This study also found that women participated at rates far below those of men during the 20-year period. However, participation rates rose rapidly since the early 1990s. In the 1980s, off-farm participation rates of men (more than 25 percent in 1981) far exceeded those of women (less than 5 percent) (Zhang, De Brauw and Rozelle, 2004: 236). Throughout the 1980s, less than 1 percent of women left the farm and worked for a wage. Since 1990, however, the rate of growth of the migrant labor force has been higher than any other category of job types for both men and women. By 2000, nearly 7 percent of the female labor forces were working as wage-earning migrants.

Table 4.1 Off-farm labor participation rates by gender for selected age cohorts in rural China, 1990 and 2000

Age cohort	Off-farm labor participation rates, 1990 (%)				Off-farm labor participation rates, 2000 (%)			
	Total	Men	Women	Men/ women	Total	Men	Women	Men/ women
16–20	24	30	13	2.3	76	75	76	1.0
21–25	34	47	13	3.6	67	79	54	1.5
26–30	29	48	9	5.3	53	73	34	2.1
31–35	27	45	7	6.4	48	71	23	3.1
36–40	21	37	4	9.3	43	70	20	3.5
41–50	21	33	5	6.6	38	61	19	3.2

Source: Adapted from Zhang, De Brauw and Rozelle (2004: 234).

One of the most striking features of the feminization of migration, moreover, is the increasing participation of young women, particularly teenagers and women in their early twenties (ibid.: 234). Although women still lag behind men, access to off-farm jobs has increased much more quickly for women than men (see Table 4.1). By 2000, over 30 percent of women had jobs off the farm, up from only 10 percent in 1990. In the youngest age cohorts, this trend is further exaggerated. Most strikingly, in the case of 16- to 20-year-old cohort, the level of participation is higher (more than 75 percent) than that of young men (ibid.: 231). In 2000, young workers in the 16- to 20-year-old cohort participated at rates more than three times (75.8 percent) those in the same age group in 1990 (23.7 percent). Those in the 21- to 25-year-old cohort and those in the 26–30 doubled the off-farm participation rates of their 1990 cohorts.

In contrast, older workers, while still increasing their participation rates significantly (by 17 percentage points), worked off the farm at less than half the rate (only 37.6 percent) than those in the 16–20 cohort. Thus, younger women are beginning to specialize by working solely in the off-farm sector. While participation rates among all women are still lower than rates among men (by 32 percentage points – 63 percent for men and 31 percent for women) in 2000, this trend disappears for younger age groups. Both men and women in the younger cohorts are solely employed in the nonfarm sector. Fifty-nine percent of young women who were employed in the nonfarm sector in 2000 did not engage in any farm-related work (Zhang, De Brauw and Rozelle, 2004: 237). The shift toward young migrants who specialize in off-farm work contrasts sharply with the situation in 1990, when "most off-farm workers continued to work on the farm on a part time or at least seasonal basis" (ibid.).

The migrant population, therefore, tends to be young with more females than males. This observation is confirmed by other studies. The 1995 Ministry of Agriculture household survey data for Sichuan and Anhui, for example, showed that of migrants in the 18 and below age group, almost 66 percent were women in Sichuan and 56 percent in Anhui (Gaetano and Jacka, 2004: 23). Young female migrants, moreover, tend not to be married. Indeed, the strategy for many migrants appears to involve one of moving to urban areas in early adult life and returning to their hometowns during their twenties (ibid.). Clearly, the current patterns of migration have had implications for the sex industry and more widely the HIV/AIDS epidemic, both in terms of supply- and demand-side conditions.

Pull factors

Despite high rates of migration among women, employment opportunities are less favorable in comparison to their male counterparts. There is evidence of considerable job segmentation between male and female migrants. Census data from as early as 1990 found that although migrants in general were mainly engaged either in industry or in the service sector, women migrants were "overwhelmingly concentrated in the service and retail sectors, most as housemaids and restaurant workers" (Gaetano and Jacka, 2004: 25). A later survey, from four counties in Sichuan and Anhui in 2000, showed that women also were recruited to the manufacturing sector, although the service sector remained more important for females. About 40 percent worked in retail or restaurants, and 40 percent in factories (Lou *et al.*, 2004: 213). Popular forms of employment are in the service sector and in particular light manufacturing activities in certain coastal development zone regions: "young single women are the preferred labor for the transnational apparel, textile, toy, and electronics industries … in the Shenzhen Special Economic Zone in 1996, 69 percent of migrants were women" (Gaetano and Jacka, 2004: 21).

A Chinese Academy of Social Sciences survey found during the early 1990s that women were highly concentrated in the low-skill and low-wage industries with an average of 12 working hours a day and salaries ranging from 300 to 500 RMB per month (ibid.: 26).[10] Migration itself, of course, exerts great downward pressure on nonfarm wages in unskilled and low-skilled occupations in urban areas. Over the 1990s, it was found that there was no increase in the real wage of unskilled labor in the Pearl River Delta, a popular destination for female migrants. It has been estimated that there are around 150 million surplus workers in the agricultural sector (UNDP/CDRF, 2005: 40). Fierce competition, therefore, will maintain downward pressure in conventional areas of employment. As a result of the large supply the female migrant labor force, according to one commentator, remains "hardworking, tolerant, cheap, and disposable" (Fan, 2003: 27). As a large surplus labor force still exists within China's rural population, it is predicted that it will be many years before it is absorbed into the labor market, and hence in turn before wages will be competed upward.

Across Chinese society, the World Bank also finds evidence of occupational segregation. Women are "disproportionately represented in lower-paying jobs" (World Bank, 1997: 40). There is also evidence that women are paid less in the same jobs as men and that this "unexplained wage gap is high by international standards" (ibid.). This income difference between men and women was explored in Chapter 3. However, it is worthwhile to note again that the gender inequalities are particularly relevant in explaining why the commercial sex industry has expanded so rapidly in the last 30 years. Women are also more adversely affected by layoffs resulting in dramatic increases in prostitution in northern China, the heartland of old state enterprises. The wage gap between men and women, furthermore, appears exaggerated among the migrant population. In a 1995 survey, a male migrant earned a monthly income of 642 RMB per month compared to 355 RMB for migrant women (Fan, 2004: 186). According to the World Bank (1997: 41), recent economic reforms may be "eroding the relative position of women." They argue that the "unfettered market orientation is threatening past achievements in gender equality and reinforcing a cultural predisposition toward differential treatment of men and women" (World Bank, 1997: 38). As Gil *et al.* (1996: 149) note, under these conditions: "the relatively lucrative nature of prostitution can easily combine with shifts in sexual mores to enable some women to consider prostitution as an outright economic option."

Push factors

Rural Chinese women have harder lives than men. As well as the "pull" factor of expected earning opportunities in the cities, Chinese women also experience greater "push" factors from their rural homes. The difficult living condition of rural females is reflected most glaringly in lower recorded levels of education and health. These factors as explored in Chapter 3 are important drivers for women to migrate to the urban areas in search of employment. Simultaneously, poor quality of life in rural regions as reflected in higher female suicide rates is also a factor in the decision to migrate. There are estimated value of over 150,000 female suicides per year in China, nearly half the world total of female suicide. Uniquely, however, most suicides occur among young rural women aged between 15–35 years old. About 25 percent more women than men are prone to suicide. In contrast, over three times as many men committee suicide in the West (UN Country Team China, 2004: 17). A recent survey of 24 hospitals reported over 14,000 suicide cases from emergency rooms between 1990–2003. It found that 72 percent of these suicides were from rural areas and that 71 percent of these cases were women (*China Daily*, 11 January 2004).

Lower quality of life for rural Chinese women as reflected in education, employment prospects, income, and suicide rates is important to our understanding of the commercial sex industry's expansion in China and, ultimately, linkages to the HIV/AIDS epidemic. While there are comparatively few detailed scientific studies of CSW in China, the evidence that does exist suggests that SWs are overwhelmingly drawn from the female migrant population.[11] In a survey of several thousand arrested SWs in 1990, it was found that the median age was 22 (similar to the typical age of female migrants shown in Table 4.1). Former occupations included being a "peasant" or farm laborer (41.5 percent), a factory worker (28.5 percent), or "cadre leader"[12] (less than 1 percent) (Gil *et al.*, 1996: 144). What emerges is "a strikingly consistent picture of the prostitute ... the 'average' prostitute depicted by these data confirm that she is a ruralite, usually prostituting in a city, young but surprisingly well educated" (ibid.: 145).[13] According to Gil *et al.*, 50 percent of their respondents' primary motivation to enter prostitution was financial (ibid.: 144).[14]

The origins of the surveyed CSW in Guangdong province by van den Hoek *et al.* (2001) showed that the majority came from poorer inner provinces of China, with only 14 percent from Guangdong. The remaining came from across the country but most notably from Hunan (35 percent) and Sichuan (16 percent). On average, women work and live in Guangzhou for 1 year. For 92 percent of the women, Guangzhou was the first and only city where they had worked as a SW. The majority of the women (45 percent) solicited their clients in massage and sauna locations. Forty-six percent of the women did not have an additional income from a regular job. A checkup for STD in the year preceding the intake was reported by 35 percent of respondents (van den Hoek *et al.*, 2001: 755). Such statistics demonstrate that the low-entry barriers to CSW for migrant women place them in greater danger of HIV/AIDS infection. Given the rapidly changing attitudes to sex, in combination with other factors, the spread of the epidemic may well be promoted by the large CSW industry that has now developed.

Migration and expected incomes

The sex industry now flourishes in most Chinese cities. The Harris–Todaro economic model of migration can help in part explain the high estimates of numbers working in CSW. As in the rest of Asia, there is evidence to suggest prostitutes generally prefer not to engage in CSW in their own hometowns or villages (although, of course, this does obviously also take place). They may often, however, be procured or move from "rural areas or small towns for the cities or, as young, first-time job-seekers new to urban areas, are vulnerable to being drawn into the sex sector" (Lim, 1998: 18). The feminization of migration, as shown in the previous section, has arguably fueled the commercial sex industry.

Economic models are useful in understanding migration of women for CSW. Such models argue migration is driven by rational economic considerations of relative benefits and costs (mostly financial but also psychological) and by *expected urban–rural real-wage differentials* (Harris and Todaro, 1970). In such models, migration rates in excess of urban job opportunity growth rates are "not only possible but also rational and even likely in the face of wide urban–rural expected income differentials" (Todaro, 1997: 38). Even by 1998, China's urban unemployment rate had reached 8 percent with the prediction that unemployment would rise in the wake of its entry into the World Trade Organization and continued state sector restructuring (quoted in Nolan, 2004: 19). Urban employment averaged 10 percent or more for some places (Giles, Park and Zhang, 2005). Unemployment, therefore, is already a feature of the Chinese urban sector. Indeed, it is only via excessive rural–urban migration, in the face of possible unemployment, that rural and urban *expected incomes* are forced closer together. This is because "expected incomes are defined in terms of both wages and employment probabilities" (Todaro, 1997: 35). It is therefore possible and even normal to have continued migration despite the existence of sizable rates of urban unemployment.[15]

The insights of the Harris–Todaro model are relevant for understanding rural–urban migration of women for two reasons. First, the model explains that unemployment is likely to be a feature of urban areas in developing countries, particularly if wages in the urban sector are considerably greater than the rural sector. With high levels of unemployment, it might be expected that at least some female migrants will migrate despite the unpromising prospects and some will consider CSW. Second, financial remuneration in sex work, by comparison with most other service or manufacturing employment, is generally considered to be very high.[16] While data for China is very limited, international studies show this to be the case. In Vietnam, for example, SWs reported earning up to seven times the average income of the general population (quoted in MAP, 2004). In Nepal, SWs earned more than six times the average annual income nationwide (an annualized income of over US$1,500). In Cambodia, SWs earned US$122 a month on average, compared with a national per capita income of just US$25 a month (quoted in MAP, 2004).[17] Compared with other forms of employment, the Harris–Todaro model predicts that a disproportionately large number of women will be attracted to the profession, driving down expected incomes to levels nearer to those found in alternative forms of employment.[18] There is indeed evidence to suggest high levels of underemployment in outlets for CSW.[19] It is typical that SWs may work in outlets such as KTV bars, giving any individual only a small chance of employment in an evening's work. While wages are high, the large numbers drive down expected incomes, as predicted in the Harris–Todaro model.

Demand growth

The growing feminization of migration explains, in part, the growth of the sex sector. Considerations of the demand side, however, are also central to explaining its growth. Some evidence suggests that China's red light areas are often located in relatively affluent neighborhoods and upmarket hotels, reflecting the clientele. What evidence there is in China as well as elsewhere suggests that relatively wealthy sections of the urban male population disproportionately drive demand in the sex sector. This is clearly important, as the middle and upper classes are growing fast and will continue to grow for a long time to come. It is interesting to note that, in general, the demand-side conditions for expansion of CSW have received far less attention than the economic reasons for why women become prostitutes. Yet for every heterosexual contact by a female CSW, there is a male partner. Such contacts facilitate the spread of HIV/AIDS from the CSW community and into the general population. In the better-researched case of Thailand, some experts note that there is still insufficient research on how economic development influences demand for CSW (Boochalaksi and Guest, 1998: 135). Much of the research undertaken on the demand side of the problem, moreover, has tended to focus on the role of foreign men, despite the fact that such demand constitutes only a small proportion of the customer base (ibid.). Not surprisingly, undue attention through the state media has also conveniently focused on the relatively few cases of foreign involvement in the Chinese sex industry. While as yet there remains less research on the reasons for women engaging in prostitution in China than in Thailand, it is also true that the demand side has been overlooked. This has arguably led to a misunderstanding of the current situation. One result of this misunderstanding, for example, is that the migrant population is frequently discussed as creating demand for CSW when much of the evidence suggests other types of population groups may actually be more important.

Despite relative neglect in understanding the demand side, it is evident that the commercial sex sector in China has been fueled by massive internal demand growth. A disproportionate share of this growth originates from the wealthier sections of the population. This is reflected in both survey and epidemiological evidence. A study of Dalian's CSW customers in KTV bars notes that customers were "mainly middle-aged businessmen, male government officials, entrepreneurs, the nouveaux riches, policemen, and foreign investors" (Zheng, 2004: 85). Early evidence from one of the few large-scale surveys of arrested prostitutes undertaken as early as 1990 also revealed that although demand came from a variety of customers, wealthy social groups were more important: 37 percent of customers were self-employed (likely to be wealthy), 20 percent were factory workers, 17 percent were drivers, and 8 percent were cadre leaders (Gil *et al.*, 1996: 145). Even at this time, by far the largest group, proportionally, was the "self-employed" group. A more recent report on self-employed entrepreneurs (*getihu*), a growing social class in China, found that "*getihu* young men are frequently identified as spreading [sexually transmitted infections] and engaging in HIV-related risk-taking sexual practices" (Gill, Chang and Palmer, 2002: 4). A national survey conducted by the Renmin University Sexology Institute suggested that enterprise managers and government officials are ten times more likely than male manual urban workers to patronize SWs (quoted in Xiang, 2004: 10). More recent surveys of the sexual behavior of the wealthier urban classes also reveal the scale of demand for the commercial sex market in China. An internet poll of nearly 3,750 adults in urban areas (of which two-thirds were male and nearly half were married) showed that 37 percent of those surveyed patronized CSWs (*Reuters*, 4 August 2006). The survey also found worrying levels of awareness of HIV. Only one-third discussed HIV and sexually transmitted infections (STIs) with their partners. Interestingly, a national behavioral survey of Thai men also found that 37 percent of men aged 20–24 years had visited a SW in the previous year (UNDP, 2004a: 11). According to another survey of Chinese males, it was found that men in the upper 5 percent of income earners were 33 times more likely to use prostitutes than people in the lowest 40 percent (*China Daily*, 2 August 2005). In China, as in earlier periods in Thailand, research on the sexual behavior of Chinese men, despite its obvious importance, still remains largely "the stuff of anecdotes, assumptions and motley, small-scale studies" (UNDP, 2004a: 11). Such observed trends are by no means exceptional as these trends are reflected in countries such as Vietnam. In southern Vietnam, surveys of SWs have found that over one-third of clients were businessmen or white collar workers (UNAIDS, 2004: 41). In a study of close to 500 men in the Vietnamese capital Hanoi, businessmen were nearly twice as likely to buy sex, compared with factory workers. In the northern provinces, over half were government officials highlighting the participation and complicit nature of many state bodies – a phenomena also observed in China (MAP, 2005: 5). In Indonesia, Laos, and Pakistan, sex workers have also reported that civil servants and businessmen were among their most frequent clients. In India, surveys show over one-quarter of CSW patrons were businessmen or service sector employees (ibid.; UNAIDS, 2004: 41). Similarly, in earlier historical periods, such as in Victorian Britain, it was "changing patterns of urban consumption between 1896 and 1913 spurred the expansion of unregulated prostitution" (Gilfoyle, 1999: 121). The changing attitudes to sex and sexual behavior are linked with China's economic development, indicating that the combination of these factors will have a tremendous impact on the future of China's HIV/AIDS epidemic.

Male migrants, of course, also create demand for CSW. Their participation, however, is somewhat limited by their wealth. Male migrants work hard and for long hours with an average annual income of 2,000 RMB, approximately "equivalent of a year's net income for a rural household in the central region" (Zhu, 2003: 495). The average price of sex, therefore, even at the lower end of the market, may represent a significant share of a male migrant's income. The household strategy of the male migrant can be understood as a strategy of "earning money in the city while spending in the village" (quoted in Zhu, 2003: 495). As Zhu points out, the "ultimate goal for most of them is to bring back money to their families and to return home to a better life later" (Zhu, 2003: 495). Renmin University Sexology Institute's national survey suggested that migrant workers make up only a minor part of commercial sex clients. On average, migrants buy sex more often than rural residents but less than urban dwellers (quoted in Xiang, 2004). Despite such evidence, some speculate that migrants contribute to the spread of HIV as they more frequently buy commercial sex owing to separation from families and the local society. While this is not proven, migrant workers are probably more vulnerable to STDs in individual cases, due to their lower usage of condoms (Hansen and Li, 2002). What then do epidemiological investigations into STD and HIV prevalence reveal about who pays for sex? As it happens, the biomedical evidence is imperfect and quite difficult to interpret. According to a survey of more than 600 STD patients conducted by the STD Branch of the Guangdong Province Police Hospital in 2000, 70 percent of the patients were migrants (*Xinhua*, 27 October 2000). Based on a review of 11 studies on STDs conducted in different provinces in China, X.S. Yang (2004) suggests that migrants' share in reported STD cases varies considerably from a low of 7.5 percent in Jiangsu to a high of 69.0 percent in Shenzhen. Of the 236,188 cases of STDs reported in all the studies in China, an average of 36.8 percent involved migrants. The considerable variation across the studies, however, also reflects differences in the structure of the general population, with some areas having more migrants. Due to the uncertainty across the studies, it is difficult to ascertain to what extent the migrant population is more susceptible than the nonmigrant population to STDs, and ultimately HIV. Indeed, of the only study that has scientifically compared migrant and nonmigrant groups (in an urban region of Eastern China), it was found that syphilis infections were higher among the nonmigrant group, although not at a statistically significant level (Hesketh *et al.*, 2006).

The correlation between migration and HIV appears stronger than that of STDs. A study of a northern province showed that migrants accounted for between 17.7–31.5 percent of infections in 1996–2000. In this study, migrants constituted only 1.8 percent of the general population covered in the survey (X.S. Yang, 2004). They have also reviewed 15 studies on HIV in different parts of China and found that on average 42.4 percent of HIV-positive cases were migrants. With the exception of the year 2000, migrants' share in the HIV-positive population has generally been on the rise. Higher prevalence among migrants may also reflect a general lack of medical care as opposed to more risky behaviors. Despite the strong statistical association between migration and HIV and STDs, the underlying mechanism between the two is far from clear. Generally, the epidemiological evidence is not as strong as it might be. While there are studies on migrants, equal attention needs to be drawn to the wealthy urban male population (mobile men with money). As there is "no formal survey of this kind of group" according to Wu Zunyou, representative of the China Center for Disease Control and Prevention (quoted in *China Daily*, 2 August 2005), it is therefore premature to conclude that the male migrant population are more likely to be harbingers of HIV than their wealthier urban counterparts.

Much evidence suggests that demand is disproportionately driven by the wealthier male sections of society. Although epidemiological data are currently incomplete, it nonetheless points to the overemphasis on migrants to the exclusion of nonmigrant groups (Hesketh *et al.*, 2006). As noted earlier, in one of the few scientific studies on HIV in migrant populations, in a comparative study of 6,000 migrant and urban workers, no statistically significant difference in HIV/AIDS prevalence existed (ibid.). Syphilis prevalence, however, was higher in urban workers as opposed to migrants (although not at a statistically significant level). These observations, of course, have important implications for the mixing pattern of HIV. It is not simply that migrants are prone to high-risk behavior. This is reflected in some medical surveillance studies which show that among the migrant population, prevalence of HIV is no higher than among nonmigrant classes.

Conclusion

Generalized epidemics, in which more than 1 percent of the adult population is HIV positive, normally require that widespread heterosexual transmission takes place. In East and Southeast Asian nations, the sexual mixing pattern responsible for risky sexual behavior is reliant upon CSWs. This chapter has asked what forces may be behind the growth in CSW in China. It has argued that the growth of the sex industry cannot be put down to chance, nor can it be attributed solely to changes in sexual tastes and attitudes (the liberation of women or the "hyper-sexuality" of men, for example). Instead, it appears a number of structural reasons related to economic and social development can help explain the massive re-emergence of sex work in China today.

Examples from the economic and social history of today's developed economies, as well as numerous examples from the late-industrializing nations of Southeast Asia, are useful in illustrating this phenomenon. More specifically, in the case of China, economic development has led to increasing gender-related income inequalities. Females now typically earn less than males. They have started, moreover, to migrate to urban areas at ever younger ages. They are also less likely to be married than male migrant counterparts and, on top of this, also have lower levels of education. Both push and pull factors, moreover, cause females to migrate. Surveys show that pull factors are typically more important for men, reflecting the often precarious positions China's rural females may find themselves in. Migrant females have typically been employed in service sectors or menial low-paid manufacturing jobs. Work conditions are generally poor and female migrants are literally "at the front line of both domestic and global capitalist development, working for the lowest wages in poor and often unsafe conditions and in occupations that urbanites shun" (Gaetano and Jacka, 2004: 2). As inequalities between males and females continue to grow and wealthier urban classes emerge, male urban demand has increased greatly, so increasing the rewards to CSW. Female migrants' employment opportunities, age, marital status, and destination of migration, therefore, may incline them toward considering CSW. Combined with rapidly changing social norms, such work is often considered "an outright option" (Gil *et al.*, 1996).[20] While most women migrants may migrate without the explicit purpose of entering the sex trade, many are subsequently attracted to it. It is likely then that "the nature and pace of development in these countries has influenced both the supply of workers to, and the demand for, the services of the sex sector" (Lim, 1998: 11).

When we think of the "deeper undercurrents" and the "terrain" in which China's HIV/AIDS epidemic is emerging, it is important to look beyond the domain of individual agency. Nowhere is this better illustrated than in the case of CSW. A set of structural forces, closely related to gender and income inequalities, has led to the re-emergence of sex work in China. CSW has grown rapidly and now exists on a massive scale. Other authors, looking at other countries in Southeast Asia, have also concluded that without addressing the underlying economic and social forces driving prostitution, steps to target individual prostitutes "are not likely to be effective or may even be inappropriate" (Lim, 1998: 2). In Thailand, hailed as East Asia's most successful HIV-prevention success story, behavioral indicators also now suggest that as prevalence has fallen, individual risky behavior is again on the rise. The Thai example shows that persistent educational campaigns directed at males can be very effective. It also shows, however, that unless they are pervasive and long term, high-risk behaviors may well end up re-emerging among the very large population groups that are at risk. Similar patterns to those in Thailand have also been witnessed in Laos. Similarly, among females, with millions of SWs and ease of entry and exit to the sex sector creating a constant turnover, some argue "individualized services based on outreach are simply not practical" (MAP, 2005: 16). Large education and information campaigns, therefore, may not even be sufficient in China. "Structural interventions," according to one source, have the advantage that they avoid having to work at the level of the individual (MAP, 2005). From a policy perspective, increasing the economic opportunities and social power of females, for example, also "should be seen as part and parcel of potentially successful and sustainable AIDS strategies" (UNAIDS, 2004: 11). Clearly, a balance between the two will be required in order to address the problem of CSW in China.

As one of the few detailed studies on the bases of the sex sectors in Southeast Asia has commented: "Unless policy makers deal with the economic and social bases of prostitution, sanctions and measures targeted at individual prostitutes are not likely to be effective or may even be inappropriate" (Lim, 1998: 2). Attempting to target individuals in the hope of curbing CSW is unlikely to be entirely successful. By extension the same arguments may be made for the HIV/ AIDS epidemic, given behavioral campaigns will never be entirely effective. Policy-makers need to ask themselves why so many young women, and often also girls, willingly enter the sex industry. As this chapter shows, a whole range of factors drives the commercial sex industry, many of them deeply entrenched in China's particular economic and social conditions.

5 Migration

Introduction

China's HIV/AIDS epidemic has entered its third phase, moving from "entry," "spreading," and is now in its "expansion" stage, according to some (Wu, Rou and Cui, 2004). Previous chapters detailed the role of intravenous drug use (IDU), commercial sex work (CSW), men who have sex with men, and demographic factors, particularly the gender imbalance among younger age cohorts in the spread of HIV. However, the ever growing migrant population is singled out as a key driver of HIV/AIDS in China during this expansion stage. In Chapter 4, we argued that the increasing feminization of migration is also linked to the growth of China's commercial sex industry and has, consequently, become an important bridge for the spread of HIV/AIDS to the general population. This chapter considers more broadly the process of migration with a particular emphasis on national-level patterns of migration. China's economic reforms have had a large impact on the movement of people in search of better opportunities. Such large-scale movements of people have historically played an important part in disease transmission:

> The link between commercial activity and transmission of infectious disease has a long history. Because epidemics depend on the introduction of a pathogen into a susceptible population, it is not surprising that global events associated with mass movements of people and goods have seen the concomitant emergence of new threats of infectious disease. Major historical challenges to public health and subsequent advances in the control of communicable disease frequently emerged in important trading centres – eg, 14th century Venice, Italy; 19th century London, UK; and 20th century New York, USA. Current challenges in Chinese population centres fit this pattern.
>
> (Fisman, 2007: 84)

In this chapter we specifically consider and analyze data on long-distance interprovincial migration, comparing this migrant data with sentinel surveillance data with the aim of investigating whether migrants typically originate from high- or low-prevalence regions. The Chinese HIV epidemic is "characterized by a wide disparity between high and low prevalence regions" (State Council AIDS Working Committee Office and the UN Theme Group on HIV/AIDS, 2004). The question of whether outward migration takes place from high-prevalence regions appears to be particularly important. If migrant risk behaviors also increase after migration, as some studies suggest, the high prevalence coupled with risky behavior would imply that migrant population groups may be particularly important in fueling China's HIV epidemic. This perspective also illustrates how a different approach to considering the migration problem and its interaction with HIV/AIDS, from the broader national perspective, can further illustrate important national determinants driving HIV/AIDS in China.

Before assessing the relationship between migrants and the HIV/AIDS epidemic, a brief summary of rural–urban migration over the last 30 years in conjunction with growing income inequality is required. This is followed by an analysis of the national-level data on the origins and destinations of China's migrant population and comparing it with sentinel surveillance data. The results point to an important conclusion, namely that China's migration patterns may indeed favor the rapid national spread of HIV. This is because regions with large net outward migration also appear to have more severe HIV/AIDS epidemics.

This chapter also draws indirectly from insights made during fieldwork in Beijing, Yunnan, and Sichuan in August and September 2005. Representatives of various UN agencies (UNAIDS, UNDP, UNESCO, UNFPA) and Chinese academic institutions were interviewed (Renmin University, Beijing University, and Kunming University). Individuals in the Departments of Health responsible for HIV/AIDS policy in both Yunnan and Sichuan Provincial Governments were interviewed. It also utilizes public security data as reported by Zhu (2003) and Chinese sentinel surveillance data as reported by UNAIDS.

HIV/AIDS and migration

Worldwide, there is considerable interest in the relationship between HIV/AIDS epidemics and migration. The Partnership on HIV/AIDS and Mobile Populations, International Organization for Migration (IOM), and Regional Office for Southern Africa and the Southern African Migration Project recently met to consider the linkages between HIV/AIDS, population mobility and migration in Southern Africa (IOM, 2005). This gathering of researchers found that despite there being a number of important factors in the rapid spread of HIV in Africa, *"perhaps the key neglected factor in explaining the rapid spread of HIV over the last decade is population mobility"* (IOM, 2005: 10). They concluded, however, that we are still far from understanding just how mobility and HIV interact.

As in southern Africa, the migrant population is now seen as a key factor in the spread of HIV in China. It is speculated that greater geographic mobility, lower levels of education, limited HIV/AIDS knowledge, and separation from partners and families make migrants more prone to high-risk behavior. Similar to southern Africa, the migrant population in China still remains quite poorly understood. A number of studies focusing on different aspects of migration and HIV in China have emerged. Case studies have considered local regions and areas of

China with a view to understanding how mobile populations interact with the virus at a local level (du Guerny, Hsu and Hong, 2003; UNDP/UNOPS, 2001). Additionally, epidemiological studies have been undertaken, though with differing degrees of scientific rigor. Complementing epidemiological studies, behavioral studies have also investigated how migrant risk behaviors may change after migration (Andersen *et al.*, 2003; Lin *et al.*, 2005; Yang, Derlega and Luo, 2007). There has also been a focus on "surplus men" and the migrant population (Tucker *et al.*, 2005). Most of the behavioral studies provide empirical evidence to show that migrant risk behaviors are greater than those of the general population. Implicitly, many argue that migration may lead to higher HIV prevalence among the migrant population. The epidemiological studies that do exist, moreover, would seem to suggest HIV prevalence is higher among the migrant population and thus confirm findings such as two-thirds of seropositive cases between 1995–2000 in the provinces of Shanxi and Zhejiang and in Shanghai were migrants (Lin *et al.*, 2005: 104).

Based partly on the behavioral and epidemiological evidence, some scholars have been quite vocal as to the increasingly important role they believe migrants will play in the spread of HIV in China. At a recent international conference, for example, it was argued that the growing migrant population in China "may be the 'tipping point' in China's battle with the AIDS epidemic" – an analogy that has now gained acceptance (e.g., see Andersen *et al.*, 2003). Other researchers, however, remain slightly more circumspect as to what can actually be deduced from the epidemiological evidence. They point to the shortage of behavioral studies and weakness with current epidemiological knowledge:

> very little is known about HIV prevalence, knowledge, and attitudes towards HIV among migrant workers in China. Routine reports from a number of cities suggest that they are at greater risk of acquiring HIV. For example, 52% of all HIV reports in Beijing, 61% in Xian, and 66% in Shanghai in 2000 were in migrant workers but without denominator figures, and given that migrants are predominantly in sexually active age groups, these figures are impossible to interpret.
>
> (Hesketh *et al.*, 2006: 11)

The assumption that migrant workers may become drivers of the HIV epidemic in China is based on the observation of large numbers, reports of high prevalence among migrants in some cities, and on the basis that migrant workers in other regions of the world have played an important role (Hesketh *et al.*, 2006). In one of the few scientifically rigorous epidemiological comparisons of HIV in migrant and urban populations, however, no statistically significant difference in infections was found between the two populations. These findings suggested that HIV was not spreading among migrant workers in one region of eastern China (ibid.). Behavioral data, moreover, showed that tendencies to migrate with partners and families and traditional attitudes to sexual relationships may have explained why migrant workers were in fact at low risk for engaging in casual sex in this region.

Reviews of the Chinese HIV epidemic generally emphasize the important role of the migrant population (Gill, 2002; Qian, Vermund and Wang, 2005). There is, however, conflicting evidence and views on the possible role of the migrant population in the spread of HIV in China. Here we attempt to contribute to this debate, taking a slightly different approach to previous research undertaken in this area. To date, no studies have examined national-level data on interprovincial migration patterns and HIV prevalence so as to ascertain whether there are any particular trends in outward/inward migration and HIV prevalence. As noted, however, a feature of HIV/AIDS in China is the geographical concentration of its epidemics: by the end of 2006, over 70 percent of China's infections originated from only five provinces. Do migrants, therefore, typically originate from high- or low-prevalence areas? This question would seem of particular relevance given the scale of outward flows and in light of some evidence that finds increasing high-risk behaviors after migration. Before addressing this important question, we briefly return to the recent trends in Chinese income inequality as the process of migration has exacerbated the situation and thus a crucial component of the third phase of China's HIV/AIDS epidemic.

Rural–urban income inequality

The large migrant population is a product of unbalanced economic development. The direction of migration is also a function of this imbalance. Few countries have experienced China's sustained economic growth. Rural reforms spurred China's growth in the early 1980s and rural incomes grew rapidly in this early period. By 1985, however, rural incomes stagnated and began to trail the increases in urban incomes which continued to grow quickly. This trend reversed only briefly in 1995 (Table 5.1). Between 1997–2002, however, farm prices fell an estimated 22 percent. Real farm incomes may actually have declined between 1998–2001 (Nolan, 2004: 17). From 2000 to 2005, the negative trend in relative farm incomes (*vis-à-vis* urban incomes) continued, despite an increasing emphasis on policies favorable to the rural sector. In 2004, average per capita income grew by a healthy 6.8 percent in the farm sector (to US\$353.70). This was the fastest annual growth since 1997. Simultaneously, urban residents per capita incomes rose by 7.7 percent (to US\$1,135). According to the most recent estimates by the National Bureau of Statistics, urban incomes stand at around 3.2 times those of a typical rural dweller.

China's officially recorded rural–urban income ratio is reflected in Table 5.1, but it is probable that it fails to capture the full extent of disparities in living standards between city dwellers and rural residents. This is because publicly provided services such as housing, pensions, health, education, and other entitlements increase urban income estimates substantially.

Economic incentives to migrate from rural to urban areas have greatly increased. The number of migrants in China has increased with close correspondence to the rural–urban income gap. A significant share of the Chinese population still lives in the countryside but rural incomes are likely to remain depressed

Table 5.1 Rural/urban income ratios and migrant population

Year	Column A – per capita annual net income of rural household, RMB	Column B – per capita annual disposable income of urban households, RMB	Column C (B/A)	Estimates of migrant population in millions
1982	...	...	...	30
1985	397.6	739.1	1.9	40
1989	601.5	1,373.9	2.3	60 +
1990	686.3	1,510.2	2.2	Stagnant
1991	708.6	1,700.6	2.4	65
1992	784.0	2,026.6	2.6	...
1993	921.6	2,577.4	2.8	80
1994	1,221.0	3,496.2	2.9	...
1995	1,577.7	4,283.0	2.7	80–100
1996	1,926.1	4,838.9	2.5	80–100
1997	2,090.1	5,160.3	2.5	...
1998	2,162.0	5,425.1	2.5	80–100
1999	2,210.3	5,854.0	2.6	...
2000	2,253.4	6,280.0	2.8	...
2001	2,366.4	6,859.6	2.9	...
2002	2,475.6	7,702.8	3.1	...
2003	2,622.2	8,472.2	3.2	150

Source: State Statistical Bureau (2004: 357); Zhu (2003).

and incentives to migrate grow: "it will be many decades before China's rural surplus labour supply is exhausted" (Nolan, 2004: 63). It is no wonder then that great interest is now focused on the role of Chinese migrants in the country's economic and social development, including the spread of HIV/AIDS.

HIV and migration trends in China

As already noted, one feature of the Chinese HIV/AIDS epidemic has been its concentration in certain geographical areas. Another is the vast pool of migrant laborers living and working in China's urban areas. These two factors combined, beg the question of whether Chinese migrants, in general, can be said to originate from areas of high- or low-HIV prevalence. Unfortunately, data on both HIV prevalence and the migrant population are both still rather limited and imperfect. This makes examining the relationship between the two slightly problematic. Nonetheless, relevant data does exist and for the late 1990s a fairly accurate picture can be drawn.

Data

The Ministries of Labor and Social Security and Public Security collect data on migrants who register as temporary dwellers in their place of origin. The problem with this data, of course, is that many migrants simply do not register. Migrants who move shorter distances for shorter periods of time are less likely to register due to the financial and time costs involved in registration. The number of registered migrants stood at approximately 46.5 million in 1998. This compared with some unofficial estimates of approximately 80 million, doubling the official registered number (Zhu, 2003: 490). Official statistics, therefore, may give only a rough estimate of the migrant population. However, it is reported with such statistics the "problem of under-numeration is a less serious problem in the case of long-distance migration" (ibid.). Longer distance interprovincial migrants, it appears, are more likely to register than short-distance migrants. Of the 46.5 million registered rural laborers at the end of 1998, approximately 30.5 million were "interprovincial" migrants. The majority of China's registered migrants are therefore interprovincial migrants. For this reason, and also because long-distance migration is more important in the national spread of HIV in China, Tables 5.3 and 5.4 concentrate solely on data for "interprovincial" migration.

Columns 3–6 in Tables 5.3 and 5.4 are based on year-end data for 1998 for registered interprovincial migrants in China. This is the most recent year for which it is available. Ideally, interprovincial migration patterns from earlier years should be examined to see if origin and destination trends have significantly changed over time. Such data, however, owing to the paucity of relevant census and public security data, are only fragmentary. The information that does exist, however, strongly suggests the trends seen in the late 1990s probably existed throughout the much of the late 1980s and also into the 1990s "expansion stage" of the epidemic. Data from the interprovincial migration matrix of China (based on retrospective questions in the 1990 census) show that China's six largest migrant-supplying provinces in the late 1990s (Anhui, Henan, Hunan, Sichuan, Guizhou, and Guangxi) were also among the largest suppliers in the 1985–1990 period (State Statistical Bureau, 1990). This should not come as a surprise as these provinces are relatively poor. There is a close relationship between the relative wealth of a province and migration (outward in the case of poor provinces, inward in the case of rich). Patterns of migration, generally from western to eastern regions, do not appear to have changed significantly during the past two decades, even if the scale has. Column 2 of Tables 5.3 and 5.4 present per capita wealth by province (for 2003) as well as the ranking of the provinces in order of wealth (1 equals the wealthiest province, 31 equals the poorest). As well as showing the share of the origin of registered interprovincial migrants for China (column 3), column 4 also shows national interprovincial migrant share relative to the provinces' share of China's total population. It thus indicates an average propensity to migrate for any individual in that province. Again, it is unsurprising that the poorer provinces exhibit a greater average propensity for migration. Finally, column 5 shows the destination of migrants as a share of the national total. It is unsurprising that the wealthier provinces attract migrants (Beijing and Guangdong in particular).

The remaining columns of the tables provide information on the extent of HIV/AIDS epidemics in the different provinces. The HIV data is based on that of sentinel surveillance sites taken from the Chinese Centre for Disease Control and published by UNAIDS and the Chinese Ministry of Health. There are problems with China's sentinel surveillance program (CDC China, 2002). It is, however, the only available epidemiological data. It therefore gives the best indication of regions with more serious outbreaks, sufficient for the purposes of this investigation. Coupled with anecdotal and media reporting, discussed in subsequent sections, a fuller picture of each provincial situation and their current trends can be fairly accurately made.

HIV and outward interprovincial migration

It should first be noted that of the registered 30.5 million interprovincial migrants recorded in 1998 in the tables, roughly 70 percent were from counties that were considered "mostly rural" (Zhu, 2003: 490). It is also significant to bear in mind that an estimated 80 percent of China's estimated 840,000 HIV-infected individuals lived in rural areas during the late 1990s (Wu, Rou and Cui, 2004: 8). Indeed, as noted, one factor that makes the epidemic in China different from other regions is that "the epidemic of HIV among intravenous drug users (IDUs) began in the rural areas and then spread to urban areas" (ibid.). Even today, approximately 50 percent of all HIV infections are attributable to IDU (MOH/UNAIDS/WHO, 2005: 1). Unfortunately, the most recent China HIV/AIDS epidemic update gives no breakdown between rural and urban infections and more generally the geography of the current epidemic (ibid.). In many previous reports, however, the rural nature of the epidemic (and its relation to IDU) has been stressed.

Closer observation of Tables 5.3 and 5.4 reveals that a relatively small number of provinces have supplied a large number of China's officially registered interprovincial migrants. These provinces also have experienced more severe HIV/AIDS outbreaks. Table 5.2 is based upon the data provided in Tables 5.3 and 5.4 and complemented with data on the number of reported HIV infections by province. Table 5.2 summarizes some of the main findings from Tables 5.3 and 5.4 as well as illustrating that six provinces have supplied a substantial share of long-distance outward migrants. According to sentinel surveillance, these are also the very provinces that have experienced either former plasma donor (FPD)- or IDU-related outbreaks. The number of reported cumulative infections (number per 100,000) is also higher than in other provinces. This is a reflection of higher overall prevalence in these regions. The reported number of cumulative infections is also very high in these six provinces. Indeed, there were about 65,000 reported infections of a national total of 166,000 in these six provinces by the end of 2006. These six migrant-supplying provinces therefore accounted for 45 percent of China's reported HIV infections by 2006, a reflection of the early outbreak of HIV epidemics in these regions. It should also be noted that Yunnan and Xinjiang, while reporting almost 34 percent of China's total reported infections by 2006, did not appear to be large migrant-supplying provinces.

The following section briefly reviews the migration and HIV/AIDS situations for the six largest migrant-supplying provinces: Henan, Anhui, Sichuan, Hunan, Jiangxi, and Guangxi as shown in Table 5.2.

Table 5.2 China's largest migrant-supplying provinces

Province	Per capita gross regional product RMB/person, 2003	Origin of registered interprovincial migrants (% share of national total)	Number of registered interprovincial migrants (millions)	Average propensity to migrate	Cumulative infections per 100,000 by the end of 2004	Total cumulative reported HIV infections by the end of 2006	Cumulative reported infections as share of national total by the end of 2006 (%)	Cumulative reported infections, national ranking by the end of 2006	IDU infection rate > 5% at one sentinel surveillance site or more	FPD-driven epidemics (provinces with average 10–20% infection among FPDs)
Anhui	6,455 (26th)	13.9	4.2	2.77	3.01–10	3,828	2.7	7th		Yes
Jiangxi	6,678 (24th)	8.1	2.5	2.38	0.11–0.50	513	0.4	20th	Yes	
Henan	7,570 (17th)	14.94	4.5	1.98	10.01–30	30,820	21.4	2nd		Yes
Hunan	7,554 (18th)	10.11	3	1.92	1.01–3	2,694	1.9	10th	Yes	
Sichuan	6,418 (27th)	13.66	4.1	1.99	3.01–10	6,524	4.5	6th	Yes	
Guangxi	5,969 (28th)	5.3	1.6	1.4	10.01–30	17,619	12.2	3rd	Yes	
Guizhou	3,603 (31st)	4.16		1.39	1.01–3	3,608	2.1	8th	Yes	Yes
Total		70%	19.9			65,066	45.2			
Yunnan	5,662 (29th)	0.28	…	0.08	30.01–44.17	37,456	26	1st	Yes	
Xinjiang	970 (12th)	0.02	…	0.01	30.01–44.17	11,924	8.2	5th	Yes	

Source: Tables 5.3 and 5.4. Columns on cumulative infections (columns 7, 8, and 9) taken from UNAIDS/WHO (2005b). Columns 10 and 11 are taken from sentinel surveillance reporting reported by UNAIDS China.

Note: The average propensity to migrate is estimated as column 3 divided by the province's percentage share of China's total population (for 1998 as reported by Zhu, 2003).

Table 5.3 Central and Western regions

Province	Per capita gross regional product (RMB/person), 2003	Origin of registered interprovincial migrants (% share of national total)	Column 3/ province's % share of total population	Destination of registered interprovincial migrants (% share of national total)	Cumulative infections per 10,000 cases 1985–2003 and reported infections in 2002 (China HIV/AIDS case report)	IDU infection rate > 5% at one sentinel surveillance site or more	HIV detected among STD patients in sentinel sites (year 2000)	CSWs 'never use condoms' above 50% once in years 1998–2000 (and 3-year average where available)	Blood plasma-driven epidemics (provinces with average 10–20% infection among FPDs)
Shanxi	7,435 (19th)	0.25	0.1	1.83	1.01–3			Yes (91.5%)	Yes
Inner Mongolia	8,975 (15th)	0.54	0.28	0.93	0.11–0.5			Yes (72%)	
Jilin	9,338 (13th)	0.07	0.03	0.57	1.01–3			...	
Heilongjiang	11,615 (10th)	0.1	0.03	1.52	0.11–0.5			...	
Anhui	6,455 (26th)	13.9	2.77	0.59	3.01–10			Yes (84.5%)	Yes
Jiangxi	6,678 (24th)	8.1	2.38	0.39	0.11–0.50	Yes		...	
Henan	7,570 (17th)	14.94	1.98	1.19	10.01–30		Yes	No (32.5)	Yes
Hubei	9,011 (14th)	4.12	0.86	1.65	1.01–3			Yes (66.5%)	Yes
Hunan	7,554 (18th)	10.11	1.92	1.05	1.01–3	Yes		Yes (63.5%)	
Total for the central region		52.12	1.46	9.72	...				
Chongqing	7,209 (21st)	6.02	2.43	0.42	0.51–1.00			...	
Sichuan	6,418 (27th)	13.66	1.99	1.2	3.01–10	Yes		No (35.5%)	
Guizhou	3,603 (31st)	4.16	1.39	0.63	1.01–3	Yes		Yes (61%)	Yes
Yunnan	5,662 (29th)	0.28	0.08	3.05	30.01–44.17	Yes	Yes	No (36.5%)	
Tibet	6,871 (22nd)	0	0	0.47	0.11–0.5			...	
Shaanxi	6,480 (25th)	3.42	1.18	0.94	0.11–0.5			Yes (71.5%)	Yes
Gansu	5,022 (30th)	3	1.46	0.3	0.11–0.5			...	
Qinghai	7,277 (20th)	0.19	0.46	0.37	0.51–1.00			...	
Ningxia	6,691 (23rd)	0.7	1.59	0.27	0.51–1.00			...	
Xinjiang	970 (12th)	0.02	0.01	2.95	30.01–44.17	Yes		Yes (54.5%)	
Total for the west region		31.47	1.36	10.6	...				

Sources: Qian, Vermund and Wang (2005); UNAIDS China (2005); Zhu (2003).

Note: The average propensity to migrate is estimated as column 3 divided by the province's percentage share of China's total population (for 1998 as reported by Zhu, 2003). Columns 7–10 based on UNAIDS China (2005).

The provinces

Henan

Henan was China's most populous province in 1998 accounting for 7.5 percent of China's total population (Zhu, 2003). It also supplied the greatest share of registered interprovincial migrants in China (15 percent of the total). Relative to its overall size, it still supplies a disproportionately large number of migrants. The ratio expressing the percentage share of outward migrants to the province's percentage share of China's total population is also among the highest in China (see column 4). Only several other provinces have higher average migration propensities (Sichuan, Chongqing, Anhui, and Jiangxi). This indicates not only large numbers, owing to the size of the province, but also a greater propensity to migrate for people among these provinces. These high-average migration propensities appear, unsurprisingly, to be quite closely related to the relative wealth of these regions. Henan, Sichuan, Chongqing, Anhui, and Jiangxi are ranked as the seventeenth, twenty-seventh, twenty-first, twenty-sixth, and twenty-fourth wealthiest provinces (out of 31 in total).

Henan's HIV/AIDS outbreak as a result of unofficial and official plasma collection, starting as early as the 1980s, was underestimated until recently. According to Ministry of Health (2003) data, only 1,001–5,000 HIV cases were reported by December 2002. This did not place Henan within the top tier of infected provinces (there being eight provinces with over 500 reported infections in December 2002). A more recent survey by Henan provincial health authority in 2004 suggests that the actual situation is far worse. The survey covered over 50,000 villages and 280,000 people identified as having used the illegal blood banks. Of these 25,000 tested HIV positive, nearly 10 percent prevalence (*China Daily*, April 14, 2005). Among those found infected, more than 97 percent came from rural areas (*China Daily*, February 26, 2005). FPDs were mainly poor farmers (both male and female), the groups most likely to participate in migration.

The true scale of the HIV epidemic in Henan is still unknown. International nongovernmental organizations suggest as many as 1.2 million people are HIV positive (Gill, 2002). By the late 1990s, sentinel surveillance was starting to detect HIV among sexually transmitted disease (STD) patients in six provinces, including Henan (at less than 1 percent), indicating that the virus had spread into other high-risk groups. The number of cumulative reported infections stood in the range of 10.01–30 per 100,000, placing it among a few provinces with levels of identified cases over 10 per 100,000.

Of an approximate 93 million people in Henan, 6.5 million were registered migrants at the end of 1998 (Zhu, 2003: 491). Of these a large share was also reported as interprovincial migrants (4.5 million). These figures are likely to underestimate the true number of migrants, owing to the problems with official registrations already mentioned. If official statistics underestimate the actual number of migrants by at least one half, which is quite plausible given estimates of the migrant population above 80 million at this time, a more realistic but still conservative estimate would place the number of interprovincial migrants from Henan at around 9 million and among the highest in the country.

Anhui

Anhui with a population of about 62 million was the second largest supplier of registered interprovincial migrants with 4.2 million in 1998, leaving it just behind Henan. Again, like Henan, relative to its share of China's total population, the number of outward migrants is large (see column 4). It was the highest in China in the late 1990s (at 2.8).

The problem of HIV transmission through plasma collection is not found exclusively in Henan. Indeed, according to MOH and UNAIDS joint assessment, a large share of China's population has sold plasma. Among adults under the age of 60, it is reported that 21.6 percent have donated plasma (MOH and UNAIDS, 2003: 10). Tables 5.2 and 5.3 show that at least eight provinces may have experienced such outbreaks, with high levels of infection among FPDs. Anhui has also experienced a severe FPD-related outbreak. In an independent medical survey undertaken in Anhui province, it was found that HIV infection in a group of former commercial plasma donors "was alarmingly high," standing at 12.5 percent and 2.1 percent among FPD spouses (Wu, Rou and Detels, 2001: 45). Anhui had reported between 501–1,000 HIV cases by December 2002 (MOH and UN Theme Group on HIV/AIDS in China, 2004). This placed it among a third tier of the eight most infected provinces in China. Anhui was among a small number of provinces that detected HIV in STD sentinel surveillance sites during the late 1990s. Sex workers (SWs) in the province have low condom use even by Chinese standards, with three-quarters of SWs "never using" condoms in areas covered by sentinel surveillance data (Table 5.4). It also had a serious STD outbreak, with the incidence of STDs in 1999 placing it in fourth position among China's provinces (with an incidence of 570 per 100,000 in 1999, the Chinese average for this year was 325) (UNAIDS China, 2005).

Anhui provides a significant share of China's long-distance migrants (14 percent). It also has a more serious HIV/AIDS outbreak related to plasma donation. Identified reported cases stood at 3.01–10 per 10,000 by 2002 (Table 5.4).

Sichuan

With a population of 85 million, Sichuan was the third most populous province in China in the late 1990s. It supplied about 4.1 million officially registered interprovincial migrants (the third largest in absolute terms, after Anhui and Henan) with 13.7 percent of the national total. It is another province with high prevalence that has been mainly IDU driven. The HIV epidemic is now generally believed to have started on the main road between Kunming and Chengdu. This is a major route for drug trafficking from Myanmar. By the end of 2000, the major HIV transmission route was still IDU (68 percent of all cases). Blood (transfusion/

Table 5.4 Coastal regions

Province	Per capita gross regional product (RMB/person), 2003	Origin of registered interprovincial migrants (% share of national total)	Column 3/ province's % share of China's total population	Destination of registered interprovincial migrants (% share of national total)	Cumulative infections per 10,000 cases 1985–2003 and reported infections in 2002 (China HIV/AIDS case report)	IDU infection rate > 5% at one sentinel surveillance site or more	HIV detected among STD patients in sentinel sites (year 2000)	CSW's 'never use condoms' above 50% once in years 1998–2000 (and 3-year average where available)	Blood plasma-driven epidemic (provinces with average 10–20% infection among FPDs)
Shanghai	46,718 (1st)	...	0	6.82	?			...	
Jiangsu	16,809 (6th)	2.71	0.47	6.56	0.51–1		Yes	...	
Zhejiang	20,147 (4th)	1.88	0.52	8.94	1.01–3			...	
Fujian	14,979 (7th)	0.72	0.27	3.56	1.01–3			Yes (78)	
Guangdong	17,213 (5th)	0.45	0.08	37.64	3.01–10	Yes	Yes	No (12.5%)	
Shandong	13,661 (9th)	2.36	0.33	2.15	1.01–3			Yes (64.5%)	Yes
Hainan	8,316 (16th)	0.02	0.03	0.51	1.01–3			Yes (32%)	
Beijing	32,061(2nd)	0	0	7.47	?	Yes	Yes	No (36.5%)	
Tianjin	26,532 (3rd)	0.05	0.06	1.91	1.01–3			Yes (59.5%)	
Hebei	10,513 (11th)	2.66	0.5	1.52	0.51–1			...	Yes
Liaoning	14,258 (8th)	0.27	0.08	1.67	0.51–1		Yes	Yes (72%)	
Guangxi	5,969 (28th)	5.3	1.4	0.94	10.01–30	Yes	Yes	Yes (61%)	
The coastal region		16.42	0.4	79.68	...	...	...	...	

Sources: Qian, Vermund and Wang (2005); UNAIDS China (2005); Zhu (2003).

Notes: The average propensity to migrate is estimated as column 3 divided by the province's percentage share of China's total population (for 1998 as reported by Zhu, 2003). Columns 7–10 based on UNAIDS China (2005).

products)-related HIV cases represented 23 percent of all HIV infections and sexual transmission 6 percent (UNAIDS, 2002: 23).

Over 50 percent of prostitutes in Sichuan never used condoms according to sentinel surveillance data. Heterosexual transmission is therefore likely to become more important in this province (ibid.). Sichuan stood in the second rank of four provinces (including Henan, Guangxi, and Guangdong) with between 1,001–5,000 HIV cases reported by December 2002 (MOH and UNAIDS, 2003). It has a serious HIV/AIDS outbreak with higher than average reported infections (3.01–10 per 10,000) and is also a large migrant-supplying region.

Hunan

Hunan has a population of 65 million, supplying approximately 3 million interprovincial migrants making it China's fourth largest supplier of registered interprovincial migrants (with 10 percent of the national total in 1998). Accounting for its population size, it is still a comparatively large supplier of migrants, with a higher relative share of outward migrants than all but five others.

No HIV cases were found among sentinel surveillance STD patients in the late 1990s. However, condom use remained very low among SWs with nearly 90 percent "never using" condoms in 2000. More importantly, Hunan had detected HIV among IDU populations. As a result, it had reported between 501–1,000 HIV cases by December 2002. This placed it within a third tier of the eight most infected provinces in China for this period (MOH and UNAIDS, 2003). While the epidemic does not appear to be as serious in Hunan as in the other provinces already mentioned, detection of HIV in IDU groups is often associated with rapid rises in HIV prevalence among other high-risk populations (MAP, 2004).

Jiangxi

Jiangxi provides 8.1 percent of China's interprovincial migrants, China's fifth largest supplier of migrants. One possible reason why Jiangxi has a high level of outward migration is that it borders three important migrant receiving provinces: Zhejiang which received 9 percent of China's total according to Tables 5.3 and 5.4, Fujian at 3.5 percent, and Guangdong at 38 percent. Unlike the other provinces mentioned so far, Jiangxi had a lower amount of cumulative recorded cases in China (0.11–0.50 per 10,000). Jiangxi had no HIV cases in sentinel surveillance STD patients by 2000. Jiangxi had reported less than 100 cases by December 2002 (MOH and UNAIDS, 2003). The IDU infection rate, however, had exceeded 5 percent in at least one surveillance site.

Injecting drug use was reported to be common among drug users in this province. Jiangxi was the sixth province to find HIV among IDUs. Over a number of years, the sentinel surveillance system has indicated high injection and needle sharing rates among drug users, with 85 percent of drug users doing so intravenously (UNAIDS, 2002: 27). Needle sharing rates among IDU were 74 percent in 1998, 93 percent in 1999, and 70 percent in 2000. Gonorrhea, condyloma (genital warts), and chlamydia have been the leading sexually transmitted infection (STI) as well as rapidly increasing rates of syphilis (ibid.). Jiangxi is one of China's more seriously affected provinces, though not in the top tier, conditions favorable for the further spread of HIV exist.

Guangxi Zhuang autonomous region

Guangxi has large numbers of IDUs and a rapidly growing HIV/AIDS problem. It was also the sixth largest provider of interprovincial migrants (5.3 percent) in 1998 (with 1.6 million). Guangxi sits on China's south eastern border and IDU is common. In Guangxi, approximately 90 percent of all drug users were reported to be IDUs and more than half shared injection equipment (UNAIDS, 2002: 24). During 1998, five out of seven sentinel sites reported increasing HIV rates among IDU in this province.

HIV positivity also increased at the CSW sentinel site in Guangxi from 0 percent at the beginning of 1998 to 5 percent at the end of the year (ibid.). Many involved in CSW in this region also have histories of drug abuse. Moreover, 63 percent of SWs reported never using a condom during sex. HIV infections are common among noninjecting STI patients (infections have also been growing at around 20 percent per annum). According to UNAIDS and the MOH, all of these factors "make the risk of an impending heterosexual HIV epidemic in Guangxi very real indeed" (UNAIDS, 2002: 24). Guangxi stood among a second tier of four provinces (including Henan, Guangxi, and Guangdong) with between 1,001–5,000 HIV cases reported by December 2002 (MOH and UNAIDS, 2003).

Discussion and conclusions

In China the migrant population is now generally considered to be a key factor in determining the future scale of the HIV epidemic. Exactly how this group is likely to contribute to the epidemic still remains slightly unclear owing to a dearth of research, as well as at times seemingly contradictory findings (Hesketh *et al.*, 2006). Studies have considered, among other things, how behavior may change after migration and whether there is higher HIV prevalence among migrant groups. Some regional case studies have also been produced. As yet, however, the broader national patterns in migration and HIV prevalence have not been closely analyzed.

This chapter, in contributing to this important subject, has examined whether there are any particular patterns in outward migration and HIV prevalence. Do provinces with more severe HIV/AIDS epidemics supply more or less migrants? As noted, this is particularly relevant in China's case owing to the high-regional concentration of infections: by the end of 2006, over 70 percent of cumulative reported infections were found in just six provinces (Table 5.2). Evidently it is a concern if migrants are more likely to originate from high-prevalence regions. Such patterns may facilitate the spread of the virus nationally. Many studies also show that risk behaviors do increase after migration. This would further imply then that this population group may act as an especially potent force in the unfolding HIV epidemic.

Examining official migration data from the Public Security Bureau for 1998 and sentinel surveillance data for this period, China's six largest migrant-supplying provinces were Henan, Anhui, Sichuan, Hunan, Jiangxi, and Guangxi. These provinces alone accounted for over 65 percent of registered outward inter-provincial migrants, totaling nearly 20 million registered migrants in 1998. Sentinel surveillance data accompanied by further investigation into each of these six provinces, moreover, show that these regions had more advanced epidemics. Examination of more recent data on cumulative infections also confirms the high prevalence in these regions: by the end of 2005, these migrant-supplying provinces had recorded among the highest number of reported HIV infections in China, accounting for over 45 percent of all reported infections. This suggests that the six migrant-supplying provinces have epidemics that started earlier than in other regions and are also more severe. Furthermore, evidence taken from earlier population censuses indicates that current patterns of migration have been in existence since the early 1980s and continue today. It is likely that official figures from public security departments seriously underestimate the true number of migrants, possibly by as much as one half, suggesting at least 40 million migrants may have left these provinces in 1998 alone. The underreporting of actual number of migrants originating from these six provinces has serious consequences to obtaining a relatively accurate account of not only changing demographics but also the interrelationship between migration and HIV.

Is it so surprising that greater outward migration takes place from high-prevalence regions? Given the close match between outward long-distance migration and higher HIV prevalence, it would seem unlikely that chance alone can explain the pattern. The evidence presented here also shows that these high-prevalence regions are also among the poorest in China. This should not come as a surprise, as it is well established that migration is driven by expected earning differentials and we would expect outward migration from poor regions. Interestingly, and of relevance to the current discussion, it has also been hypothesized that in general susceptibility to HIV is also greater in poor regions (Stillwaggon, 2006). In poorer regions, knowledge of HIV, nutritional intake, and health standards all tend to be lower and gender inequalities are greater. The relatively impoverished nature of these migrant-supplying regions may also in part explain higher prevalence in these regions. In China, the tendency of higher prevalence within poorer regions has been particularly compounded by the fact that IDU has also been more common in the poorer south western regions of China. This is partly because drug trafficking routes exist in these regions. It has also been exacerbated by unsafe plasma donation, more widespread in poor rural areas, such as those found in central areas of China like Henan and Anhui. Adding to the more general tendencies that may favor HIV infection in poor regions, China's lower income regions have also experienced additional unfavorable influences. This might suggest that the migrant population could play an important part in the spread of HIV in China, via its role as a conveyor of HIV from relatively high-prevalence rural regions to other, as yet, low-prevalence urban areas where jobs can be found. The Chinese example as such may also point toward an important underlying dynamic between HIV, poverty, inequality, and outward migration. This relationship is one in which high-prevalence poor regions are more prone to the outward migration of people, and as a result of migration these groups are also prone to high-risk behavior, which in turn makes them more likely to transmit HIV.

The question of where migrants go to and what they do after migration is also important to consider. Tables 5.3 and 5.4 indicate that the destinations of a large share of migrants are several coastal regions, including Guangdong and Beijing. Interestingly, these areas also have higher than average prevalence. Li, Morrow and Kermode (2007: 1290) found in their study of male migrant workers in Chengdu of Sichuan province, more than half of all respondents had migrated and worked in three or more cities prior to Chengdu. In addition, the migrants surveyed displayed significant gaps in HIV knowledge, such as the belief that one can contract HIV through sharing food (Li, Morrow and Kermode, 2007: 1290). Coupled with high mobility and lack of HIV knowledge, various studies have also found that migrants are more prepared to take greater sexual risks. Yang, Derlega and Luo (2007: 284) concluded from their research that migrants are four times more likely to have unprotected sex than their nonmigrant counterpart; and more than six times likely to have three or more lifetime casual partners. In a survey by Yang and Xia (2008: 335) of both male and female nonmigrants and migrants in a southern province, they found that female migrants (not HIV positive or drug users) were 15 times more likely to have multiple sexual partners than their male migrant counterparts. The gender differences in migration are clearly pronounced, as explored in Chapter 4. However, in understanding risk-taking behavior, we must consider the social, cultural, economic, and political environments in which these situations occur. In the case of female migrants, Yang and Xia (2008: 342) observe with great clarity:

> To reduce female temporary migrants' risky sexual behavior, it appears necessary to improve their economic well-being and social integration in cities. Policy measures to alleviate social, cultural, and institutional constraints that limit female temporary migrants' equal access to urban employment are urgently needed.

Nonetheless, there is still only a limited understanding of how mobility and HIV interact. It is probably also fair to agree with the IOM's view that "today it is certainly much more difficult to map the connections between disease and mobility than it was in the past" (IOM, 2005: 11).

Finally, in understanding the linkages between HIV and migrants, it is worth stressing that we should not be solely confined to a particular category of migrants that is so often portrayed in the media, the migrant toiling "the bitter, dirty, arduous, and low prestige work denigrated by urban residents" (Solinger, 1995: 129). As we have noted earlier, mobile men with money are also likely to be an important group. Other studies have also shown that those in positions of wealth and power are also mobile when it comes to employment. They are also important to any analysis of mobility and HIV. Uretsky (2008: 803), for example, also believes that China's economic development has empowered men in the upper echelons of society to engage in risky sexual practices, but such practices are steeped in "particular set of socio-cultural and politico-economic factors that converge within their work-related roles and duties." Changes in pattern of sexual behavior including the increasing commodification of sex will have tremendous impact on the HIV/AIDS epidemic in China. Uretsky's research further indicates the complexities of grasping the connections between HIV and migration.

This chapter notes hitherto overlooked trends in current migration patterns in China. On average, Chinese migrants are more likely to already have contracted HIV, even before migration, than other population groups. This finding contrasts with that of many studies on migration and HIV, where emphasis is on the increased susceptibility only after migration, owing to behavioral changes. As such they overlook the important role migrants may play as a conduit of the virus. They also overlook the added potency this brings to the migrant population as contributors to the HIV epidemic. It is behavioral change coupled with already high prevalence that makes the migrant population in China such an important component of the HIV/AIDS epidemic. From a policy perspective this finding also has important implications, namely that targeting migrant population groups only after migration may already be too late. To achieve a holistic understanding of the HIV/AIDS epidemic in China and thus appropriate policy measures, it is clear that that our frameworks must be broadened to include the social, cultural, economic, and political contexts in which the epidemic occurs.

6 Healthcare

Introduction

This chapter investigates and summarizes reforms in healthcare and considers how these have impacted on delivery of important public health services. It also looks in detail at one related area of public health, the emergence of sexually transmitted diseases (STDs). The number and kinds of STDs in China have grown dramatically since reforms started. Their dramatic re-emergence, particularly since the mid-1990s, is also linked to the weaknesses now found in China's healthcare system. There are a number of further reasons why exploring the nature and trends of STD infections is important. First, evidence on STD infections provides insights into how heterosexual transmission networks are evolving. As more HIV infections are via sexual transmission, as most evidence suggests is the case, this mode of infection has become an ever more important component of the epidemic. In fact, widespread generalized epidemics (exceeding 1 percent of the adult population), require widespread heterosexual transmission within the general population. As such, gaining further insights into the forces driving heterosexual transmission dynamics is important. Second, by focusing on the epidemiological evidence we have on STDs, we may also be able to better understand the particular groups in society that are most affected, as well as the factors that place them at risk. Third, this may help put together a more comprehensive picture of the particular forces, or undercurrents that are currently and in future will drive the epidemic forward. Examination of the evidence on STD infections may therefore help us better understand the economic and social determinants of sexual transmission networks. The epidemiological and medical evidence, in this regard, may provide some useful insights.

STD infections have grown rapidly in part because of the inadequate healthcare system. This has led to ineffective treatment policies for a number of public health problems, particularly in rural areas where incomes are lower. An official national survey in 2003, for example, showed that around half of all patients needing treatment did not visit a doctor. Nearly one-third of all patients needing hospitalization, moreover, refused it because of cost (Kaufman, 2005: 4). Public contributions to hospital running costs, moreover, have decreased from about one-third in the 1970s to under one-tenth in 2000 and the growing funding shortfall is basically funded by patient fees (Kaufman, 2005). This general pattern of inadequate treatment is quite more pronounced in the area of STDs. Owing to stigma, lack of accessible treatment centers and the asymptomatic and self-limiting nature of some STDs (e.g., chlamydia and syphilis), many patients are not properly treated. In one study of a rural county outside Beijing, for example, it was found that 80 percent of women with symptoms of STD did not seek treatment because of the high costs and their own lack of knowledge about their illness (Chen *et al.*, 2007: 134). Given these various problems, the emergence of STDs is now very much a major public health problem and one related, to among other things, the way in which healthcare is provided. Active STD prevention, testing, and treatment policies must play a vital role in reducing sexual transmission of HIV. This is because STDs also work to increase the probability of transmission of HIV/AIDS and are an important cofactor in its transmission. Understanding the nature of STD epidemics is therefore of central importance to understanding the spread of HIV.

This chapter first considers the nature of China's evolving healthcare system. By looking at the capacity of the health system, we can get a clearer picture of China's capacity to manage not only the increase in STDs but also the HIV/AIDS epidemic. Second, we then look in more detail at the evidence on China's STD epidemics, so as to provide more insights into some of the fundamental drivers of sexual transmission networks. Interestingly, evidence from a number of epidemiological studies supports some of the arguments made earlier, regarding, for example, the drivers of commercial sex work (CSW) and the possible role of migrant populations.

The healthcare system

Economic reforms have severely weakened China's healthcare system. Prior to 1978, the rural cooperative medical scheme (CMS) served the majority of China's rural population as the provision of care was available through communes. The CMS operated the village and township clinics with staffing by barefoot doctors. While having only basic training and facilities, these barefoot doctors were largely successful in meeting the medical needs of the rural population. The CMS emphasized preventive health coupled with patriotic health campaigns. The health apparatus achieved significant gains, including, as it happens, the near eradication of STDs. China's primary healthcare system, at this time, was held up as the model to emulate (Kaufman, 2005). Since the health system came under review and restructuring in the 1980s, however, the responsibility for health provision has shifted dramatically toward local governments. The central government's share of national healthcare spending has, correspondingly, also decreased, from around 40 percent in the early 1980s to around 18 percent in 2005 (Tang *et al.*, 2008: 1497).[1] Because of this, access to healthcare services has fallen dramatically and access for China's rural population, in particular, has fallen dramatically (Brown, de Brauw and Du, 2009). As Liu, Hsiao and Eggleston note:

The number of outpatient visits made by both rural and urban residents has increased during the reform era, partially due to increased incomes. Yet there has been a relative decline in use of hospital services by the rural population in recent years. Between 1985 and 1993 annual inpatient days per 1000 urban residents increased by 12.8%, whereas the rural population experienced a 10.3% decline.

(1999: 1352)

The distribution of resources across China's healthcare system is now "decidedly pro-rich" (Wagstaff, Lindelow, and Wang, 2009: S13). Of the total government spending on health services in 2005, a full 25 percent went to four of China's wealthiest provinces and municipalities: Jiangsu, Zhejiang, Beijing, and Shanghai (Kaufman, 2005). Within provinces, moreover, spending is heavily in favor of urban residents, in particular the provision of subsidies for urban health insurance schemes. According to the Ministry of Health's (MOH) National Health Account, over 40 percent of government spending in 2002 went to urban health insurance programs (quoted in Wagstaff, Lindelow and Wang, 2009: S13). While city hospitals received 50 percent of the subsidies in 2002, county hospitals received just 9 percent and township healthcare centers received only 7 percent (ibid.). This lack of funding severely undermines China's ability to address a variety of health problems at the rural level. Indeed, rising health costs are also one of the most important factors in pushing households beneath the poverty line. The National Bureau of Statistics reported that of the 592 poor counties in 2004, one-quarter of the households that fell into poverty suffered a severe loss of income associated with a major health shock. By 2000, it is reported, China ranked 188 out of 191 countries in terms of fairness in financial contribution to health (Kaufman, 2005: 2).

Coupled with poor financing of rural health services, out-of-pocket health expenses for individual patients have also increased exponentially. With fiscal decentralization, hospitals saw a sharp decline in state financing, although this was in part offset by local government subsidies. For rural hospitals where government revenues were restricted, the cost of care has been pushed down to the individual level. In response to declining subsidies, hospitals were encouraged to raise revenue through patient fees, including such things as diagnosis fees and mark-ups on drugs. Although basic service costs and standard medication are controlled by the state, this has not stopped some creative solutions. Moreover, "[o]veremphasis on cost recovery, through user fees and drug sales, has skewed health institutions towards providing curative services," as opposed to preventive measures (Fang and Kaufman, 2008: 1619). This situation contrasts strikingly, of course, with the earlier approach of the barefoot doctor. Out-of-pocket medical fees, it has been found, now have the greatest impact on forcing people into poverty (van Doorslaer *et al.*, 2006). A Health Ministry survey in 2004 found three-quarters of rural patients declined the recommended hospital treatment owing to financial reasons. Unsurprisingly, children living in the poorest provinces and in rural China face the highest death risks. Child mortality levels in urban areas average about one-third of those in rural areas. Under-five mortality rates range from 8 per 1,000 live births in Shanghai and Beijing (comparable to the US) to 60 in the poorest province of Guizhou (comparable to Namibia) (UNDP, 2005: 63). There is now also a danger that China will miss the Millennium Development Goal target for child mortality. Deepening inequalities, moreover, may slow progress toward other health goals (ibid.).

Due to the increased costs of health, those in need of care are also much more likely to forgo treatment. There is evidence also to suggest that women and girls have been more adversely affected by these reforms. It has been found, for example, that women in rural areas were less likely to seek assistance for reproductive issues, received less prenatal care, and 94 percent gave birth at home (Kaufman, 2005: 115). The gender aspect of healthcare, or lack of, is further noted by Guan *et al.* (2009: 446), who found women with symptoms of STDs would, on average, spend less than their male counterparts on treatments. The focus on cost recovery by healthcare practitioners and institutions sharpens not only unequal access to health between the rich and poor but also between male and female. The gender dimension is clearly present when we consider reproductive tract infection (RTIs), STDs, and HIV/AIDS. In a study of rural women's access to reproductive healthcare in Yunnan, Tian *et al.* (2007: 292) observed that the women who did seek treatment for RTIs were prescribed medication for trichomonas without any diagnosis by the practitioner. While this shows the agenda for generating revenue, Tian *et al.* (ibid.) also suggested that the practitioners were limited in their health knowledge. Participants of their study voiced their lack of choice and concern in accessing healthcare, particularly as practitioners provided very limited treatment options for their patients (Tian *et al.*, 2007). The perception of poor quality of healthcare is supported by Tang *et al.* (2008). Their study showed that 55 percent of respondents from both the lowest and highest income quintile of the 2003 national household survey were dissatisfied with inpatient services; and 40 and 45 percent (respectively) were unhappy with outpatient services (Tang *et al.*, 2008: 1499). The weakened health system not only sharpens rural–urban divide but also gender inequalities. It is therefore of enormous concern for a number of public health issues. In the case of HIV/AIDS, the ability for those to afford care, especially those impoverished both pre- and post-HIV/AIDS, such as former plasma donors (FPDs) from rural regions, will face further economic hardships in managing their health.

The affordability of healthcare is of particular concern to HIV/AIDS patients, many of which to date have been in poorer rural regions. The average per capita expenditure on "medical care" in the urban areas of low and medium human development provinces affected by HIV averaged around 390 RMB per capita. In the urban areas of the higher human development index regions (Beijing, Shanghai, and Tianjin), per capita spending stood at 728 RMB. In the low HDI high HIV provinces, per capita rural expenditure on medical care fell to about 79 RMB, compared with almost 250 in the rural areas of high HDI regions. This suggests that the relative medical expenditures between rural and urban regions fall dramatically in the worst affected regions of China. On average, rural expenditures on medical care were about one-fifth those of urban counterparts in low HDI high HIV provinces. In the medium HDI group, this rose to about one-quarter and in the high HDI group this rose further still, to about one-third. The disparities in healthcare rise significantly as one moves to the worst affected regions of China. In Yunnan, for example, rural residents spend about 15 percent of their urban counterparts on medical costs. In Henan, rural residents spend about 21 percent of their urban counterparts and in Guangxi rural residents spend about 24 percent of their urban counterparts.

The extent and potential of China's HIV/AIDS epidemic has led to some positive responses from the government in terms of financial support for those in poverty and suffering from HIV/AIDS. The Chinese government has pledged to assist in the provision of health services for FPDs, with many in advanced stages of HIV/AIDS through the Four Free One Care policy. The four free and one care includes: free antiretroviral treatment for rural AIDS patients or urban residents with financial difficulties; free voluntary counseling and testing; free testing services to newborns and to prevent mother-to-child transmission; AIDS orphans are provided with free schooling; and households of people living with HIV/AIDS (PLWHA) are provided with care and economic assistance. While patients may have access to discounted medication subsidized by the government, the cost of long-term healthcare may still be unaffordable. In a study by Meng *et al.* (2006: 215) in a rural Jilin province, the researchers found that the average health expenditure for participants with HIV/AIDS was 1,800 RMB per annum (US$225). These expenses were particularly high given that their estimated average annual income was only 2,936 RMB (US$355). The burden of the direct financial costs that fall on HIV/AIDS patients is very large. The indirect costs incurred by the loss of time and income for family members required to care for their relatives are also significant. Aside from the subsidization of medical costs, it is these other costs that are also crippling for HIV/AIDS patients. The cost of transportation to clinics, the cost of hospitalization, including meal and bed fees, all come into consideration for those deciding whether to seek assistance or not (Moon *et al.*, 2008). The Chinese government has made substantial inroads in the provision of care for those impoverished and HIV positive. However, it would appear that heavily subsidized medication may not be enough, as it is the peripheral costs, such as hospitalization, that also contributes to the overall financial burden.

Given the numerous factors such as underfunding of rural health services, urban bias, increasing out-of-pocket expenses, and gender inequality in access – China is poised to face the challenges of the provision of medical care to its citizens with great difficulty, not to mention the HIV/AIDS epidemic. All these extraneous factors serve to work against stemming the tide of the epidemic. Furthermore, the inequalities that we see within China, as discussed in Chapters 2 and 3, between rural and urban and men and women, in areas such as education, income, and health, are further exacerbated as China's health system fails to address basic health needs. There may be some changes on the horizon. With the central government announcing in April 2009 to spend an additional 850 billion RMB (US$125 billion) on healthcare, it is a step in the right direction.

Additionally, the introduction of the New Medical Cooperative System will ensure greater numbers of rural residents with medical insurance (see Brown, de Brauw and Du, 2009). Nonetheless, the health system is reliant on a joint funding system from both the central and local governments which will result in great variations in the quality of care being provided, as so much is dependent on local governments having the revenue base to support the health system. Whether these steps will mean greater capacity to address the HIV/AIDS epidemic and the return of STDs remains to be seen.

The re-emergence of STDs

The breakdown in healthcare provision has had important implications for a number of public health issues in China. The re-emergence of STDs, however, is one very striking example of how inadequate services have led to an unprecedented explosion in STDs.

While progress has been made globally in combating many infectious diseases during the twentieth century, such as polio and smallpox, at the same time a number of infectious diseases have continued to expand. This includes, among other things, TB, multidrug-resistant TB, and also HIV/AIDS. STDs, moreover, have also seen considerable global growth in this period. Morbidity attributed to STDs, when compared to other infectious diseases, has also grown during this period, despite the relative low costs of treatment and possibilities for adequate prevention via promotion of condom use.[2] Today over 20 microbial agents and parasites can be transmitted by sexual contact. Around 330 million people worldwide contract an STD each year compared with the approximately 3 million that contract HIV (Family Health International, 2011). Around 236 million people, for example, are estimated to have trichomoniasis, with 94 million new cases a year. Chlamydia affects around 160 million people, with 97 million new cases annually. Approximately 30 million new cases of genital warts and about 78 million new cases of gonorrhea occur each year. Genital herpes infects 21 million and syphilis infects 19 million people. More than 9 million people are infected with chancroid annually (UNAIDS/WHO, 2000; Family Health International, 2011). The majority of these infections, moreover, are in developing countries, where STDs are nearly as common a disease as malaria. STDs, unsurprisingly, rank among the top five diseases for which adults in developing countries seek healthcare, as well as ranking among the five most important causes for loss of healthy reproductive life (ibid.). Such STDs, moreover, greatly facilitate the transmission of HIV and constitute an important cofactor.

STDs may increase individual susceptibility to HIV infection by two mechanisms. Genital ulcers (such as those caused by syphilis, herpes, or chancroid) result in breaks in the genital tract lining or skin. These breaks create an entry point for HIV. Nonulcerative STDs, on the other hand (such as chlamydia, gonorrhea, and trichomoniasis), are likely to increase the concentration of cells in genital secretions that can serve as targets for HIV (CD4+ cells). Medical research shows that when HIV-infected individuals are also infected with other STDs they are more likely to have HIV in their genital secretions. It has been found that men with both gonorrhea and HIV, for example, are more than twice as likely to shed HIV in their genital secretions compared with those who are only infected with HIV. The median concentration of HIV in semen, moreover, is much higher in men who are infected with both gonorrhea and HIV than in men infected only with HIV. Despite the obvious significance of STDs and their impact on health in developing countries, it is only in quite recent times that governments and international organizations have started paying more attention to them. This is mainly because their important role in promoting HIV infection was recognized.

STDs in China

STDs were probably introduced into China around 500 years ago by European traders, via Guangzhou in the early 1500s (Abrams, 2001). By the time the Communist party assumed power in 1949, however, STDs had become endemic and were a very serious problem. Widespread poverty, inequality, a broken health system, and failed governments, accompanied by decades of civil war, left an estimated 10 million Chinese infected with an STD. By the 1950s, for example, it was reported that syphilis was present in 84 percent of prostitutes and 5 percent of the general population in some large cities, as well as 2 to 3 percent of rural residents (Chen *et al.*, 2007: 132). China had one of the largest such epidemics in history of mankind. By the mid-1960s, however, hard hitting public health measures, along with significant changes in people's lifestyles owing in large part to a radically changed socioeconomic system, had led to a remarkable reversal. As economic reforms started to unfold in the 1980s, however, and lifestyles again changed, a number of powerful economic and social forces again led to the dramatic re-emergence of STDs.

It was only in 1998 that China's public health reporting system again started to track eight types of STDs. Data are collected quarterly from all provinces, autonomous regions, and municipalities. The surveillance system requires that all cases of clinically diagnosed STDs, as well as the source of infection are reported by doctors.[3] Overall, the rate of infection for these eight STDs increased fourfold from 1990 to 1998, from 14 cases per 100,000 persons to 51 cases per 100,000 (Remez, 2000). The incidence of gonorrhea tripled over the period, from 9 to 24 cases per 100,000, and that of genital warts quadrupled to 11 cases per 100,000. The infection rate with syphilis, considered in more detail shortly, rose even more dramatically, experiencing a 20-fold increase according to official data, from 0.2 to 4.3 infections per 100,000. Throughout the 1990s, the rate of infection with any STD increased by an average of 17 percent annually. Syphilis had average annual increases of 20 percent (ibid.). In spite of these rapid increases, by 2000 the reported annual incidence for all eight infections was only 0.07 per 100 persons for the general population (ibid.). More recent estimates, however, also show a continued growth in these STDs. For syphilis, for example, it is reported that the total rate of cases of both primary and secondary syphilis had reached 5.7 cases per 100,000 persons by 2005 (Chen *et al.*, 2007: 132). It stood at 0.2 cases per 100,000, in 1993, by contrast. The rate of congenital syphilis, which is passed from mothers to unborn infants, had increased even more rapidly, with an average yearly rise of around 70 percent [from 0.01 cases per 100,000 live births in 1991 to 19.68 cases per 100,000 in 2005 (ibid.)].[4] The effects of STDs on women are particularly serious. Untreated RTIs can lead to serious health problems, such as cervical cancer, fetal loss, and the increased risk of HIV transmission. In a study of over 2,000 rural women in Yunnan province, it was found that 42 percent had one infection and 9 percent had two (Kaufman *et al.*, 1999: 115).

Despite the rapid growth in these reported cases, it is also highly likely that such estimates have significantly underestimated the real number of STD cases to date. There are a number of reasons why this is so. First, it is widely believed that important centers of treatment may severely underreport cases. Hospitals, family planning centers, gynecological clinics, pharmacies, and private practitioners are the main culprits. For example, in Shenzhen and Guangzhou, around 30 percent of STD patients sought initial care at a site other than a government center. If these are underreporting then estimates will be inaccurate. In studies undertaken in Chengdu and Hangzhou, approximately 18–40 percent of patients sought care from private doctors and pharmacists. In an internal but unpublished quality-control study carried out in 1999, STD surveillance officials found that in one province over three-quarters of STD cases were not reported. Private practitioners were the least reliable (reporting under 1 percent of cases), followed by district-level hospitals (7.9 percent), provincial-level hospitals (15.4 percent), and city-level hospitals (35.5 percent) (Chen *et al.*, 2007: 135). Second, in many cases, asymptomatic infection may lead to underreporting (particularly of chlamydial infections). Third, there is also evidence to suggest many STDs are often misdiagnosed and therefore also underreported.

An indication of how severe the underreporting of STDs may be is given by the fact that the official 26 sentinel sites reported about 18 percent of the nation's aggregate syphilis cases from 1995 to 2001. These sites, however, cover only 3 percent of the population (about 35–40 million people). Such results imply that nonsentinel sites are massively underreporting the actual scale of the epidemic (Chen *et al.*, 2007: 134). Despite universal reporting requirements, underreporting remains a problem, and many STD-infected patients who seek care from nongovernment sources are missing from the official data. Consequently, the data indicating sustained growth in STDs are still conservative estimates. By 1999, for example, there were 837,357 officially reported infections of STDs according to China's MOH (Abrams, 2001: 434). Experts estimate that actually more than 8 million Chinese citizens (10 times higher than reported) had contracted STDs in 2002. The majority of individuals with STDs in China displays no symptoms, have not been identified, and also therefore have not been appropriately treated.

International comparisons

The rapid growth of STDs means that infection rates in China today are far higher than those found in many other countries, including both the developing and developed world, as well as those countries with the most severe HIV/AIDS epidemics. Recent epidemiological research, for example, shows that the incidence of primary and secondary syphilis in 2005 was 5.67 cases per 100,000. By comparison, there were 2.7 cases of primary and secondary syphilis per 100,000 individuals reported in 2004 in the United States (Chen *et al.*, 2007: 135): "In both relative and absolute terms, the 25 times increased risk of syphilis reported by Chen and colleagues dwarfs that seen in the USA, Canada, and Europe" (Fisman, 2007: 84). As well as syphilis, chlamydial infection in urban China is "as high as or higher than among urban groups in developed western societies" (Parish *et al.*, 2003: 1271). Comparing studies that used similar sampling techniques and looking at similar population groups (based on sexual experience, comparable residence), recent research shows that such infection rates among women aged 20–44 years in China were nearly five times those of similar individuals in Britain (1.5 per 100 in Britain compared with 7.4 in China). Among men, prevalence was 2.2 in Britain and 3.0 in China (per 100). In another study, comparing North America with China, female prevalence stood at 4.3 in the former and 7.6 in the latter. For men, prevalence decreased to 1.6 in the former and 2.2 in the latter (quoted in ibid.). Another study comparing the Netherlands with China, looking at women who reported having sex in the previous year (in the age groups 15–40 years), found a prevalence of 2.8 per 100 in the Netherlands and 9.0 in China (quoted in ibid.).

Some studies have found that prevalence rates of certain STDs among China's rural population may be comparable with those of rural Africa, the region at the epicenter of the global HIV/AIDS pandemic. Large regional differences aside, Chinese rural chlamydial infection prevalence for those aged 20–59 years were 1.7 for women and 2.2 for men. In a region of Uganda among individuals aged 15–59 years, rural prevalence were 2.1 for women and 2.4 for men (ibid.). Uganda had a national adult HIV prevalence of over 4 percent in 2004 (UNDP, 2005: 248). Other studies looking specifically at commercial sex workers (CSWs) reached similar findings. According to Gil *et al.* (1996), a comparison of bacterial STD rates in sex workers from four counties of China's Sichuan province and in the city of Chengdu in the mid-1990s found 48.8 percent of all Chinese prostitutes carried one or more bacterial STD infection, compared to global prevalence rates ranging from 8.3 percent in Taiwan to 51.2 percent in central Africa. Syphilitic infections, ranged from between 0.8–6.8 percent, lower than that in both African and US samples, although the rapid growth of syphilis in China recently has reversed this situation (ibid.: 147). Trichomoniasis, stood at 38.5 percent prevalence in this sample and was higher than both Central Africa (6 percent) and the US (7.8 percent) samples studied (ibid.). Consequently, the rate of STD infections across China is an important indicator, if not a worrying one for China's HIV/AIDS trajectory.

Risk factors and high-risk groups for STDs

A number of recent epidemiological studies are also useful in helping to further understand the dynamics of STD emergence in China. There are now a variety of studies that provide insights into STDs in different social and economic groups, such as migrants and sex workers, as well as providing comparisons with the general population. Some of these studies also provide quite detailed information on socioeconomic status, education status as well as the knowledge, attitudes and behaviors of different groups. Two epidemiological studies, for example, look at specific STDs among migrant populations (including in one case also HIV), so providing insights into the nature of sexual transmission networks in these groups. These studies were both undertaken in developed regions of eastern China's Yangtze River Delta, which has among the highest reported prevalence of STDs in China. One was for Hangzhou, in Zhejiang province (Hesketh *et al.*, 2006) and the other in Shanghai (He *et al.*, 2005). These studies, unlike those based on officially reported data, also included coverage of social and economic factors that may be associated with STD infection. In addition, other studies have also looked at different population groups, including STDs in sex workers in various parts of China, incorporating those regions with high HIV prevalence, such as Yunnan, (Hesketh, Zhang and Qiang, 2005: 961) and also those with lower HIV prevalence but high STD prevalence, as in the case of Guangzhou (van den Hoek *et al.*, 2001). These types of epidemiological studies provide useful insights into the nature of risky sexual behaviors and the dynamics of STD transmission in particular population groups (often those at high risk). They also allow comparisons to be made against the general population. As such, they can also provide further insights into the nature of some of the deeper undercurrents driving China's HIV/AIDS epidemic. These studies also therefore provide an opportunity to reconsider and explore arguments considered in earlier chapters.

Most studies considering CSW find, unsurprisingly, that the spread of STDs is quite closely related to the commercial sex industry. Sex workers in general have very high levels of infection. This is also despite the fact that many sex workers see such work as only a temporary solution and turnover within the industry is accordingly high. In a study of 1,000 sex workers in Guangzhou, the median duration of employment was 1 year. Yet syphilis was present in 14 percent, chlamydia 32 percent, gonorrhea 8 percent, and trichomoniasis 12.5 percent of the workers (van den Hoek *et al.*, 2001: 753). Similarly in Yunnan STDs were reportedly common (Hesketh, Zhang and Qiang, 2005). Despite the short duration of prostitution then, and the low number of clients, the prevalence of STDs was high (van den Hoek *et al.*, 2001: 758). In another study of chlamydial infections, a substantial prevalence of chlamydia infections was found among female sex workers (Chen *et al.*, 2006: 284). Unsurprisingly, knowledge about STD/HIV transmission and condom use has been poor. Perhaps unsurprisingly, a strong association between STD infection and visits to CSWs is also found within male populations in most of the epidemiological studies to date.

High-risk groups

Is it possible to identify any other social groups affected by STDs? If so, this may provide evidence on which to base future policy. Earlier chapters argued there were a variety of reasons, particularly if the experiences of other Southeast Asian nations hold any lessons, to suggest that demand for sex work originates disproportionately from the relatively wealthier social groups. It was also argued that growing inequalities also help to explain the rapid growth in the commercial sex industry. Does any epidemiological evidence support this argument?

Income, wealth, and demand for CSW

In one study of chlamydia infections, using a sample of over 3,000 individuals representing the general public, only 110 men and 45 women had had sex with two or more noncommercial sexual partners in the previous year (Parish *et al.*, 2003: 1271). These individuals had low rates of infection and in general the findings pointed toward a low rate of transmission of chlamydial infections through lateral, casual sex networks. Indeed, the findings strongly supported the argument that chlamydial infections were more often passed through commercial sex networks, particularly involving men with high incomes, who traveled and socialized frequently, exactly those who have the greatest opportunity for commercial sex. In another study of an eastern Chinese city which had reported more than 10 percent STD prevalence rate, the authors also concluded that having more discretionary income was significant predictor of visiting entertainment venues (Li *et al.*, 2009). Furthermore, visiting entertainment venues was also correlated with unsafe sex and STD infection (ibid.: 818). Women married to men in these groups were also more often infected, providing further circumstantial evidence of one of the most common STD infection paths.

Research on chlamydia infections has also showed that successful men who earned higher incomes were more likely to engage in unprotected commercial sex. The fact that wealthier groups are disproportionately engaged in commercial sex is corroborated by other research into the clientele of Chinese sex workers (Gil *et al.*, 1996: 147; Pan, 1999). It has also been found that in other parts of the world some of the more educated population groups with higher incomes are more sexually active. In the early stages of the sub-Saharan African epidemics, for example, wealthier social groups, such as school and university teachers, were more adversely affected. In China, a lot of evidence now suggests these wealthier groups are more prone to engage in unprotected commercial sex. Similarly, women in relationships with such men are also more likely to be infected. By contrast, as yet there is comparatively little evidence to suggest that the poorer migrant groups are adversely affected by STDs. On average, migrant groups have lower levels of education, are less able to pay for treatment or receive subsidized treatment, and have far greater psychosocial stresses, which may lead to riskier behaviors. There are a number of reasons for believing migrants therefore may be at high risk to STDs. Only several scientific studies of STD prevalence within migrant groups, however, have been published to date and concerns have been voiced with some of the unsubstantiated reports claiming high prevalence among migrant populations (Hesketh *et al.*, 2006: 11). Some city reports, for example, suggest greater risk of acquiring HIV among migrants: 52 percent of all HIV reports in Beijing, 61 percent in Xian, and 66 percent in Shanghai in 2000 were in migrant workers. But as Hesketh *et al.* (2006) point out, without denominator figures and "given that migrants are predominantly in sexually active age groups, these figures are impossible to interpret". Their own study, using one of the largest samples (of 6,000 people in eastern China in 2004) found that the prevalence of syphilis was similar in migrants and urban workers and that the use of sex workers was no more common in the migrant group (ibid.). Migrants, despite having consistently less education, actually had similar rates of syphilis infection. One possible explanation for this was that an increased tendency to migrate with partners and families, and traditional attitudes to sexual relationships, placed migrant workers at low risk for engaging in casual sex (ibid.). Another explanation, of course, is that their relatively lower income also precludes frequent visits to sex workers. In another study of 1,000 migrants in Shanghai, it was also found that the prevalence of STDs among males was relatively low (He *et al.*, 2005: 286). Interestingly, within the different migrant groups studied by He *et al.* (2005: 288) there was also evidence to suggest higher earning groups had greater levels of STDs. Thus prevalence was lowest for construction workers (3.2 percent) but higher for market vendors and factory workers (5.6 percent). A higher proportion of market vendors (10.2 percent) made 1,500 RMB or more (US$187) per month and factory workers were also better educated and earned more than those in construction. Longer duration (and with it presumably higher income) in Shanghai and more frequent home visits (again related to income) were associated with greater chance of infection. Many of the migrants, moreover, including those working in construction sites, were married (market vendors had the highest percentage at 88 percent). Although most were married, only 13.5 percent of married construction workers were currently living *with their* wives, compared with 89.7 percent of married market vendors and 61.7 percent of married factory workers (He *et al.*, 2005). STD infection was as common in migrants who lived with partners, disputing the earlier suggestion that migration with partners may reduce visits to sex workers and hence STDs.

Within migrant groups there is some evidence for a gradation, with higher infection rates among wealthier groups. Other studies, looking at the general population, also find evidence of an association between wealth and STD infection. Another study found that risk factors for chlamydial infection among men, for example, were unprotected commercial sex, less education, and recent sex with their spouse or other steady partner. The activity of unprotected commercial sex, however, was more common when the men "earned a high income, socialized often, and travelled frequently" (Parish *et al.*, 2003: 1270). Some of the risk factors for chlamydial infection among women were having less education, living in a city or along the southern coast, and having a spouse or other steady sexual partner who earned a high income, socialized often (ibid.). Again, this would seem to support the view that greater wealth allows consumption of sex in the commercial market. Additionally, Li *et al.* (2009) found that in a sample of over 4,500 food market workers in an eastern city in China, over 30 percent of those in the income brackets of 501–1,000 RMB and over 1,000 RMB monthly incomes had visited an entertainment venue at least once in the last 30 days. Visiting entertainment venues, as mentioned previously, was correlated with unprotected sex and STD infections.

Age groups

Many of the victims of Asia's HIV/AIDS epidemics are young and more likely to take risks (MAP, 2005: 8). In most Asian countries, the majority of sex workers and injecting drug users are younger than 25 (ibid.). It is interesting to note, however, that some evidence suggests that the age profile in China of some STD infections appears to be somewhat different to this. While more than 70 percent of reported cases of syphilis in China in the past 10 years, for example, were in people aged 20–49 years, the average age of all cases was found to be in the mid-thirties. The mean age of people with syphilis in 2005 ranged from 37 to 39 years (Chen *et al.*, 2007: 134). This is clearly a high average age and also one that does not correspond to the age profile of the migrant population, which is younger on average. It would, therefore, seem unlikely that the majority of those with syphilis are migrant workers. It is also interesting to note that the mean ages were slightly higher in northern and central China than in other regions of the country (ibid.).

While there is substantial research conducted on CSW in large and populous cities such as Shenzhen, China's first Special Economic Zone (Lau *et al.*, 2002) and Guangzhou, capital of southern province of Guangdong (van den Hoek *et al.*, 2001), comparatively little research has been done on the industry in more remote and regional areas of China. Subsequently, as Fang *et al.* (2008) suggest, there is insufficient evidence to provide a profile of female CSWs, which is likely to vary by working environment. Additionally, Hong and Li's literature survey (2008) of behavioral studies of female sex workers concludes that existing studies were heavily concentrated in the south and southwest regions of China. Nonetheless, what evidence there is, would suggest the average age of sex workers is considerably lower than the average male customer, ranging from teens to early twenties (Hong and Li, 2008).

The relatively slow acquisition of income that can be used for commercial sex one factor that leads to the relatively older age at which STDs are contracted by the general population. Other studies confirm this observation. Chlamydial infection is considered a disease of youth in developed countries. Screening concentrates on those younger than 25 or 30 years old. In China and other Asian societies, however, sexual activity typically begins with a spouse or fiancé and it takes time for the acquisition of income for use in commercial sex. As a result, some believe the onset of STDs could be particularly late in China. Chlamydial infection in China, for example, is actually concentrated among those aged 25–44 years rather than among those younger than 25 years (Parish *et al.*, 2003: 1271):

> The researchers speculate that the rise over time in the proportion of infections acquired outside of marriage reflects an "evolution of sexual beliefs and behaviors" in China, and that the relatively high mean age of Chinese

STD patients compared with patients in other countries reflects an older age at sexual initiation.

(Remez, 2000: 142)

The changes in sexual behavior and attitudes witnessed in China are partly a result of greater economic wealth. This partly explains the rise of STDs among comparatively older cohorts in the Chinese population.

As well as evidence pointing toward wealth as important determinant for high-risk behavior, there is also worrying evidence of high concentration of STDs in the core risk groups for transmitting HIV. One systematic review of published work on syphilis in specific populations found the highest prevalence of syphilis in remunerated blood donors at 2.86 percent; possible female sex workers 0.83 percent; incarcerated female sex workers 12.49 percent; drug users 6.81 percent; and men who have sex with men 14.6 percent. Moreover, in the past 5–10 years, annual syphilis rates seem to have increased most among drug users (0.96 percent), incarcerated female sex workers (1.41 percent), and men who have sex with men (4.5 percent) (Chen *et al.*, 2007: 135).

Gender dimensions

STDs have spread quickly to the female population. Although overall trends among men and women were similar, according to Remez (2000: 142), the annual average increase among women was higher than that among men. Women also accounted for a significantly higher proportion of STD infections in 1998 than in 1989. In 1989, women represented just 33 percent of new STD cases, but in 1998, they accounted for nearly 43 percent of all diagnoses (ibid.). Both male and female STD patients were significantly older in 1998 than in 1995 (mean age of 31.9 and 30.7, respectively), and the vast majority (93 percent) were between ages 20–49 (ibid.). Moreover, in the mid-1990s, the proportion of STDs that were acquired outside of marriage increased significantly in China (from 55 percent of new cases in 1995 to 72 percent of those diagnosed in 1998) (ibid.). Meanwhile, syphilis ratio for male to females declined from 2.0 to 1.0 between 1988–2000 (Chen *et al.*, 2007: 134). Again, this change is of interest, as it also corresponds to trends seen in HIV infections, with a shift from male to female populations. Parish, Laumann and Mojola in their survey of sexual behavior in China conclude that "significant transformation" has taken place for men and women in their twenties and thirties (2007: 750). Yet, what is most interesting are the authors' findings that it is after marriage that "couples are increasingly at risk should a generalized HIV epidemic take hold" (Parish, Laumann and Mojola, 2007: 750), thus affirming factors such as commercial sex, lax condom use, and prevalence rates of STDs in both men and women in their twenties and thirties.

The role of education

It is widely considered that education, or lack of it, is an important factor driving HIV/AIDS epidemics. What can we learn about education and its impact on the

Chinese HIV/AIDS epidemic from the studies on STDs? The few epidemiological studies undertaken on STDs, as well as those on CSW, are useful in shedding more light on this question.

Some of the statistical analyses that examine the various individual risk factors suggest education is important factor in contracting an STD. On the one hand, education seems associated with an increased chance of any individual undertaking risky behavior. This appears to be because in general wealthier groups have better education. It is also these wealthier groups that are more predisposed to travel and frequent socializing, particularly among men with higher socioeconomic status (Uretsky, 2008). Such behaviors are also associated with unprotected commercial sex. On the other hand, while relatively well-educated individuals may be important in driving the demand for commercial sex, there may also be greater potential to bring about rapid behavior change with appropriately targeted information and education campaigns in this group. To illustrate, one study showed a risk factor for chlamydia, one of China's most common though least reported STDs, is having high income and traveling frequently. However, further statistical analysis also showed that the better educated individuals were also less likely to be infected. Thus education can also confer some protection. Looking at a sample of both men and women in the age group of 20–44, chlamydial infections were also associated with less education for both groups (Parish *et al.*, 2003: 1270). Furthermore, a study of STDs by Guan *et al.* (2009: 445) of market vendors in Fuzhou showed that the highest prevalence rate of self-reported STDs were among the 20- to 30-year-old age group, those who were married or living with a partner, and with the least education. Education, therefore, "may confer unspecified advantages that public health campaigns could build upon" (Parish *et al.*, 2003: 1272).

Another group, the large migrant work force, has comparatively lower levels of education. One investigation into this group showed that about one-quarter of the subjects had received, at most, a primary school education (He *et al.*, 2005). According to Hesketh and Lu, only 28 percent of migrants in their survey knew the use of condoms could protect against the transmission of HIV (and thus STDs), compared to 56 percent of urban workers sampled (2005: 1550). Sex workers from lower class brothels were also less likely to use condoms and had, in general, worse educational backgrounds, in spite of good access to condoms (Hesketh, Zhang and Qiang, 2005). A number of statistical analyses reveal that low levels of education predispose individuals to infection (both among migrant and nonmigrant groups).

It is perhaps unsurprising that education may provide individuals with the knowledge required to avert transmission. At the same time, however, it is interesting that education is also associated with a number of other risk factors, such as access to higher incomes and opportunities to travel.

The geography of STDs

The geographical distribution of China's STD epidemic is of great concern as the overlap between the major HIV/AIDS outbreaks and China's STD epidemics have not been, to date, particularly close. If further bridging between higher pre-valence HIV regions and those areas with more severe STD epidemics takes place, HIV will be able to quickly spread within those regions with the more severe STD epidemics that exist across China. In the case of syphilis, for exam-ple, all of China's 2,882 counties have reported outbreaks in recent years. There is, however, a much greater number of reported infections in the more developed coastal regions, those in general that are wealthier (such as Beijing, Shanghai, and other large cities) (Chen *et al.*, 2007). While the detection rate is likely to be higher in such regions, population-based studies of individual risk factors (not relying on officially reported data) also strongly suggest higher prevalence in the wealthier eastern provinces. Parish *et al.* (2003), for example, found that one risk factor for chlamydial infection for women was living along the southern coast. Another study (of syphilis) also found higher prevalence among the urban popu-lation when compared with migrants in China's Hangzhou region (Hesketh *et al.*, 2006). This is corroborated by other studies of migrants, as mentioned, that find relatively low prevalence among male migrants, the majority of which come from poorer inland regions (He *et al.*, 2005: 288).

If official data are used, prevalence and incidence both appear to increase in the east of the country, with the seaboard regions having the most severe prob-lems. In 2005, using syphilis again as an example, Chen *et al.* (2007) found the highest prevalence rates were reported in Shanghai (55.3 cases per 100,000 indi-viduals), Zhejiang (35.9 per 100,000), and Fujian (26.8 per 100,000), which together with Jiangsu (13.0 per 100,000) form China's prosperous eastern sea-board. Beijing municipality had the next highest rate (24.9 per 100,000), fol-lowed by the southern Zhujiang River Delta (Guangxi, Guangdong, and Hainan provinces, reporting 14–21 cases per 100,000 individuals). Chen *et al.* (2007), by contrast, reported much lower syphilis rates in the northeast provinces of Jilin, Liaoning, and Heilongjiang and the far western provinces of Qinghai and Xinjiang with rates of 5–12 cases per 100,000 individuals. Interestingly, in land provinces such as Henan, Anhui, Sichuan, and Hunan had substantially low inci-dence rates, ranging from 0.1 to 4.99 cases per 100,000 in 2005 (ibid.: 134).

It is highly significant that rural regions with higher HIV prevalence, to date, have not experienced such severe STD outbreaks. Although the situation appears to be changing quite quickly, most HIV infections so far have occurred in more isolated rural areas where CSW is not as common as in urban areas. During the late 1990s, an estimated 80 percent of China's estimated 840,000 HIV-infected individuals lived in rural areas (Wu, Rou and Cui, 2004: 8). Indeed, as already noted, one factor that makes the epidemic in China different from other regions of the world, is that "the epidemic of HIV among IDUs began in the rural areas and then spread to urban areas" (ibid.). In part, this is because drug use is more common in rural areas, such as in Yunnan and Sichuan. The estimated 50,000 new HIV cases in 2007, 42 percent of cases were transmitted through intrave-nous drug use (IDU), with heterosexual transmission the highest at 44.7 percent (Wang *et al.* 2009: 417). The distribution of HIV was most concentrated in Yunnan, Guangxi, Sichuan, Henan and Xinjiang (ibid.). A number of high

HIV prevalence provinces, therefore, do not appear to have such severe STD outbreaks.

This evidence suggests the potential for growth of the Chinese STD epidemics in hitherto less-affected regions is large. Many agree that the social conditions exist for explosive growth, particularly as the sex industry has grown throughout China's regions. There is also evidence of lower condom use in poorer regions as well as lower levels of education, leading to riskier behaviors. Long distance movement of HIV-infected individuals from the interior also appears to be taking place. Many migrants are moving to wealthier coastal areas where STDs are more common. Some migrants may become sex workers, buy sex, or engage in homosexual sex. The meeting of HIV-infected individuals with the widespread STD epidemic that exists in the more developed regions presents a favorable environment for the spread of HIV in these areas. Sentinel surveillance evidence would suggest this is already happening, as HIV prevalence is increasing in urban areas that are the centers of CSW.

Conclusion

China has one of the fastest growing STD epidemics in the world which looks bad even when compared with some of the worst affected countries elsewhere in the world. The STD epidemics, moreover, are highly dynamic and evolving quickly. The majority of studies conclude, however, that there is greater potential for the further spread of HIV/AIDS via the sexual transmission networks that have developed: "The pandemic of STDs in China strongly suggests the potential for an explosive epidemic of HIV infection through heterosexual transmission" (He *et al.*, 2005: 286). The largest STD outbreaks to date, moreover, have predominantly been concentrated in China's wealthier regions, where the commercial sex industry is more active. Most HIV infections, by contrast, have been found in the western and interior regions of China. This suggests that once HIV establishes itself more firmly in the transmission networks related to CSW, found in greater intensity in the coastal regions, there may well be rapid spread of HIV within these networks. Indeed, if HIV is to spread at similar rates as some STDs, a generalized epidemic could emerge in a relatively short-time period. The exponential growth of syphilis provides just one example of how rapidly STDs may spread. The available evidence suggests that this process is already underway, as the number of female infections and non-IDU and plasma donation-related infections is increasing rapidly.

China's healthcare system, which has undergone some dramatic changes since China's reform and opening, is not capable of dealing with this important public health issue. The reforms undertaken in healthcare have meant access to preventive medicine has decreased. Treatment costs have also risen sharply, leading to the under provision of necessary treatment and to the sharp increase in the number of STD cases. It is now also very ill-equipped to deal with the rising STDs infection rates, especially in rural areas where healthcare costs constitute an even larger burden on the population.

As well as the geographical aspects, details from STD studies provides evidence that CSW is also of central importance to the spread of STDs. The epidemiological studies into STDs, moreover, confirm some of the findings of earlier chapters. In particular, they suggest that it is the wealthier economic groups that disproportionately create demand for CSWs. It also supports the view that focusing purely on prevention efforts aimed at female sex workers are unlikely to be entirely successful. Issues related to their clients and the broader context in which sex takes place must also be addressed. Those prevention efforts that do not do so, it is argued, "are among the least successful in reducing unprotected commercial sex" (MAP, 2004: 36).

7 The role of civil society organizations

Introduction

Civil society organizations (CSOs) today and in the past have played and continue to play a key role as advocates in promoting positive social change. This chapter addresses the question of what role China's civil society has played and will play in the struggle against China's rapidly growing epidemic. The role of civil society is especially important as we have seen in Chapter 6 given the failure of the Chinese government to provide an adequate health system to meet the needs of its citizens, namely in the rural areas. Thus, there is substantial room for CSOs to offer their expertise in areas such as health education. There are over 50 nationally registered Chinese CSOs targeting HIV/AIDS and perhaps hundreds of thousands more (registered and unregistered) focusing on a wide range of issues from basic health to environmental issues. Accordingly, the central question of concern here is the extent to which these CSOs can contribute to the curbing the HIV/AIDS epidemic. The growth of civil society and organizations within this sphere is certainly encouraging. Nonetheless, due to government regulations, this nascent sector still faces significant challenges.

Interestingly, the resurgence or rediscovery of civil society as an analytical tool for understanding social and political change can be largely attributed to system changes of the 1980s in Eastern Europe. The emergence of social organizations or CSOs[1] in opposition to the state during Eastern Europe's transition was interpreted within the civil society framework. Since the 1980s, civil society has been deployed across the social sciences to explain, comprehend, and justify the need for a people- or society-centered approach to solving developmental problems of a nation or community. Civil society and the organizations within and across nations have proved an essential force in meeting the needs and representing the interests of the people due to the failure of many states to adequately do so. As a result, CSOs are at times seen as "gap fillers," providing social and welfare services to its constituencies precisely because of state failure. In this context, the role of civil society and CSOs is vital in the health sector, particularly with regards to HIV/AIDS for many developing countries where the resources and capabilities of the state are limited. The possibility of HIV/AIDS becoming an epidemic and thus a potential hindrance to China's economic development has forced the state to acknowledge its own shortcomings in sufficiently managing the effects of HIV/AIDS. Consequently, the state has expressed an interest in working with CSOs to address the issue. If civil society is viewed to be a force for sociopolitical change as in the case of Eastern Europe then it is necessary to frame this analysis within a wider context. Accordingly, an understanding will begin to emerge in the development of CSOs in China and ultimately their potential not only to successfully tackle HIV/AIDS but also affect existing institutions.

The specific aim of this chapter is therefore to provide an understanding of civil society in order to analyze its impact on the health sector, particularly with reference to CSOs undertaking advocacy work in HIV/AIDS issues in China. Based on research and interviews conducted between March and August 2005 with a wide range of CSOs, this chapter will place the context of HIV/AIDS CSOs within the wider background of civil society development in China. The first section provides a general but concise overview of how civil society has been interpreted by Western scholars. It also considers how this is applicable to the health sector. Second, civil society emergence within China is examined in greater detail. Scholarly debates regarding the conception and understanding of civil society in China will provide context to assess the importance of HIV/AIDS CSOs. Third, the focus shifts to the development of CSOs in China and the possibilities of making an impact in stemming the effects of HIV/AIDS. The fourth section will draw together the analysis of the previous section by reflecting on the actual possibilities for Chinese CSOs in the fight against HIV/AIDS.

The effectiveness of CSOs with regards to HIV/AIDS in China is dependent on the relationship between state and society. The role of the state cannot be ignored whether the attention is on HIV/AIDS, development of China's civil society, or sociopolitical change. This is because the Chinese state is still very much present in many sectors of society. As a consequence, the impact that HIV/AIDS CSOs have on the epidemic is likely to be restricted by what the government deems as acceptable. The significance of this will reverberate and affect the development of a functioning civil society.

Civil society and HIV/AIDS

The deployment of civil society as an analytical framework to identify and understand sociopolitical change has given recognition to forces within society as agents of change, including that of CSOs. This is particularly relevant to the health sector, where initiatives of the state have failed and thus CSOs have taken on a greater role to provide for the community. While realigning the focus of analysis to that of civil society is indeed positive, it must also be used with caution as the state, in the case of China is still central to any study.[2] This first section will offer a foundation in grasping the concept of civil society followed by its applicability to HIV/AIDS.

Understanding civil society

The notion of "civil society" within the Western/European sense is the space between state and society where each is largely autonomous of the other. Edward Shils writes:

> The idea of civil society is the idea of a part of society which has a life of its own, which is distinctly different from the state, and which is largely in autonomy of it. Civil society lies beyond the boundaries of the family, the clan and beyond the locality, it lies short of the state.
>
> (Shils, 1991: 3)

The autonomy from the state is an aspect of civil society theory that has been constantly re-emphasized as this is seen as a crucial element for nondemocratic countries in the process of political transition.[3] The fall of communism in Eastern Europe in the late 1980s is seen as a triumph for both civil society and democracy. Furthermore, writers such as Vladimir Tismaneanu (1992) argued that the surfacing and ultimately the force of CSOs such as Solidarity in Poland and the Hungarian National Forum undermined the authority of the state, thus suggesting this division or difference is necessary for civil society to be effective. Furthering the separation of state and civil society, theorists such as Daniel Bell (1989) and Michael Edwards (2007) advocate a return to the "local" in which individuals and their communities are promoted as the principal factor in dealing with social issues, such as inequality. This individualism echoes Hegel's belief that civil society is the realm where individuals can pursue their interests.

The understanding of civil society is often split between the sociological and political interpretation. Sociologists regard civil society as an intermediary between state and family and would thus include all social organizations. This space allows individuals to come into cooperative relationships with others based on the requirement to satisfy certain needs, thus resonating Hegel's notion of civil society. Hegel's *Elements of the Philosophy of Right* has been instrumental in shaping the Western conception and function of civil society. Hegel regarded civil society as the realm where individuals exist and are able to pursue their private interests and satisfy their own livelihoods. In recognizing our own needs and finding ways of meeting them, we are faced with the same desires as others, hence mutual relationships between individuals are formed and in what Hegel refer to as "universality" or the "quality of being recognized" (1991: 22). Consequently, *"subjective selfishness turns into a contribution towards the satisfaction of the needs of everyone else"* (Hegel, 1991: 233). Hegel's notion of civil society therefore implies a certain universality of the human condition. In the political sense, the notion of civil society is derived from Anglo-American liberal political theory, where it sees civil society as a relationship between state and society embodied in citizenship rights, representation, and the law.

Regardless of any conception of civil society that one may ascribe to, civil society is not entirely separate from the state, no matter how much some have tried to force this distinction. Even where social and political change has occurred as in the case of Eastern Europe, both the state and civil society contributed to a system change. Shils (1991: 4) sees the state as defining the boundaries of autonomy for civil society to operate and in return, civil society establishes the limits of state action. For example, the Chinese state has sought to demarcate the boundaries of civil society through laws and policies, as will be discussed in the Civil Society and HIV/AIDS section. Nonetheless, where there seems to be consensus is in the fact that civil society must be different from the state in order to generate social change and influence the state.

The role of civil society in HIV/AIDS

Public health and healthcare reforms have always benefited from civil society. Individuals such as Florence Nightingale and Edwin Chadwick of the Victorian era were instrumental in transforming the healthcare system. Nightingale's involvement in the Crimean War and subsequent career pioneered modern day nursing. The high death tolls of British soldiers in hospital barracks during the war led Nightingale to believe that poor living conditions were the major cause of death. Upon her return to Britain, she advocated for sanitary living conditions, thus helped to reduce death rates in the Army during peacetime. Chadwick similarly argued that sanitary living conditions would not only improve life expectancy but would be an economic benefit for society, as a healthier population would be more productive. His 1842 *Report into the Sanitary Conditions of the Labouring Population of Great Britain* showed that life expectancy was much lower in towns than in the countryside thereby challenging the government to improve people's lives by bringing about reforms (Chadwick, 1842). In 1848, the British Parliament passed the first Public Health Act which enabled the creation of central and local Boards of Health. From the Victorian era we see that civil society and healthcare are not opposing forces but complimentary with strong possibilities of bringing about positive social changes.

The activism of modern day civil society and CSOs in the health sector can in part be attributed to the weakening capacity of the state to adequately provide for its citizens. However, it can also be attributed to people's growing concern of the need to have a more participatory process in planning and policy-implementation procedures which affect their daily lives. Thus, the call for governments to be more accountable and transparent not only in the health sector but in all its workings is in part spearheaded by CSOs. Community-based healthcare in the 1970s and 1980s was an expression of disenchantment with the state and thus developing parallel systems was a method in which healthcare professionals could express this sentiment. The World Health Organization's Alma-Ata declaration of 1978, "Health for all by year 2000" was a realization of the need to provide access to health for all but this goal was unachievable without partnerships between governments and CSOs. Since the late 1970s, CSOs in the health sector have tended to work with the marginalized and poorest sector of society through the provision of primary healthcare. CSOs often act alone but have developed key networks and alliances including "The Milk War" of the 1980s. The International Baby Food Action Network was founded to support activists wanting a monitoring and regulatory system for the sale of baby formula foods. While "The Milk War" achieved substantial successes in forcing standards onto major companies producing baby formula foods, one of the major criticisms of CSOs working in the healthcare sector is their autonomy and thus the scale of their projects is often limited to the local level. This prevents successful projects from being shared as lessons learned.

In terms of HIV/AIDS, the outlook on the role of civil society and of CSOs is one that is regarded as essential in order to successfully combat its spread and effects on society. The *2006 Report on the Global AIDS Epidemic* believes that in order to address the long-term challenges of AIDS, countries need to think beyond the short term (as dictated by election cycles). And thus, civil society is able to assist in looking at the long-term impacts and challenges. Civil society has traditionally been at the forefront in combating the stigma and discrimination caused by AIDS and also reaching to other marginalized groups within society. Consequently, CSOs have built up an "unrivaled" understanding of the epidemic and needs of those who are affected by it (UNAIDS, 2006a: 221). Thus it would be a pity not to harness the knowledge and capabilities of CSOs' to address the impact of AIDS. A study by the Global Fund of its 25 recipients showed that financial disbursements to civil society had better rates of targeting beneficiaries of 85 percent compared to 57 percent for national governments (Halmshaw and Hawkins, 2004: 38). The accumulated knowledge of CSOs and their ability to assess the situation and thus distribute the money, where it is most needed, suggest that CSOs are able to respond at a faster rate to an impending epidemic, whereas governments are often hampered by their own bureaucracy. The proliferation of finances from Northern to Southern governments to combat HIV/AIDS, although needed, creates a concern at another level. To allocate these resources, international donors are relying on Southern governments to help distribute the money and this leads to questions of capacity. Halmshaw and Hawkins (2004: 37) express unease as to whether Southern governments are able to effectively disburse the money on a large scale and then to provide the technical assistance, monitoring, and evaluating to ensure appropriate use of the finances. Although CSOs are proving to be an indispensable part in the fight against HIV/AIDS, the role of the state is still essential in successfully addressing the impacts of HIV/AIDS on a national and eventually global scale.

Successful responses: Brazil and Thailand

The success of Brazil in preventing HIV/AIDS from becoming a full-blown epidemic can largely be attributed to the role played by the Brazilian civil society (see Oliveira-Cruz, Kowalski and McPake, 2004). However, it is also with the action of the government by instituting universal healthcare to all in its constitution that has ensured its success. Nonetheless, the achievements of Brazilian CSOs in influencing policy and evaluation are due to their active presence on national steering committees. CSOs also exist outside of formal structures where they can exert pressure. For example, in 1999 when financial constraints jeopardized the purchase of antiretroviral (ARV) drugs, demonstrations and street marches were organized by CSOs to send a message to the government. Since such outpourings and demonstrations by the public, the Brazilian government has sought to manufacture generic ARV drugs within Brazil or source components of the medication from developing countries, such as India, to avoid the high cost of patent drugs of major multinational drug companies. The Brazilian government's foresight and response to civil society pressure led to the free treatment for HIV/AIDS patients, implemented in the early 1990s. This guarantee for HIV/AIDS patients became formalized in the Congressional Bill 9113 (November 13, 1996) which ensures all AIDS patients for free access to medication and treatment. The Brazilian response has halved AIDS mortality from 12.2 deaths per 100,000 in 1995 to 6.3 deaths per 100,000 by 1999 (Hsu, 2004: 12).

In the Brazilian case, CSOs have confirmed their position as advocates of change and pushing the government to take action with regards to HIV/AIDS. The government in turn has responded to the point where infection rates across Brazil have dropped sharply. This indicates not only the need and importance of civil society in combating such an issue but that the partnership between civil society and state is key in drawing out a balanced response. Agencies such as UNAIDS have emphasized the need and role of CSOs in combating HIV/AIDS, this is most evident in recent documents such as *The 2006 Report on the Global AIDS Epidemic*.

Similarly, Thailand's coordinated response has ensured a substantial decrease in infection rates since the start of the epidemic in the late 1980s. The Thai case differs to that of Brazil in that the Thai state responded relatively more decisively and with less pressure from civil society. The Office of the Prime Minister subsumed direct responsibility of the HIV/AIDS challenge, which complemented the important and personal involvement of the well-known national cabinet member Mechai Viravaidya of the family planning department. Nonetheless, the participation of CSOs has made considerable inroads into the fight against epidemics. In addition, CSOs have offered those marginalized by HIV/AIDS a voice and representation in society. Well established development CSOs such as Population and Community Development Association, Thai Red Cross Society were able to speak on behalf of the marginalized. These CSOs were subsequently joined by newly emerging ones, specifically targeting AIDS such as EMPOWER. The number of CSOs involved increased from 23 to 184 between 1992–1997, and self-organized groups of people living with HIV/AIDS (PLWHA) also expanded from 11 to 108 between 1994–1997 (Ainsworth, Beyrer and Soucat, 2003: 17). The work of CSOs in Thailand is coupled with a government commitment to increasing civil society's participation and this is reflected in the allocation of financial resources. The Thai government increased its financial contribution to CSOs from US$480,000 in 1992 to US$3.2 million in 1996 (Hsu, 2004: 14). The recent activism of Thailand's HIV/AIDS organizations has resulted in the new military interim government announcing the compulsory license for the manufacturing of efavirenz, an ARV drug produced by pharmaceutical company, Merck.

The Ministry of Health believes that it can have the drug on the market by the middle of 2007, thus increasing the number of patients having access from 20,000 to 100,000 (quoted in Levett, 2006). Thailand's multisectoral response has significantly reduced infection rates from 149,000 in 1991 to 29,000 in 2001 (Hsu, 2004: 13). Regardless, it is no time for complacency. Thailand is entering a new phase, where those infected at the very start are now showing signs of symptomatic diseases and this requires continuing vigilance by all sectors. The cooperation between the Thai government and CSOs indicates that it is possible for the two to work successfully together and reduce the overall risk of HIV/AIDS.

State and civil society partnership

In understanding civil society as a space between state and society, the possibility emerges of seeing how civil society and various actors within it can be effective agents for change. However, it would be a disservice to any analysis of sociopolitical change if the separation between state and society is forced. It has been argued thus far that while civil society and CSOs are indispensable in both the health sector and in HIV/AIDS, it needs to be coupled with an understanding of the state. Certain states are weak and lack capabilities as well as resources to respond to the impact of HIV/AIDS, and thus CSOs are taking on roles where the government is incapable of doing so. CSOs are indeed service providers but we must not simplify our analysis by only considering CSOs as operating within this role. As in the Brazilian case, CSOs act as an influential force in advocating for policy change. The need for government to respond to the threat of HIV/AIDS is just as important, as we will see in the next section. The role of Chinese civil society will be closely considered in conjunction with the state's response to the HIV/AIDS threat.

Chinese civil society

Civil society is often seen as the catalyst for system and social change, as in the case of Eastern Europe, but in China, the transformation that is occurring is of a much more muted nature. We will consider the development and usage of civil society to understand China's transition. This then provides a solid basis for analyzing the emergence of CSOs in China today and its potential to influence change. The role of Chinese CSOs in curbing the effects of HIV/AIDS is one that is given much hope by an array of international civil society actors including bilateral, multilateral agencies, and nongovernment groups, but it is a hope that must be tempered by a realistic outlook on the capabilities of Chinese CSOs. Simultaneously, the Chinese state is in the position to limit the role and strength of CSOs, which ultimately will have bearing on the potential for sociopolitical change.

Civil society and China

Since the early 1990s, scholars and observers concerned with China have deployed the concept of civil society to explain the pluralization of Chinese society indicated by the growing numbers of CSOs. Furthermore, the Tiananmen Square incident of 1989 and the fall of communism in Eastern Europe stimulated academic enquiries into China's social, political, and economic transition and this was translated into civil society agitating for political change. While there seems to be genuine social change in terms of state–society relationship and also increasing numbers of CSOs dedicated to various social concerns, including HIV/AIDS, the concept of civil society is often used with caution. It is used with caution because of the Western/European origins of the concept. Nonetheless, the interest in using civil society as a framework can be partly explained by the events in Tiananmen in June 1989. The scholarly works that emerged immediately after the incident demonstrated the desire to comprehend the nature of China's social transition and state–society relationship.[4]

The primary concern here is not the events of 1989 or whether the presence of civil society leads to democracy *per se*, the concern here is to consider the applicability of the civil society framework in the context of socioeconomic change and its consequences, including HIV/AIDS. Scholars such as Brook and Frolic believe that using civil society framework to understand China highlights the social changes that have occurred since the introduction of economic reforms in 1978. They note that "civil society serves as a heuristic device for thinking through certain changes that China is currently undergoing, but neither reproduces nor fully explains that reality" (Brook and Frolic, 1997: 8). Similarly, D. Yang (2004) believes that the civil society framework provides a useful analytical tool for emphasizing certain facets of change within China.

Béja (2006) argues the importance of the Chinese state in the shaping of civil society. However, he emphasizes the partnership between Chinese academics and the state, with academics serving as a proxy for CSOs. Academics have utilized CSOs as an indicator of change and development of civil society, hence the heavy focus on the counting and cataloging of CSOs. The government on the other hand regards academics as an important element in the development of civil society and in designing new policies. The continuation of the household registration or *hukou* – which once prevented the free movement of people and greatly disadvantaging rural residents with regards to access to social welfare – is one of the many policies that have drawn widespread criticisms within the academic circle. Academics argue that the policy prevents the integration of the labor market and distribute the labor where there is demand. As a result, some local governments have taken heed and established pilot projects allowing labor migrants near same benefits as urban residents. Nonetheless, academics "intervene as experts inside the system" (Béja, 2006: 67). Although academics have pushed hard for social policy change in some areas, and also with many CSOs consulting them in the hope of being represented in the eyes of the government, many have not pushed for further policy changes relating to CSOs. Many have remained silent or have not supported social organizations in their quest for an autonomous voice, as they are well aware of the government's intolerance of such actions. Their silence is also due to the elitism of intellectuals, believing that the current "quality" of the population is unable to deal with such issues.

With such assessment of China's CSOs, one that is partially being represented by academics and consequently without an independent voice, it leads to the question: To what extent will China's civil society and CSOs be effective in the fight against HIV/AIDS? Despite civil society's premature state, exploring the above question from a civil society perspective will allow the observer to study horizontal relationships, such as that between CSOs. In the following section, we will reflect on this question by tracing the development of Chinese CSOs.

The development of Chinese CSOs

CSOs in China are increasingly becoming a significant part in the changing social landscape. They have benefited from the government's liberalization policies, with the state permitting greater space for their development. The state's recognition of CSOs' positive social contribution in terms of welfare provision has prompted the state to become more actively engaged with new social actors and groups. This section will further draw out the relationship between the Chinese state and CSOs as this will provide insight into the response from both parties to HIV/AIDS. Undoubtedly, the state is in a position to direct and control the space that CSOs currently occupy through various laws and policies. An exposition of the laws and regulations relating to CSOs will thus provide an important understanding into the functioning of the state. The roles and operations of CSOs must first be examined before confidently claiming that CSOs are the new contributors to the Chinese society and thus the solution to China's potential HIV/AIDS epidemic. Similarly, the capacity of CSOs requires analysis in order to determine their potential for affecting change.

Laws and regulations pertaining to CSOs

China's CSOs have multiplied since the economic reforms of the late 1970s. There are some 415,000 registered organizations with the Ministry of Civil Affairs (MCA) in 2009 (World Bank, 2009). Notwithstanding the quantity and diversity of CSOs, the involvement of the state in the affairs of CSOs has prompted the rise of various terminologies in the Chinese language. CSOs in China can be registered with the MCA under the following categories: social organizations (*shehui tuanti*), nonprofit organizations (*feiyingli*), foundations (*jijinhui*), educational institutions (*xueshu*), or corporations (*gongsi*). In general, *shehui tuanti* is most commonly used to denote any social organizations that are nongovernment. The classification system alone suggests that the government is able to target any particular category of CSOs fairly quickly depending on their threat to the state.

The reach of the government extends to the formation and supervision of CSOs through the MCA. The MCA is responsible for the registration management of CSOs and is given the authority to issue warnings, orders, cancel, or change an organization's status. As a result of the 1989 Tiananmen incident, numerous government documents have emerged detailing the management of CSOs. Prior to 1989, there were no universal regulatory systems for the management of CSOs. Immediately after the Tiananmen events, the State Council issued the Movement Regulations on Registration of Social Organizations in October 1989. This required all social organizations from henceforth to find a willing government department or professional leading units (*yewu zhuguan danwei*) to sponsor the organization. To find a sponsoring government department is a difficult process as there are no incentives for government departments to take on the extra administrative work, thus preventing many organizations from completing the registration step. Thus, as a method to become registered and avoid the lengthy bureaucratic process, many organizations have decided to register as a commercial or business entity. The development of CSOs is unfortunately affected by the immature legal system, where loopholes do exist. Chen argues that a "disconnect exists between policies and regulations and the objective, practical requirements" (Chen, 2001). We can see that the government is attempting to create a balance of maintaining control through policies and the law, meanwhile wishing to harness the energy of social organizations. This disconnect may prove to be an obstacle for both the government and CSOs for the near future because the pursuit of both goals by the government could lead to the sending of conflicting messages to CSOs.

The registration process remains a lengthy and arduous process. To further limit the scope, CSOs cannot establish regional or branch offices. Such government policies will curb the possibility of many organizations to scale up their services. Additionally, only one type of each organization may be established in any given region.

The limitation that the government places on CSOs in China has restricted the development of CSOs and essentially its effectiveness at a wider, national level. In assessing the development of CSOs from this regulatory perspective, it indicates that the Chinese trajectory of social and associational development is state directed. Yet where we see control on the part of the state, there is on the other hand a weakening at the same time. With the various limitations and restrictions placed on the development of CSOs kept in mind, it is interesting to ask: just what is the role of CSOs in Chinese society and more specifically with regards to HIV/AIDS?

The severe acute respiratory syndrome (SARS) epidemic in 2003 brought to the forefront the role of CSOs in potentially mitigating a health crisis. Social community organizations provided counseling hotlines, information dissemination, and provision of basic medical supplies, such as masks. The public viewed these groups as better providers of much needed information and social services. Chinese media saw the potential for China's social organizations to contribute positively to the fight against SARS. However, the role of CSOs was perceived to be a supporting one. The SARS epidemic had a tremendous impact on how the government responds to health crisis. Realizing the damage incurred to the government's credibility from the initial cover-up and denial of the epidemic, the lessons learned from the 2003 situation would appear to have affected its response to HIV/AIDS. The potential disaster of SARS provided the government with strong incentives to take action. Since SARS, the Chinese government has taken more decisive actions and initiative in addressing the impact of HIV/AIDS and has shown interest in working with CSOs. While there is a call for greater autonomy for CSOs, this is largely framed in the context of a crisis and to lessen the burden of government duties. The series of government regulations enforced for the management of CSOs outlined above would tend to suggest that the autonomy of CSOs from the government is still very much in the future. Nonetheless, Chinese CSOs do have the potential to become active along with the government to affect social change. Such changes would include the enlargement of space for CSOs to conduct their work and provide various social services and also be effective partners with the state in the social transition process, especially in the precarious situation of HIV/AIDS.

What role for Chinese civil society in HIV/AIDS?

Chinese CSOs have an important and indispensable role to play in facing the challenges posed by HIV/AIDS. However, to effectively respond to the challenge and preventing an epidemic, a multisectoral response is required. It is a response that requires coordinated action and partnerships between the various stakeholders including Chinese CSOs, the government, and international donors. In this section, due consideration will be given to each of the stakeholders and their response to China's HIV/AIDS situation.

The beginnings of an active civil society

The number of CSOs has increased sharply since liberalization including the number of CSOs addressing the HIV/AIDS issue. There are over 50 registered CSOs working nationwide on HIV/AIDS in 2006. The emerging activism of HIV/AIDS CSOs can be accredited to the Henan blood scandal of the 1990s, which triggered international outcry at the attempted cover-up by local government officials. The selling of blood by poor farmers in villages of Henan to subsidize their incomes, encouraged by local government officials without proper hygiene standards, led to many villages to become afflicted by HIV/AIDS. Such a cover-up forced Drs Gui Xien and Gao Yaojie to take a moral stand and publicly expose the provincial government's exploitative efforts in August 2001. While there is such role for individuals to take lead and initiative in advocating for the government to take more decisive actions against HIV/AIDS, the work of CSOs in this area is still predominantly on a small scale or at the community level. The emphasis from international donors and governments involved in HIV/ AIDS in China is now shifting and they are encouraging the participation of civil society actors, but it is still heavily focused, however, on targeting the government to be more active, as shall be addressed in due course.

CSOs involvement and role

HIV/AIDS CSOs across China are providing essential services to marginalized groups of people and are essential to effectively respond to the challenge. CSOs have marked several areas where there is heavy involvement of civil society. The provision of services such as counseling and information to the gay community is predominantly the work of CSOs. In many larger Chinese cities, hotlines have emerged to provide advice on HIV/AIDS testing and safe sex advice. Peer education is another area where CSOs are active. The Institute of Contemporary Observation (ICO) based in Shenzhen is conducting peer education programs in factories. Migrant workers are seen as high-risk groups because of their mobility and by providing reproductive health programs to such target groups is likely to reduce the risk. CSOs have also been hard at work in campaigning for compensation for hemophilia patients infected with HIV through contaminated blood. The organization Hemophilia Home of China based in Shanghai has successfully advocated for 50 patients, receiving compensation from the municipal government of Shanghai. Such activities and activism are at times seen as at odds with the government's aim. The work of CSOs with drug users is a particular example whereby the government has thwarted past achievements. Injecting drugs is one of the primary vehicle of HIV transmission, particularly in southern China, thus the work of CSOs in harm minimization, methadone clinics, and outreach programs is essential in reducing the risk of infection rates. The targeting of drug users by the government's Strike Hard Campaign clearly indicates that there is inconsistency within government ranks regarding HIV/AIDS and various issues surrounding it. The central government has contributed large amount of resources such as the building of new detention facilities for drug offenders and the deploying of police for regular raids on well-known drug areas. Where authorities directly target drug users, clinics and services, hampers any attempts that CSOs may undertake to prevent the spread of HIV/AIDS. Such government actions denote a disinterest in the work of CSOs and are unwilling to cooperate with CSOs to alter the situation. The invaluable contribution of CSOs can be compromised by government actions, at times contradictory to other policies. On the one hand, the government sees the work of CSOs in the arena of HIV/AIDS as reinforcing lax moral standards, on the other CSOs are seen as competitors to government fee-for-service providers. In areas such as condom distribution, the government providers are supplying to users at a fee whereas the majority of CSOs provide it free of charge. Accordingly, government healthcare providers feel a level of threat from the CSOs: "Government departments, particularly at local levels perceive NGOs – particularly in the health sector – as competitors for delivery of fee-for-service programs and react by suppressing the private sector actors" (Thompson and Lu, 2006: 37). Hence, the various challenges that beset CSOs not just in the HIV/AIDS arena but across the health sector seriously inhibit the growth and potential of these organizations to provide quality care to the community. Nonetheless, the government is not the only hurdle for CSOs to overcome. The recent disputes between CSOs have raised doubts about the capabilities of Chinese CSOs in overcoming the HIV/AIDS challenge.

Civil society representation on the Global Fund's Country Coordinating Mechanism (CCM) highlights the friction among local CSOs. The election of Jia Ping, Development Director of Aizhiyuanzu based in Shenyang as the CSO representative on the CCM board, has proved contentious. Challenges were directed at some CSOs in attendance regarding the organizations' authenticity or whether they were simply hospitals or local health authorities in the guise of a CSO (China Development Brief, 2005). Beijing-based Aizhixing has encountered partnership problems with other CSOs because of their working style (Personal communication, July 25, 2006). This particular organization is open with their criticisms of other HIV/AIDS organizations and this creates discomfort among project partners. According to the founder, his criticisms are often seen by other organizations as an attempt to discredit them – his "competitors" – rather than as an attempt to assist in the improvement of CSOs. Regardless of how it is perceived, this "competition" among CSOs is distracting them from the primary task of uniting together to work against the threat of HIV/AIDS. The value of CSOs working on HIV/AIDS should not be overlooked despite the disputes. Although in conjunction with government forces, China's response to the health and social problems caused by HIV/AIDS is likely to be fractured. Nonetheless, the power of the state may yet be useful in confronting HIV/AIDS.

A closer look at CSOs in the HIV/AIDS sector

In this section we will look at a few CSOs in greater detail to understand the range of projects and activities carried out to confront China's potential epidemic. As mentioned earlier, there are over 50 registered CSOs working nationally, however, it does not account for the numerous local groups with or without registration as a "social organization."[5]

AIDS Care China located in Guangdong province was founded by Thomas Cai in 2000. It started off as a modest counseling service for those with HIV/AIDS. Its operations now cover Guangdong, Guangxi, Hubei, and Yunnan. Its main focus includes assisting poor PLWHA by providing generic ARV drugs and providing a supportive environment for PLWHA and their families. As the aim of the organization is to improve the living standards of PLWHA, it seeks to provide more personalized care and counseling in addition to what the patients receive from the hospitals. It directly helps PLWHA by assisting them with employment and provides training to improve their employment prospects. It also seeks to bridge the gap between patients and society by raising awareness and it is doing this by working with university students and healthcare professionals and also by publishing a series of news booklets. AIDS Care China received its first funding from the United Nations in 2003 and has since received support from a host of international organizations including UNAIDS, Ford Foundation, Treat Asia, among others.

Aizhixing Institute of Health Education based in Beijing is one of the country's better known CSO, founded by former state health official, Wan Yanhai.[6] This organization started up with an initial grant from the Elizabeth Taylor AIDS Foundation. Its operations have expanded to the point where it is now allocating some of its own funds to nurture grass roots CSOs. However, the main focus of its work remains with advocacy work, training, education, organizing support groups for PLWHA in rural areas, and legal support for PLWHA in rural areas. In the area of advocacy, Aizhixing has proved to be relatively vocal in comparison to other organizations and this openness when addressing the government Wan Yanhai believes will bring about change much more quickly as the government will realize sooner the needs of the CSOs (Personal communication, July 25, 2005). They have advocated for changes to the pricing of ARV drugs and policies affecting gay men and women of China. The organization has received funding from the National Endowment Fund for Democracy and the Soros Foundation. As these foundations have proved quite sensitive for the Chinese government, Aizhixing has been very open with their finances and work undertaken using external funding.

Beijing Loving Source Information Consulting Center also based in Beijing was founded in 2003 by Hu Jia. Due to the difficulties in finding a government sponsor, it has had to register as a business thus making it liable for taxes. The organization focuses on assisting AIDS orphans by arranging one-on-one care from volunteers. Donations of goods are also made to AIDS orphans living in poor remote areas. In order to arrange volunteers for the AIDS Orphan program, Loving Source organizes volunteer training on a number of areas relating to HIV/AIDS. Its annual budget for 2005 was approximately 300,000 RMB (China Aids Info, 2005: 23).

Chengdu Gay Community Care Organization is a regional CSO founded in Chengdu in 2002 by Wang Xiaodong and Jiang Hua. The organization's mission is to improve the social standing of gay men in the Chinese community. In achieving this goal, the organization has conducted a series of training programs for health officials to understand and be sensitive to the needs of gay men. In serving the gay community, it organizes outreach activities and education programs, provides a 24-hour hotline and publishes quarterly newsletters. The newsletters are distributed to 20 cities across the country and also in Chengdu's local bars and clubs along with condoms. The China–UK HIV/AIDS Care and Prevention Program has funded the organization from 2000 to 2006.

China Family Planning Association is one of the largest CSOs in China, with strong ties to the government. It was established in 1980 and its mission is to complement and implement the state's family planning policies, primarily cutting the natural growth rate to less than ten per thousand through education and strict controls. Its extensive network from cities to villages to households enables it to cover a large geographic area with its programs. The Association included HIV/AIDS in its strategy since 1996. It has worked with various international organizations including Marie Stopes International and UNFPA to implement a youth peer education program on health and HIV/AIDS. The program targeted middle schools and universities in Beijing and Shanghai

HAIKEYI is a student association established in 2003 at Shanghai's Jiaotong University. The association's main activity is its Peer Education Program conducted within the university. Student volunteers of the association conduct sexual health and HIV/AIDS awareness classes. Approximately ten classes are held each semester. It has also worked with the local district government on migrant health training programs. The students in conjunction with the local Family Planning Association conduct classes for migrant workers living in the area. Due to the nature of the association, one that is student based, the association is restricted by the University's rules and regulations in terms of activities and funding.

HomeAIDS based in Kunming, Yunnan, was jointly established by the Salvation Army of Hong Kong and Macau and the Yunnan Red Cross in 2002. HomeAIDS focuses on education, outreach, training, counseling, networking, media publicity, care and support of PLWHA. It also operates a 24-hour hotline providing AIDS-related information to callers. HomeAIDS is funded by the Australian Agency for International Development, Norwegian Agency for Development Cooperation, and UNICEF.

Mangrove Support Group based in Beijing was the first registered national support group for those living with HIV/AIDS. Founded in 2002, its aim is to improve the quality of life for PLWHA by providing skills training. The organization was founded by Li Xiang who contracted HIV/AIDS through blood transfusion. To improve communications between PLWHA, Mangrove publishes a magazine and runs a hotline.

Snow Lotus HIV/AIDS Education Institute is a university student volunteer group based in Xinjiang. Since its inception in March 2006, it has encountered trouble with the authorities. Nineteen students in Kashgar were dismissed from their public schools because they tested positive to Hepatitis B in September 2006. As such discrimination is against Chinese law, Snow Lotus revealed the news to the media in early October 2006 and this has resulted in the detainment of four of its volunteers by Xinjiang officials. Despite its shaky start, it operates a discussion forum on its website and with a grant from the Global Fund, it will carry out school-based HIV/AIDS education programs. Its education program will also target men who have sex with men and drug users.

Yunnan Evergreen PLWHA Mutual Assistance Group was founded in 1998 in Kunming. The Groups assists PLWHA who are on drug rehabilitation programs and help them reintegrate into society. The Group also offers methadone treatment services, needle exchange, as well as peer education programs. Families of PLWHA are also offered support through the group's network. There are currently 70 staff members with a budget of 800,000 yuan per year.

While this is only a brief introduction into the HIV/AIDS CSOs, it is evident that the majority of these organizations were established within the last 6 or 7 years, indicating their infancy. This is also suggestive of the time when HIV/AIDS became a concern for the Chinese government and the movement toward addressing the matter. The organizations surveyed above indicate the diversity of organizations in China. Yet, many of the organizations in the HIV/AIDS sector are based in Beijing and this raises the question of the environment and space permissible for these CSOs. The fact that so many are based in Beijing would suggest that the political environment has relaxed in the nation's capital for HIV/AIDS CSOs to do their work. Nevertheless, this relaxation is not necessarily replicated in the rest of the country, particularly in the lower levels of provincial governments. While there is a degree of openness in Beijing for HIV/AIDS CSOs to operate, if government bodies and institutions perceive threat and/or competition, this space is likely to shrink, as mentioned previously. On closer inspection of the location of CSOs, Yunnan province is also a host to many. The openness of Yunnan provincial government has long been hailed as a mini success for China's civil society development. The Yunnan Evergreen PLWHA Mutual Assistance Group was established in 1998, one of the few CSOs with a longer history and to be working on drug rehabilitation of PLWHA further signifies the openness of the Yunnan provincial government.

The surveyed organizations would suggest that HIV/AIDS CSOs are indeed broadening the social landscape. The various works and activities of the organizations, ranging from peer education to methadone treatment, demonstrate that CSOs do have the potential to make an important contribution to battling HIV/AIDS. However, the doubt arises as to how much impact these organizations can make given the state-directed civil society. As seen in the two student groups surveyed, HAIKEYI and Snow Lotus, HAIKEYI's partnership with the local government has allowed them to participate and conduct programs beyond the campus. Snow Lotus on the other hand has faced restriction due to its perceived challenge to the local government's wisdom and authority. Perhaps for CSOs to be effective and experience a certain freedom to operate, they require strategizing and cooperation with the government. This leads us to the question raised earlier of whether CSOs are unwilling to initiate change and become reliant on the government, thus reinforcing the state-directed civil society. Nonetheless, what is also evident in the student groups' example is the difference and tolerance level of local governments. China's success in curbing HIV/AIDS will largely depend on the openness and willingness of local level governments to work on the issue and work with nongovernment forces.

In looking at the catalyst behind the establishment of some of China's prominent HIV/AIDS CSOs, it is often the efforts and experiences of one individual. Chinese media reports often focus on the individual, rather than the organization and its work as a whole. Thus it would suggest that the success and potential failure of a CSO are very much tied to this one individual. And this leads to the sustainability question of CSOs, how likely will these CSOs exist after the departure of the founding member and what sort of impact would this create on its programs and constituents? Beyond the challenges posed by various levels of government to CSOs, internal structure and the politics of an organization are also likely to generate future obstacles.

If we look at the funding patterns of CSOs across the HIV/AIDS sector, the majority receive support from international organizations or governments. This matter also leads us to the question of sustainability. How sustainable is it to rely on outside funding? However, with restrictions placed on fundraising activities and lack of government finances devoted to CSOs, organizations are forced to apply for external finances. Yet where there is outside funding of local HIV/AIDS projects, the government is a close observer. CSOs in the HIV/AIDS sector, although motivated to combat the disease, face a battle that they are unlikely to resolve independently. The questions of funding and carrying out effective projects regardless of government sensibilities are issues that demand joint coop-eration of both CSOs and the government.

State-directed civil society

The strength of the Chinese state is seen as a beneficial force and international organizations have pushed the government to take on a greater role in meeting the challenges posed by HIV/AIDS. The paradigm that dominates in terms of fighting HIV/AIDS is one that is directed at the Chinese government to provide greater financial assistance and support to the rural areas in the health sector. Reducing the inequality in health spending between the urban and rural areas is seen as a precursor in fighting HIV/AIDS, where rural citizens will thereby have better access to general health education, prevention, and treatment of illness. This paradigm is promoted by organizations such as the United Nations in China, where its 2005 report, *Advancing Social Development in China: Contribution to the 11th Five Year Plan*, clearly indicating the need for the central government to curb the growing inequalities between rural and urban access to healthcare (UN Country Team China, 2005). With economic liberalization, the responsibility of healthcare has gradually been pushed down the hierarchies of the government structure and in some cases to the lowest level, being that of the rural village. Kaufman, Kleinman and Saich (2006) similarly cite the growing inequalities in healthcare as a major obstacle in tackling HIV/AIDS. While the Chinese state may be promoting greater equality in the process of social development, the incentives that drive local government officials are often out of step with this vision. The state has yet to rectify the incentive structure for the promotion of local or provincial officials (Landry, 2009). It is still largely economic achieve-ments that matter, not the number of people having access to health services or education. It is without a doubt that the need to restructure the Chinese health system is vital in order to tackle HIV/AIDS in a holistic manner with the support of both the state and local governments.

There are dual implications for Chinese civil society actors with the predomi-nance of such a paradigm in the battle against HIV/AIDS. First, with the spotlight on the state in pushing it to ensure greater equity in the provision of healthcare, the role of CSOs will inevitably be second to that of the government. While CSOs are implementing many worthwhile projects as outlined above, it is ultimately the state that has the overall strength to guarantee greater equity in terms of access to services and resources. Thus, in managing HIV/AIDS, the role of the CSOs will to some extent be a supportive one. Second, the Chinese state sees the contribution of CSOs very much as service providers or gap fillers. For CSOs to be effective in their work against HIV/AIDS, their part needs to be more than just gap fillers. With the state limiting the scope of CSOs work as dis-cussed previously, including registration difficulties, the possibility of Chinese CSOs becoming a force like those in Brazil and Thailand is questionable. The development of CSOs is controlled by the state and it will be the state that determines the level of CSOs involvement in HIV/AIDS. Space provided for CSOs to operate can be withdrawn by the state as quickly as it has been offered, through a number of punitive measures. There appears to be greater freedom for CSOs working in HIV/AIDS than other types of CSOs and perhaps this is an indication of the state showing signs of relaxing its hold on civil society. Although, what is apparent at the state level does not always filter down to local levels of government as observed by Watts (2005: 1370): "Obstruction at a local level is a major problem in implementing central government welfare policies in such a large country as China, where the health minister is outranked by the Henan provincial governor."

The disconnect between the central and local governments will likely impede on the work of CSOs, where the state may welcome their presence but treated with indifference or at worse with hostility at the local level. CSOs working on HIV/AIDS in China, while dependent on the state in granting space and permission to operate, also have a significant battle of their own in terms of becoming effective players in preventing the spread of HIV/AIDS. This is a challenge not just for CSOs as a whole but it is a challenge of legitimacy, to represent the needs of the people in an era where the powers of the state are on the decline.

International donors

Foreign assistance to China's HIV/AIDS programs and projects has increased significantly over time and this has meant greater resources to tackle various aspect of the disease. By the end of 2005, foreign assistance from the governments of the United Kingdom, the United States, Australia, the European Union, and other European governments, as well as international foundations, multinational companies resulted totaled 1.867 billion RMB (US$229 million) (Gill, 2006: 6). Although international resources have increased over time, the number of CSOs and the areas receiving assistance tends to be limited. It is not uncommon to see the same CSOs as principal recipients of major international funding but this is also related to similar types of CSOs being prevented to proliferate in the same areas. Thus, the growth of international assistance does not necessarily match the growth of HIV/AIDS CSOs in China.

The involvement of international organizations has helped reshape approaches to managing HIV/AIDS. International organizations such as the Global Fund have emphasized and require all applicant countries to establish a CCM which enables multisectoral representation, including civil society. China's initial proposal to the Global Fund was rejected because it did not have a CCM that had a broad enough representation. In 2003, a CCM was set up with representatives from government ministries, international donors, and nongovernment organizations (NGOs), with 54 members by the end of 2005. The Global Fund has so far provided over US$190 million in funds to HIV/AIDS projects in China. However, the majority of the finance is granted to the China's Center for Disease Control, a state institution and it is then responsible for disbursing the money to different implementers. The proportion of the Global Fund finances earmarked for civil society increased from 15 percent in the first round to 34 percent in the latest round.[7] As raised earlier, governments proved to be less effective in using the resources granted by the Global Fund than CSOs. With the Chinese bureaucracy so large and cumbersome, it remains questionable to what extent the resources are actually targeting those most in need.

In line with promoting a multisectoral response, the China Health Alliance is a network of government ministries, businesses, local and international CSOs, and multilateral agencies set up to ensure a well-rounded approach to HIV/AIDS in China. The participation of Accenture, China National Textile and Apparel Council, Pfizer, Marie Stopes International, UN agencies, Shenzhen-based ICO among others have agreed to provide education, tests, and support in the workplace on tuberculosis and HIV health issues. While such alliances are needed, the question arises as to whether such response is a tokenistic one or whether it will be useful and help China contain the spread of HIV/AIDS.

Conflict or cooperation?

China's response to HIV/AIDS appears to be fractured despite the dominance of the state. The slow response of the government to the potential threat shows that it is ill equipped and/or unwilling to fully address the situation with all its facets. CSOs on the other hand are divided among themselves regarding representation and competition. International donors are providing substantial resources but accountability and effectiveness of such assistance are uncertain when it is channeled into government bodies. Despite the need for civil society to help the nation meet the difficulties of HIV/AIDS, CSOs in China are weak and some are antagonistic toward each other. As pressure mounts on the government to provide more equitable development, with all benefiting across China, CSOs can be the vehicle to help the government deliver the tangible goods of an equitable society such as health, education, employment skills, and others. Rather than suppress because of the fear that CSOs may unite and create disturbances for the government, what in fact should occur is the opposite, to nurture and provide the room for CSOs to mature. Bearing the reality of China's political situation in mind, the state will continue to be present in many parts of society, politics, and economy – our expectations should be grounded in this reality. Nonetheless, the state can and ought to ensure that the current space for CSOs does not shrink and that the stance taken on CSOs ought to be streamlined.

Comparisons have been made between Britain's industrialization and China's current modernization drive. The social consequences of both are similar: major health issues appearing, worsening of the environment, growing inequality among others. However, with the activism of people such as Edwin Chadwick, and the writings of Henry Mayhew and WT Stead, the media and civil society of industrializing Britain were able to redress many of the social ills of development. Their campaigns and writings forced industrialists and politicians to take heed and action: "The public voice of civil society produced the great social reforms of the mid-19th century, from sewerage to child labour and trade union rights" (Hunt, 2006). According to Hunt, the two major differences in the comparison between Britain and China in addressing the negative impact of modernization are the free voice of civil society and a free press (ibid.). Civil society proved to be an outlet and vehicle for the British to afford social change. But as we have seen, civil society in China is under the control of the state and hindered to being an effective voice for the marginalized. CSOs in China are still developing and maturing. This should not detract from the role that they could potentially play in China's HIV/AIDS challenge. A cooperative strategy between government and civil society is required to foil HIV/AIDS and many other impacts of development. It is a cooperation that demands commitment, genuine participation from all stakeholders, and being able to look long term.

Conclusion

With such an array of issues to manage for all stakeholders, the likelihood of successfully combating HIV/AIDS in China seems bleak. Unlike Thailand, China has not shown the political leadership or will to deal with the matter at hand. The sensitivity of the government toward HIV/AIDS and sexual health cannot be more obvious when it was only in 2003 that the government lifted the ban on condom advertising. Although the Chinese government has indicated its desire to redress the problem by increasing spending on the control and prevention of HIV in 2006–2007, with a budget of 1.5 billion RMB (US$185 million), more than double the previous year. Yet the distance between the central government's desire and the willingness of local government to implement plans is enormous. Observers may say this is where CSOs should come in, to bridge that gap by offering to work with local governments but the suspicion and misunderstanding on the part of the local government is itself another hurdle. Without a doubt, there is a role for CSOs to play in China's HIV/AIDS case.

By exploring the situation from a civil society standpoint, we begin to gather a more complex perspective. The civil society framework does not necessarily mean an outlook that is positive, rather as we have seen from the Chinese case there are many barriers for CSOs to overcome and resolve, including disharmony within HIV/AIDS CSOs. Hence, the question is not about the existence of civil society in China, rather it is a question of how much contribution the current state of civil society can make to afford social change. Ultimately the answer to that question lies in the realms of state–society cooperation. Such collaboration would help redress the imbalance of power within society, where the power is predominantly in the hands of the state. By allowing civil society room to make its own choices and represent the marginalized, the state would be better served and less burdened. Where would the force come from to demand change? One of the most likely candidates is that which the state is currently trying to manage – the poor rural peasant population. Chinese academics are seen as a possible force for change as they have greater sway. Perhaps this is an underutilized vehicle. Nonetheless, academics cannot be a proxy for civil society – it can be part of civil society but not its only voice. To successfully counter an HIV/AIDS epidemic, a series of partnerships and cooperation between various stakeholders is required.

Brazil and Thailand have both demonstrated that it is possible to reduce the infection rates among its population, thanks to political leadership that incorporated all stakeholders. There are lessons for China's civil society and government in the pages of Thailand and Brazil. The first and foremost is to comprehend the danger of HIV/AIDS. In understanding the havoc that HIV/AIDS can cause upon a society, responses ought to be united. To be united requires all levels of government and CSOs working together and looking to the future. The will on the side of CSOs is present but their will and response are stunted by government bodies and institutions. Hence, the road ahead is most certainly dependent on the political resolve from both central and local governments. Building a better rapport and cooperative measures with CSOs will greatly enhance the government's position in its response to HIV/AIDS. Only when the responses from all levels of the state are coherent and coordinated can civil society do its part.

Conclusion

The microbe is nothing; the terrain, everything.

(Louis Pasteur, 1822–1895)

This book has used an alternative conceptualization of epidemic disease to try and understand the types of forces causing the emergence of an HIV/AIDS epidemic in China. The purpose has not been to provide an exhaustive account of how China's epidemic has emerged or is evolving, or what the responses have been. There are already a number of useful accounts that serve this purpose. Instead, it has been an attempt to explore the ways in which a different conceptualization of how epidemic disease is generated can be employed to explain a specific country case. What, after all, is the best way to try and understand HIV/AIDS epidemics? Are such epidemics best thought of as the product of individual risky behavior and individual action? Or, is it more useful to look at the broader social and economic forces that act on large groups of people? The first approach, to date, has undoubtedly been the dominant one taken in trying to understand the world's HIV/AIDS epidemics. The second approach, on the other hand, which considers in far more detail the type of economic and social terrain in which epidemic disease flourishes, has received far less attention. Looking at what has also been referred to as, among other things, the "biosocial," "structural," "distal," or "economic and social determinants" of disease, in this approach we have attempted to move beyond the subject of individual agency. As such, the contribution of this book to the understanding HIV/AIDS in China is somewhat novel while also being complementary to many existing studies.

In Chapter 1, we showed how HIV/AIDS epidemics have generally been seen as a medical problem. In this conceptualization, disease is generated mainly through individual risky behaviors. This sees, among other things, HIV-infected drug injectors helping to build up a "critical mass" of infections in sexual networks, from where HIV spreads across to wider society (MAP, 2005). Introduction of HIV into networks of injecting drug users can result in the rapid spread of HIV, particularly where multiple use of nonsterile needles is common. Injecting drug users may also be engaged in sex work, or become clients of sex workers. This in turn provides transmission pathways from the high-prevalence intravenous drug use groups into lower prevalence commercial sex work (CSW) groups, from where transmission to the general population may then more easily take place. In addition to IDU populations, homosexual population groups may also be important in kick-starting a generalized epidemic, as well as individuals infected through blood donation or transfusion. This conceptualization of HIV/AIDS epidemics, using a biomedical approach, tends to focus its attention on these high-risk groups and the extent to which bridging between high- and low-risk populations may take place. According to the biomedical viewpoint, therefore, at the heart of most of Asia's epidemics "lies the interplay between injecting drug use and unprotected sex, much of it commercial" (UNAIDS/WHO, 2005a: 31).

But we also noted that there is dissatisfaction and growing dissent regarding these approaches. Causes of disease, for example, can be distinct at different levels of organization. This phenomenon, some argue, can be understood through the concept of what has been referred to as "emergent group properties" (Schwartz, Susser and Susser, 1999). This idea stipulates that each level of organization has unique characteristics confined to that level. Water, for example, can be described at a molecular level as an arrangement of hydrogen and oxygen molecules. The liquidity of water, however, possesses characteristics that cannot be described by examination of its molecular components (ibid.). Studying something at a different level of analysis may yield quite different results. This led us to consider the ways in which population groups move in to more high-risk behavior as a result of economic and social changes. This observation is particularly germane for the case of China. In East Asia the HIV/AIDS epidemic has been expanding faster than anywhere else in the world (UNAIDS, 2008). Contrasting with many of the sub-Saharan African epidemics, however, many parts of Asia have seen their epidemics expand under conditions of speedy but also highly uneven economic growth. Unlike the HIV/AIDS epidemics in SSA, which have generally been associated with sluggish economic growth and considered "diseases of poverty," the fast-growing epidemics of East and Southeast Asia have occurred during periods of rapid economic growth and social transformation. Unlike in many of the other areas of human development (education, health, and the environment), however, which tend to improve with economic development, the HIV/AIDS epidemics appear to show no obvious relationship with growth and development. In fact, some evidence shows that the types of rapid but often unbalanced development processes found today in East Asia may create favorable economic and social terrain for HIV/AIDS epidemics. This includes such things as income inequality, migration patterns, and gender differences. Economic growth, therefore, may not be a panacea for HIV/AIDS epidemics, even if it may help promote other areas of human development.

An approach that considers the broader economic and social distal determinants of disease is not without serious limitations. We also noted, for example, the difficulty of specifying particular levels of analysis when moving beyond an individual level, of identifying causal variables and their various interactions, and also with dealing with the temporal and dynamic aspect of epidemic disease. Despite these reservations, however, we argued that this alternative perspective might provide useful complementary insights into China's HIV/AIDS epidemic, particularly given the extremely rapid economic and social changes taking place. The underlying terrain, so to speak, has evolved rapidly and warrants further consideration in the emergence of HIV/AIDS epidemics.

To date, many academic studies and reports, such as those produced by UNAIDS or the Monitoring AIDS Pandemic Network (MAP, 2005), provide detailed descriptions and analysis of the *individual* risk factors associated with HIV/AIDS. These publications include discussion of the behavior and action of certain high-risk population groups, such as the frequency of condom use, changes in HIV prevalence among intravenous drug users, and homosexual population groups. It is common that incidence and prevalence rates among these important risk groups, as well as some of their behavioral patterns, are monitored in detail. This general approach to understanding HIV/AIDS, as discussed, focuses much upon the risk factors than we can say with certainty cause HIV infection and transmission in individuals. The broader socioeconomic factors and trends that have also been identified as placing populations at risk, such as gender inequality, poverty and income distribution, levels of education, and political representation, are not given nearly as much attention, despite increasing lip service to their relevance. Indeed, some of these human and social indicators of development are also now included in recent UNAIDS Epidemic Updates (from 2007 onward). The explicit recognition of these reports, moreover, is that HIV/AIDS epidemics are also closely related to a country's overall economic, social, and human development levels and progress. Nonetheless, the amount of data and level of analysis undertaken, even of a simple comparative nature, are quite minimal. Human development indicators at the national level, for example, are included. Such things as the human development index, human poverty index, and an estimate of people living under US$2 a day are all included. Despite incorporating this population-level data, few comparisons are made between countries, nor are dynamic patterns and interrelationships considered over time. There is no analysis of how different poverty levels or inequalities may contribute to the different epidemics. This, of course, contrasts strikingly with the discussion of individual risk factors, where there are many comparisons (of general HIV prevalence levels and prevalence within specific groups and between countries).

With a view to better understanding this so-called terrain, and how it is evolving, the second chapter undertook a comparative analysis of China's development path. Extensive use of human development indicators taken from data collected for monitoring of the Millennium Development Goals was used to move beyond a focus on prevalence and incidence of HIV/AIDS in certain population groups. Instead, such things as gender and income inequality, urbanization and migration, education and health were considered, with a view to establishing population-level patterns in development that may provide a better understanding of the particular terrain in which HIV/AIDS is emerging. Comparisons were made with countries in SSA at various levels of human development, although also with more severe HIV/AIDS epidemics, so as to tease out similarities and differences with the Chinese example. Interestingly, it was found that China's development path, if not yet the extent of its HIV/AIDS epidemic, appeared to share a number of similarities with that of Thailand. While China's real income is still lower than Thailand's, it is catching-up quickly. They both experienced rapid average annual income growth over extended periods, both among the fastest in the sample. Both have also developed an outward international orientation and have been more open recipients of globalization processes, extensively using foreign direct investment. More importantly, their income distributions are also quite heavily skewed, with considerable shares of income concentrated in quite small segments of the population. Both countries have also seen large-scale migration, often from poorer regions with higher HIV prevalence. Each, moreover, has seen the development of a significant commercial sex industry. Worryingly, Thailand has also experienced a generalized epidemic, as well as implementing effective policies to decrease adult prevalence. The Thai case may hold lessons in terms of specific economic and social determinants. It may, possibly, also provide an indicator of where the Chinese epidemic is currently heading.

This comparative analysis revealed some interesting features concerning the terrain of HIV/AIDS in China. While, for example, absolute levels of education may be higher in China and East Asia generally than in, for example, SSA, relative inequalities in education between sexes may well be greater. Following from this broad overview, the third chapter went on to investigate in more detail the specific drivers of HIV/AIDS epidemics that have been identified at the population level in other studies. Among the most important of these, it was argued, is the role of a number of inequalities:

Models of disease emergence need to be dynamic, systemic, and critical. They need to be critical of facile claims of causality, particularly those that scant the pathogenic roles of social inequalities. Critical perspectives on emerging infections must ask how large-scale social forces come to have their effects on unequally positioned individuals in increasingly interconnected populations; a critical epistemology needs to ask what features of disease emergence are obscured by dominant analytic frameworks.

(Farmer, 1999: 5)

A number of studies have now shown that income and gender inequalities are important drivers of HIV/AIDS epidemics. Therefore, to move beyond the dominant analytic framework, a better understanding of specific social inequalities may help explain China's rapidly growing HIV/AIDS epidemic. A range of studies, spanning a variety of disciplines and using different methods, now argues that social and economic inequalities have a strong impact on population health (Farmer, 1999; Gandy and Zumla, 2002; Wilkinson, 2005). Income inequality, for example, has been found to have a particularly strong association with health in both the developed and developing world (Wilkinson and Pickett, 2006). Additionally, it is of importance to note that a growing body of recent research also finds a very strong empirical association between HIV/AIDS prevalence and income inequality (Holtgrave and Crosby, 2003; Drain *et al.*, 2004; Nepal, 2007; Talbott, 2007). Others, using slightly different approaches, persuasively argue that these types of inequalities are among the most important drivers of HIV/AIDS epidemics (Barnett and Whiteside, 2006; Craddock, 2004; Schoepf, 2004; Farmer, 1999).

Given that a strong international association has been established between income inequality and HIV/AIDS, this raised the question of whether China has a similar type of relationship and whether the unprecedented increases in income inequality in China have also been important in driving China's HIV/AIDS epidemic. Building on the work of a number of ecologic studies, which use statistical approaches to understanding these relationships, we also looked to briefly investigate the relationship between income and gender inequality and HIV/AIDS prevalence in China. By focusing on inequalities, this third chapter pointed the way for further investigation of the mechanisms whereby inequality might give rise to HIV/AIDS epidemics. Subsequent chapters, for example, considered how inequality was linked to CSW. CSW is central to understanding Asian HIV/AIDS epidemics. In the case of China, it is now also becoming a significant mode of transmission for HIV/AIDS. While HIV/AIDS epidemics may be kick-started by subpopulations (e.g., IDU populations), for full-blown generalized epidemics to take place, widespread heterosexual transmission is also necessary. The Asian countries that have experienced large-scale epidemics heterosexual transmission via CSW has been a necessary precondition. The sexual mixing pattern in Asia related to professional sex workers is also considered an efficient way for rapid spread of HIV (Grassly *et al.*, 2003). Given the far greater absolute numbers that engage in risky sexual activity, it is now predicted that heterosexual transmission will become the dominant mode of transmission in China (Wu, Rou and Cui, 2004: 10). Indeed, evidence increasingly suggests that the epidemic is already spreading swiftly from high-risk groups to the general population via sexual transmission. Corresponding to the movement out of the predominantly male IDU population, the infection rate of women has also increased.

To further explore this issue, the fourth chapter asked what deeper forces lay behind the growth in CSW. It argued that the growth of the sex industry could not be put down to a shift in sexual preferences and attitudes, such as the liberation of women or the increased appetites of men. Instead, a number of structural reasons related to economic and social development can help explain the massive re-emergence of sex work in China today. Examples from the economic and social history of today's developed economies, as well as examples from the late-industrializing nations of Southeast Asia, were used to illustrate this phenomenon. More specifically, in the case of China, it was also argued that economic development has led to increasing gender-related income inequalities. Females now typically earn less than males. They have started to migrate at ever younger ages. They are also less likely to be married than male migrant counterparts. As well as this, they also have lower levels of education. Both push and pull factors, moreover, cause females to migrate. Surveys show that pull factors are typically more important for men, reflecting the often precarious positions China's rural females may find themselves in. Migrant females have typically been employed in service sectors or menial low-paid manufacturing jobs. Work conditions are generally poor and female migrants are literally "at the front line of both domestic and global capitalist development, working for the lowest wages in poor and often unsafe conditions and in occupations that urbanites shun" (Gaetano and Jacka, 2004: 2). As inequalities between males and females continue to grow and wealthier urban classes emerge, male urban demand has increased greatly. Female migrants' employment opportunities, age, marital status, and destination of migration, therefore, may all incline them toward considering CSW. Combined with rapidly changing social norms, such work is often considered a legitimate career option. And while most women migrants may migrate without the explicit purpose of entering the sex trade, many are subsequently attracted to it. We showed in Chapter 4 that it is highly likely that the nature and pace of development in China have affected the supply of workers and the demand for CSW, including the inequalities identified in Chapter 3.

When we think of the "deeper undercurrents" and the "terrain" in which China's HIV/AIDS epidemic is emerging, it is important to look beyond the domain of individual agency. A set of structural forces and inequalities has led to the re-emergence of sex work in China. This has grown rapidly and now exists on a massive scale. Other authors, looking at Southeast Asia, have also concluded that without addressing the underlying economic and social forces driving prostitution, steps to target individual prostitutes "are not likely to be effective or may even be inappropriate" (Lim, 1998: 2). In Thailand, hailed as East Asia's most successful HIV-prevention success story, behavioral indicators now suggest that as prevalence has fallen, individual behavior is again becoming more risky among men. The Thai example shows that persistent educational campaigns can be very effective. But unless they are pervasive and long term, high-risk behaviors may well end up re-emerging. Similar patterns have been witnessed in Laos. Similarly, among females, with millions of sex workers and ease of entry and exit to the sex sector creating a constant turnover, some argue "individualized services based on outreach are simply not practical" (MAP, 2005: 16). Large education and information campaigns, therefore, may not even be sufficient in China. "Structural interventions," by contrast, have the advantage that they avoid having to work at the level of the individual (MAP, 2005). From a policy perspective, increasing the economic opportunities and social power of females, for example, "should be seen as part and parcel of potentially successful and sustainable AIDS strategies" (UNAIDS, 2004: 11). Clearly, a balance between the two will be required in order to address the problem of CSW in China.

Following from this, we then moved to the related subject of migration. There is considerable interest in the general relationship between HIV/AIDS epidemics and migration. The Partnership on HIV/AIDS and Mobile Populations, International Organization for Migration, and Regional Office for Southern Africa and the Southern African Migration Project, for example, recently met to consider the linkages between HIV/AIDS, population mobility and migration in

Southern Africa. These researchers found that despite there being a number of important factors in the rapid spread of HIV in Africa, "perhaps the key neglected factor in explaining the rapid spread of HIV over the last decade is population mobility" (IOM, 2005: 10). They concluded, however, that we are still far from understanding just how mobility and HIV interact. As in southern Africa, the migrant population is also seen as a key factor in the spread of HIV in China. It is speculated that greater geographic mobility, lower levels of education, limited HIV/AIDS knowledge, and separation from partners and families make migrants more prone to high-risk behavior. The role of the migrant population in China, however, remains quite poorly understood. Exactly how this group is likely to participate in the epidemic remains slightly unclear owing to a dearth of research, as well as to the at times seemingly contradictory findings (Hesketh *et al.*, 2006). Studies have considered, among other things, how behavior may change after migration and whether there is higher HIV prevalence among migrant groups. Some regional case studies have also been produced. A number of studies focusing on different aspects of migration and HIV in China have emerged. Case studies have considered local regions and areas of China with a view to understanding how mobile populations interact with the virus at a local level. Additionally, epidemiological studies have been undertaken. Complementing epidemiological studies, behavioral studies have also investigated how migrant risk behaviors may change after migration (Andersen *et al.*, 2003; Lin *et al.*, 2005; Yang, Derlega and Luo, 2007). There has also been a focus on "surplus men" and the migrant population (Tucker *et al.*, 2005).

Despite the range of studies to date, it is of interest that the broader national patterns in migration and HIV prevalence have not been closely analyzed. Our conceptualization of epidemic disease, in moving away from a focus on purely understanding individual behavior, directs us toward analysis of these wider national level migration trends. The fifth chapter, therefore, examined in particular whether there are any specific patterns in outward migration and HIV prevalence. Specifically, do provinces with more severe HIV/AIDS epidemics supply more or less migrants? While this might seem an obvious question, to date, in part owing to the dominance of a biomedical approach that focuses on individual behavior, studies have overlooked it. It is, however, particularly germane in China's case, owing to the high regional concentration of infections: by the end of 2006, over 70 percent of cumulative reported infections were found in just six provinces (Chapter 5). If migrants are more likely to originate from high-prevalence regions, this may have implications for the spread of the virus nationally. Many studies also show that risk behaviors do increase after migration. This would further imply that such migrant population group may act as a potent force in the unfolding HIV epidemic. To illustrate this problem we examined official migration data from the Public Security Bureau for 1998 and sentinel surveillance data for this period. We found China's six largest migrant supplying provinces were Henan, Anhui, Sichuan, Hunan, Jiangxi, and Guangxi. These provinces alone accounted for over 65 percent of registered outward interprovincial migrants, totaling nearly 20 million registered migrants in 1998. Sentinel surveillance data accompanied by further investigation into each of these six provinces, moreover, showed that these regions had more advanced epidemics. Examination of more recent data on cumulative infections also confirms the high prevalence in these regions: by the end of 2005, these migrant supplying provinces had recorded among the highest number of reported HIV infections in China, accounting for over 45 percent of all reported infections. This suggests that the six migrant supplying provinces have epidemics that started earlier than in other regions and are also more severe. Furthermore, evidence taken from earlier population censuses indicates that current patterns of migration have been in existence since the early 1980s and continue today. It is likely that official figures from public security departments also seriously underestimate the true number of migrants, possibly by as much as one half.

Because of the nature of China's development process, including growing inequalities between regions, the number of migrants, both male and female, has increased dramatically. Our conceptualization of HIV/AIDS led us to think about the larger forces driving migration, as opposed to focusing purely on the individual migration decision and how, for example, behavior may change in response to migration. As a result of our approach, we found hitherto unrecognized patterns in outward migration and its relationship to HIV/AIDS. Again, what this suggests is that our approach can provide useful complementary perspectives in helping understand HIV/AIDS in China. The Chinese example, as such, may also point toward an important underlying dynamic between HIV, poverty, inequality, and outward migration. This relationship is one in which high-prevalence poor regions are more prone to the outward migration of people, and as a result of migration these groups are also prone to high-risk behavior, which in turn may make them more likely to transmit HIV.

Following this, we considered the evolving nature of China's healthcare and how it may interact with HIV/AIDS. Health systems are vital to treatment and care, but also central to preventing the spread of HIV/AIDS. They are particularly important in dealing with public health problems related to HIV/AIDS. Tuberculosis is one such problem, as is the treatment of sexually transmitted diseases. In Chapter 6, we used the example of the STD outbreak in China to illustrate how the healthcare system is related to the emergence of the HIV/AIDS epidemic. China has one of the fastest growing STD epidemics in the world. China's healthcare system, which has undergone some dramatic changes, is in part responsible for this outbreak. It is now also ill-equipped to deal with the rising STDs infection rates, especially in rural area. The STD epidemic is highly dynamic and changing quickly. The majority of studies on STDs also conclude that there is great potential for a very serious HIV epidemic: "The pandemic of STDs in China strongly suggests the potential for an explosive epidemic of HIV infection through heterosexual transmission" (He *et al.*, 2005: 286). It is very important to note that STDs, to date, have been concentrated in China's wealthier regions where the commercial sex industry is more active. Most HIV infections, by contrast, are found in the western and interior regions of China. This suggests that once HIV establishes itself more firmly in commercial sex networks, found in greater intensity in the coastal and more developed regions, there may well be rapid spread of HIV within these networks. Indeed, if this were to happen, it is not inconceivable that a generalized epidemic could emerge in a relatively short period of time. The exponential growth of syphilis, for example, illustrates just how rapidly STDs may spread. The evidence available suggests that this process is already underway, as the number of female infections and non-IDU and plasma donation-related infections are increasing quite quickly. Finally, it is worth noting that the evidence on STDs points toward an outbreak that is serious by international comparison with STD epidemics in other developing countries. China's rates of STDs also appear high when compared to regions of the world with the highest HIV prevalence rates. Without an adequate healthcare system to address the oncoming health challenges, China may well find itself struggling to contain the HIV/AIDS epidemic.

As well as the geographical aspects, evidence from STD studies confirms the view of CSW as being central to the spread of STDs. The epidemiological studies into STDs, moreover, confirm some of the findings of earlier chapters. Epidemiological data show, for example, that it is wealthier economic groups that are important sources of demand for the services of commercial sex workers and that wealth, travel, and infection rates are also related. A growing number of epidemiological studies now provide an excellent opportunity to further study the deeper undercurrents driving sexual transmission networks. Studies, in particular, that have information on the socioeconomic background of population groups are very useful. More should be made of these going forward to identify the particular forces that lead individuals into high-risk situations.

Civil society organizations have played and continue to play a key role as advocates in promoting positive social change. Chapter 7 looks at what role China's civil society has played and may play in the future struggle against the rapidly growing epidemic. The role of civil society is especially important given the weak role of the state in a number of crucial areas, particularly healthcare. Unlike some other nations that have mounted quite effective responses (Thailand, for example), China has not yet shown the necessary political leadership or will to deal with the huge problem it faces. The sensitivity of the government toward HIV/AIDS and sexual health is illustrated by the fact that it was only in 2003 that the government lifted its ban on condom advertising. Although the Chinese government has indicated its desire to redress the problem by increasing spending on the control and prevention of HIV [with a budget of 1.5 billion RMB (US$185 million) in 2006–2007, more than double the previous year], and taken bold steps, it faces numerous challenges. The distance between the central government's desire and the willingness of local government to implement plans, for example, remains significant. Observers believe that this is where CSOs should come in, to bridge that gap by offering to work with local governments. Suspicion and misunderstanding on the part of the local government, however, is itself another hurdle CSOs must overcome.

There is, without a doubt, a role for CSOs to play in addressing the HIV/AIDS epidemic. There is substantial room for CSOs, for example, to offer their expertise in areas such as health education. There are over 50 nationally registered Chinese CSOs targeting HIV/AIDS and perhaps hundreds of thousands more unregistered organizations, focusing on a wide range of issues from basic health to environmental issues. But whether these CSOs can contribute to the curbing of the HIV/AIDS epidemic will depend upon how government agencies at different levels respond to their growing presence. The growth of civil society and organizations within this sphere is certainly encouraging. Nonetheless, government regulations and mean this nascent sector still faces significant challenges.

There are still many barriers for CSOs to overcome and resolve, including also disharmony within HIV/AIDS CSOs. Hence, the question is not about the existence of civil society in China, rather it is a question of how much contribution the current state of civil society can make to social change. Ultimately, the answer to that question lies in the realms of state–society cooperation. Such collaboration would help redress the imbalance of power within society, where the power is predominantly in the hands of the state. By allowing civil society the room to make its own choices and represent the marginalized, the state would be better served and less burdened. Countries such as Brazil and Thailand have both demonstrated that it is possible to reduce the infection rates with political leadership that incorporates all stakeholders. The lesson from these examples is that responses need to be united. This in turn requires that all levels of government and CSOs must actively work together. Building a better rapport and cooperative measures with CSOs will greatly enhance the government's position in its response to HIV/AIDS. Only when the responses from all levels of the state are coherent and coordinated can the potential of civil society be fully realized.

Implications for policy

As noted back in the first chapter, dominant conceptualizations of what causes disease and poor health have been instrumental in driving policy making, both in China and elsewhere. This is important because quite different conceptualizations have been dominant at different periods of history. In the early twentieth century, in the wake of the emergence of the germ theory of disease, for example, some public health policy makers argued that removing rubbish and investing in sewage treatment would not make a difference to a city's mortality rate (Schwartz, Susser and Susser, 1999). With their newly acquired understanding of the microorganisms, they simply believed that the broader environmental conditions no longer mattered.

Critics of HIV responses would argue that policy makers have adopted a similarly myopic approach today. Because the dominant biomedical model explains disease at the individual level, policy for the most part has looked primarily at reducing exposure of individuals to high-risk situations. As a result, attempts to control HIV/AIDS epidemics, critics argue, have been overwhelmingly medically and epidemiologically driven. They have also adopted policies that have been based on the experiences of other types of epidemic disease. Unlike HIV/AIDS, however, which is a long-wave event (with a considerable gap between time of initial infection and contraction of AIDS), these epidemics were quite different in nature. These responses, it has therefore been argued, incorporated: "a short term and conceptually limited firefighting perspective based on [the] experience of other more explosive and shorter-wave infectious disease outbreaks" (Barnett and Whiteside, 2006: 78). Little consideration, therefore, has been given to the specific contexts of particular countries or regions. Instead, the policy-making logic has been derived from an a priori reasoning which has represented best thinking available at the time (Barnett and Whiteside, 2006). Integral to these policies, as noted, has been the provision of information and education campaigns (IEC). These campaigns have looked to encourage condom use, as well as medical and other interventions, to reduce the probability of transmission from high-risk groups and within the general population. Many critics have argued that these programs are mass produced and short-sighted solutions to HIV/AIDS epidemics, which are in fact caused by complex social problems.

Given these criticisms, it is not surprising that current policies around the world have been heavily criticized. Early beliefs about the HIV epidemics in Africa, for example, focused primarily on what was perceived to be the "hyper-sexuality" common among high-prevalence populations. The spread of HIV, as one contribution to this debate notes, confirmed Western notions of African "hypersexuality." This in turn derailed investigations into other possible causes for the epidemics' rapid spread: "Deep-seated Western stereotypes of African sexuality hijacked the AIDS-in-Africa discourse, and, consequently a beha-vioural bias continues to limit AIDS analysis and policy" (Stillwaggon, 2006: 11). In other examples, similar policy-related problems emerged. In the case of Haiti, for example, it is argued that instead of searching for the underlying social and economic forces propelling the HIV/AIDS epidemics, specific cultural and behavioral explanations were sought. Paul Farmer, for example, notes how anthropologists at first misconstrued the spread of HIV as related to culture:

> When we were face to face with sexual practices or AIDS outcomes that were manifestly linked to poverty and inequality, we wrote instead about the exotic reflections of cultural difference. Animal sacrifice, zoophilia, ritua-lized homosexuality, scarification, and ritual beliefs all figures prominently in the early anthropology of AIDS. The only problem was that none of this had any demonstrable relevance to HIV transmission or AIDS outcomes, and claims to the contrary were eventually revealed to be mistaken – not, however, before a certain amount of damage was done.
>
> (Farmer, 1999: 9)

Given that individual behavior has been held responsible for the spread of HIV/AIDS in the biomedical field, it is also unsurprising that many experts have argued strongly for promoting education of HIV/AIDS transmission mechanisms. Some argue, for example, that a "major lesson" of responses to HIV/AIDS so far has been the "need to address directly and publicly the disease's existence, its modes of transmission, and the means to reduce the probability of infection: for the population's ignorance of such things is the greatest barrier to its containment" (Bell and Lewis, 2005: 26). Critics of this view again, however, point instead to the fact that despite hundreds of millions of dollars being spent on cognitive intervention (IEC and "knowledge, attitude, behavior, and practice"), there still remain only a relatively small number of examples of countries that have successfully lowered HIV/AIDS prevalence. They also point to the difficulty of placing individual agency at the heart of policy making:

> one study after another – as well as rocketing AIDS statistics – have shown that people often knowingly engage in sexual behaviour that places their health at risk. With full knowledge of the dangers of the epidemic, many people continue to have unprotected sex, often with multiple partners ... The forces shaping sexual behaviour and sexual health are far more complex than individual rational decisions based on simple factual knowledge about health risks, and the availability of medical services.
>
> (Campbell, 2003: 7)

Critics of IEC also argue that it is very difficult to prove the effectiveness of cognitive interventions, particularly among the poor, the groups often most at risk. Proof of their effectiveness requires controlling for other possible external influences, which is not straightforward. Critics therefore argue that we should not view education as the "only available vaccine." Indeed, they argue that since we cannot show that cognitive interventions have been highly effective in prevention of HIV infection among the poor – the global risk group – "it is surely unwise to rely *exclusively* on such methods" (Farmer, 1999: xxii). Others have argued that prevention programs have only worked in very specific circumstances: "The view that influencing individual choice and changing individual behaviors without transforming their social and economic context is wrong. It is a sure way to fail and waste resources" (Barnett and Whiteside, 2006: 390). Concern with promoting individual behavior change and risk reduction, it is argued, has been at the expense of the "almost total exclusion of the structural and distributional factors which result in those behaviours" (ibid.: 78).

There is considerable evidence to suggest that this biomedical conception is still dominant at all levels of HIV/AIDS-related policy making today. The 2006 annual UNAIDS Epidemic Update, a flagship report, provides a good example of this dominance. This report was published in support of the UN General Assembly Special Session held between 189 nations in 2001. A General Assembly High Level Meeting on AIDS was also held in 2006 as a key follow up session to the 2001 UNGASS special session on HIV/AIDS. The purpose of this meeting was to move the response to HIV/AIDS up another level. The report's findings, therefore, are influential and important. It summarizes data from 126 countries. For the first time, moreover, civil society was actively engaged in preparation of the reports. The report claims to provide one of the most comprehensive accounts of how the global HIV/AIDS epidemics are unfolding (UNAIDS, 2006a). It is toward policy making, however, that it is ultimately directed. In this regard, the report also raises the fundamental question of whether the correct strategies have been designed and are being followed. The head of UNAIDS remarks in it: "even though the pandemic and its toll are outstripping the worst predictions, for the first time ever we have the will, means and knowledge needed to make real headway" (Peter Piot, quoted in UNAIDS, 2006a). The report argues, therefore, that HIV can be stopped with concerted effort and "the use of evidence-based strategies" (ibid.: 3). Interestingly, the report acknowledges the important role of fundamental drivers:

> To get us to the point where future generations are free from AIDS will require that every aspect of the response be sustained over the longer term – leadership commitment, activism, financial resources, innovation in developing new medicines and preventive technologies, *and, not least, real action to tackle the fundamental drivers of this pandemic, particularly gender inequality, poverty and discrimination.*
>
> (Peter Piot, UNAIDS, 2006a; emphasis added)

Despite this acknowledgement, the report still overwhelmingly emphasizes IEC policies, particularly those addressing the most vulnerable risky behaviors and vulnerable populations, such as IDUs, men who have sex with men, and sex workers. While acknowledging that the "underlying currents" and the "terrain" in which the epidemic thrives are of great importance, policy remains driven by a biomedical conception of disease. The recent history of international policy interventions, as critics note, illustrates the continuing dominance of the "limited, clinical–medical take on how you deal with an epidemic of infectious sexually transmitted disease" (Barnett and Whiteside, 2006: 77). To this end, policy has generally focused on increasing knowledge and awareness, delaying sex, reducing the number of sexual partners and the promotion of condom use, treating sexually transmitted infections, and also protecting blood supplies. Others note that since 2000, there has been an increasing recognition that HIV/AIDS is a development issue, even if "policy prescriptions still do not reflect a development agenda" (Stillwaggon, 2006: 15).

Given the strong bias in policies noted, it is perhaps not surprising that China's responses to HIV/AIDS have also been driven by a similar conceptualization of epidemic disease. China's policy responses in China are discussed in the various UN Theme Group's HIV/AIDS epidemic updates. These reports provide concise summaries of the policy action being taken. While they highlight the increase in HIV/AIDS prevention, treatment, and care activity, they also reveal how prevention policies are dominated by IEC campaigns. Raising awareness and educating key population groups (and also local government leaders) are considered among some of the primary policy responses. For example, it is reported that a broad range of mass media education activities has been initiated across China. Over 120 million HIV/AIDS-related IEC (information, education, and communication materials) were distributed in 2005 and 35 million people received face-to-face education (UNAIDS, 2006b). As well as this, condom promotion campaigns have been launched (Yunnan Province, for example, took the lead by requiring hotels to supply condoms in rooms). Progress has been made in promoting methadone clinics and needle and syringe exchange sites. In addition, greater resources have been put into testing and creation of better surveillance mechanisms. And, of course, measures have been taken to address the problem of illegal blood and plasma donation.

The responses to the HIV/AIDS epidemic in China have largely attempted to follow internationally recognized courses of action. As already discussed, however, there is increasing debate about whether these types of responses are actually adequate to address the deep-rooted nature of an HIV/AIDS epidemic. Much policy, as in many other countries, has been motivated by conventional epidemiological and biomedical understanding of epidemic disease. Various UNAIDS publications represent this stance, as do many of the current government-led publications in China.[1] While HIV/AIDS is a disease an individual may acquire, we have argued here that an epidemic is also a disease of society. As Rudolf Virchow, a founder of social medicine, noted as far back as 1848:

> The history of epidemic diseases must form part of the cultural history of mankind. Epidemics correspond to large signs of warning which tell the true statesman that a disturbance has occurred in the development of his people which even a policy of unconcern can no longer overlook.
>
> (Quoted in Schoepf, 2004: 18)

The various chapters in this book have tried to identify some of the underlying terrain in which China's HIV/AIDS epidemic is emerging. While conventional approaches are clearly still needed and should not be abandoned, further appreciation of such things as the roles of gender and income inequalities, patterns in migration, and the role of health-care reform and civil society development is required. While it is by no means easy to understand and address the distal determinants of epidemic disease, such an approach may well provide longer term, more complete solutions to those currently being offered.

Notes

1 Understanding HIV/AIDS epidemics

1 The ideas in this section draw extensively from insights in articles in the epidemiology and social epidemiology literature, in particular those by Susser and Susser (1996) and also Schwartz, Susser and Susser (1999).
2 Early followers of the miasma model included luminaries and political activists such as Friedrich Engels, Edwin Chadwick, and Florence Nightingale.
3 The practice of epidemiology, according to Rose, concerns the question of "Why did *this* patient get *this* disease at *this* time?" (Quoted in Decosas, 2002).

2 Economic and social determinants of HIV/AIDS

1 Many of these countries have a large number of sex workers who are visited by a significant share of the male population (World Bank, 2004b). Some argue that the HIV epidemics in Asia have been driven largely by sex work and injecting drug use (Ruxrungtham, Brown and Phanuphak, 2004: 69).
2 As well as experiencing different levels of HIV prevalence, cofactors in the spread of HIV should also be considered. For example, tuberculosis is also a problem in many of these countries and sexually transmitted infections also play a very important part in speeding an epidemic. According to some estimates, coinfection with STDs may increase by as much as 50–300 times the chances of contracting HIV. Hence, these must also be considered in the biomedical approach.
3 National prevalence figures may also obscure the seriousness of the Asian epidemic in specific states or provinces. In Cambodia, Myanmar, and Thailand, a number of provinces have infection rates that are significantly higher than the national average, as is also the case for China (UNAIDS, 2005: 9). Care is required in using national averages.
4 It is notable that in Thailand and Cambodia, some quite successful measures to combat the virus have been taken. They stand out as being among the few countries to have lowered quite high national prevalence rates. Other countries in the region, particularly Vietnam, Indonesia, and China, are currently predicted to experience fast-growing epidemics (UNAIDS/WHO, 2005a: 36).
5 Asia–Pacific was home to around 60 percent of the global population in 2000 with 19 percent of those living with HIV in 2004 (MAP, 2005: 2). The general prevalence levels here are therefore still considerably lower than in southern Africa. Despite this, there were an estimated 2.3 million adults and children living with HIV/AIDS, of the global burden of 42 million by 2004 (World Bank, 2004b: 11).
6 These are estimates of prevalence.

7 Comparing female to male literacy, of course, is only one limited indicator of gender imbalance. Work opportunities, land and asset ownership, as well as a voice in determining family size, are also important indicators. Gender inequalities were reflected in employment opportunities. In SSA, 35 percent of women worked in nonagricultural wage employment in 2004, an increase from 32 percent in 1990. In East Asia, there was an increase from 38 to 41 percent over this period (UNDP, 2006: 8).

8 The Arab States were among the worst performers with a female literacy rate of 53 percent and male 71 percent.

9 The East Asia and the Pacific region averaged 86.2 percent for female literacy and 91 percent for men.

10 Indeed, by international comparison with Norway, the United Kingdom, and the United States: women first elected to parliament in 1911, 1918, and 1917, respectively, one-third of seats in parliament are held by women in Norway, but only 6 and 7 percent in the United States and the United Kingdom, these countries do not compare so unfavorably to SSA region.

3 Inequality and HIV/AIDS epidemics

1 "Ecologic" approaches, using statistical analyses, have also identified some other important variables measured at the population level that are closely related to HIV/AIDS prevalence.

2 The Gini coefficient is a measure of inequality of income distribution ranging from 0, absolute equality, to 100, absolute inequality.

3 Social capital can be conceived within Putnam's (2004) idea that "social networks have value," where essential elements include trust, reciprocity, and cooperative relationship among group members.

4 Commercial sex work

1 At the peak of the epidemic in Thailand, over 90 percent of CSWs became infected within one year of starting CSW (Grassly *et al.*, 2003).

2 This reflects in part the increase of HIV found among former plasma donors together with higher number of cases found among CSW.

3 Related activities (bars, hotels, entertainment facilities, and tourist agencies that thrive on prostitution) employ "literally millions more workers" (MAP, 2004: 37).

4 The latter, *meifating*, are particularly common throughout China and cater to the lower end of the market.

5 Interestingly, this estimate corresponds quite closely to the estimates made for urban Victorian England, of about one prostitute per 36 people (or one per 12 males).

6 Gil *et al.* (1996: 149) note that the expansion of CSW coincides with the establishment of "over 100 re-education facilities in 24 of the country's 30 provinces."

7 There are an estimated 100,000–200,000 prostitutes for Thailand's population of 60 million.

8 There are only in total about 135 million females in the 15- to 29-year age group in China.

9 In Beijing in 1997, around 34 percent of 2.3 million incoming migrant workers were women of which 46 percent were unmarried. Of these women, the overwhelming majority were between 18–20 years old. (UNAIDS, 2002: 58).

10 While there is a disproportionate concentration of young female migrant workers in the light manufacturing sector, women aged between 30–40 are heavily represented in the domestic work sector. These women are in general from the countryside and working to support their families or to pay off debts. There are tens of thousands of domestic workers across China's cities. Domestic workers earn approximately 700 RMB per

month in Beijing and from 400 to 600 RMB in Guangdong. Domestic service is less lucrative than other jobs and also stigmatized.

11 Most had STDs at the time of their arrest, with gonorrhea being the most common. In most cases, prostitutes had a history of other STDs.

12 A "cadre" is a person who holds an official position.

13 In a 1991 survey conducted by the Beijing Women's Federation of women detained for prostitution, 68 percent were between 14–25 years. In 1999, a survey of 1,293 detained women of which 83 percent were between 14–29 years old. The upper age limit of the prostitutes had also changed, becoming older (reflecting State-owned enterprises [SOEs] layoffs).

14 But a strong secondary motivation was stated to be "for sexual enjoyment (41%)."

15 The basic argument is that "As long as the present value of the net stream of expected urban income over the migrant's planning horizon exceeds that of the rural income, the decision to migrate is justifiable" (Todaro, 1997: 34–35).

16 "Hostesses earn incomes that are higher than those of most urbanites and well beyond the reach of the women working in domestic service ... some make important social connections" (Gaetano and Jacka, 2004: 7).

17 SWs in China's Yunnan province have reported that they earn on average 247 RMB (US$30). As well as making considerably higher incomes through sex work, it is also possible that certain types of SWs may

make important social connections through their clients and are able to start their own businesses, further their education, gain urban household registration, and establish enduring sexual and emotional relationships with urban men, things that other migrant women can only dream of.

(Gaetano and Jacka, 2004: 7)

18 There may be a premium that females must be paid to participate in sex work owing to its demeaning nature. Some evidence, however, suggests it may not be very large. In a survey of over 2000 arrested prostitutes, it was found that a main reason for undertaking sex work was "pleasure" (after "money"). Gil *et al.* (1996: 149) also found no "hint or remorse or of social embarrassment about being in the profession; none was self reflexive in any traditional sense."

19 Such as massage parlors, beauty salons, and karaoke bars.

20 Interestingly, and again of relevance for understanding heterosexual HIV transmission, some surveys now also show that older married women are increasingly migrating for work (and a significant share of SWs arrested in the early 1990s, about one-quarter, reported being married). As a recent study concludes, women migrants also typically return to their villages to marry: "the vast majority are young and single, and they return to the countryside upon marriage" (Fan, 2004: 177). A survey of over 1,000 female migrants in Sichuan and Anhui in 2000 found "rural women do migrate in large numbers after marriage" (Lou *et al.*, 2004).

6 Healthcare

1 While the central government's share of total health spending has decreased, however, it is important to also note that spending in real terms actually grew. From 1978 to 2003, health spending in real terms stood at 8.7 percent per annum (Wagstaff, Lindelow and Wang, 2009). This was possible due to the rapid growth of China's gross domestic product (GDP) and increasing government revenues (ibid.).

2 The cost of treating genital ulcer disease is between US$0.50–$4 per person (UNAIDS/WHO, 2000).

3 Chlamydial infection was not reported until 2006.
4 Nearly half of infants born with congenital syphilis die even though the disease can be treated with antibiotics if diagnosed early. Most untreated infants go on to suffer serious and debilitating health complications as a result of the disease. Individuals with the genital ulcers that appear in primary syphilis, moreover, are about three to five times more likely to contract HIV. The implications for HIV transmission are therefore obvious.

7 The role of civil society organizations

1 The use of the term civil society organizations or CSOs is used in this chapter as an all-encompassing term which includes a wide range of civil society actors whether non-state, nonprofit, voluntary organizations among many others. NGOs are included in the term CSOs.
2 In referring to the Chinese state, we refer to the institutions and the bodies that govern the Chinese nation. The Chinese state is very much top down and the institutions at the central level are replicated downwards to the lowest level of government. Hence, the state is present in all levels of society, regardless of their efficiency or success.
3 It is not the aim of this paper to ponder the likelihood of democracy in China, given the presence of CSOs. The interest here is in the evolving nature of state–society relationship, not political transition.
4 For analysis of Tiananmen Square incident of June 1989 and the role of the state and society, see, for example, Wasserstrom, J and Perry, E (eds.) (1994), *Popular Protest and Political Culture in Modern China*. Second Edition. Boulder, CO: Westview Press; Calhoun, C. (1994) *Neither Gods Nor Emperors: Students and the Struggle for Democracy in China*. Berkeley, CA: University of California Press, and the articles in the *Australian Journal of Chinese Affairs*, No. 124, 1990.
5 For a comprehensive list of local and international CSOs working in HIV/AIDS sector, as well as bilateral/multilateral initiatives, see *China HIV/AIDS Directory 2005*.
6 Wan Yanhai, the founder fled China in May 2010 due to increasing government pressure on his work and fears for his safety (see 'AIDS Activist Leaves China for US, Citing Pressure', New York Times, May 10, 2010).
7 The 35 percent is 10 percent higher than the average of all nations receiving support from the Global Fund (UNAIDS, 2006a).

Conclusion

1 See UN Theme Group and Chinese Ministry of Health, for detailed descriptions of aspects of individual risk behaviors and the hard epidemiological evidence.

Bibliography

ADB. (2007) *Key Indicators 2007*. Manila, Philippines: ADB.

Abrams, H.K. (2001) 'Resurgence of Sexually Transmitted Disease in China', *The Journal of Public Health Policy*, 22(4): 429–440.

Ainsworth, M., Beyrer, C. and Soucat, A. (2003) 'AIDS and Public Policy: The Lessons and Challenges of "Success" in Thailand', *Health Policy*, 64(1): 13–37.

Andersen, A.F., Qingsi, Z., Hua, X. and Jianfeng, B. (2003) 'China's Floating Population and the Potential for HIV Transmission: A Social Behavioural Perspective', *AIDS Care*, 15(2): 177–185.

Barnett, T. and Whiteside, A. (2006) *AIDS in the Twenty-First Century: Disease and Globalization*. New York: Palgrave Macmillan.

Béja, J.P. (2006) 'The Changing Aspects of Civil Society in China', *Social Research*, 73(1): 53–74.

Bell, C. and Lewis, M. (2005) 'Economic Implications of Epidemics Old and New' (February). Available at: http://ssrn.com/abstract=997387 (Accessed 23 January 2011).

Bell, D. (1989) 'American Exceptionalism Revisited: The Role of Civil Society', *The Public Interest*, 95: 38–56.

Benjamin, D., Brandt, L. and Giles, J. (2005) 'The Evolution of Income Inequality in Rural China', *Economic Development and Cultural Change*, 53(4): 769–824.

Boochalaksi, W. and Guest, P. (1998) 'Prostitution in Thailand', in L.L. Lim (ed.) *The Sex Sector: The Economic and Social Bases of Prostitution in Southeast Asia*, 130–169. Geneva: International Labour Organization.

Brook, T. and Frolic, B.M. (1997) 'The Ambiguous Challenge of Civil Society', in T. Brook and B.M. Frolic (eds.) *Civil Society in China*. Armonk, NY: M.E. Sharpe.

Brown, P.H., de Brauw, A. and Du, Y. (2009) 'Understanding Variation in the Design of China's New Cooperative Medical System', *The China Quarterly*, 198: 304–329.

Campbell, C. (2003) *'Letting Them Die': Why HIV/AIDS Intervention Programmes Fail*. Bloomington, IN: Indiana University Press.

CDC China. (2002) *Joint China CDC – U.S. CDC HIV Surveillance Assessment*. Beijing: CDC China.

Chadwick, E. (1842) *Report on the Sanitary Condition of the Labouring Population of Great Britain*. Available at: http://www.deltaomega.org/ChadwickClassic.pdf (Accessed 4 October 2011).

Chen, G.Y. (2001) 'China's Nongovernmental Organizations: Status, Government Policies, and Prospects for Further Development', *The International Journal of Not-For-Profit Law*, 3(3). Available at: http://www.icnl.org/JOURNAL/vol3iss3/ar_guan-gyao.htm (Accessed 10 August 2007).

Chen, X.S., Yin, Y.P., Mabey, D., Peeling, R.W., Zhou, H., Jiang, WH, Wei, W.H., Yong, G., Shi, MQ, Chen, Q. and Gao, X. (2006) 'Prevalence of Chlamydia trachomatis

Infections among Women from Different Settings in China: Implications for STD Surveillance', *Sexually Transmitted Infections*, 82(4): 283–284.

Chen, Z., Zhang, G., Gong, X., Lin, C., Gao, X., Liang, G., Yue, X., Chen, X. and Cohen, M. (2007) 'Syphilis in China: Results of a National Surveillance Programme', *The Lancet*, 369(9556): 132–138.

China AIDS Info. (2005) *China HIV/AIDS Directory 2005*, Beijing: China AIDS Info.

China Development Brief. (31 May, 2006) 'Governance Splat Plagues Coordinating Board of Global Fund, Divides NGOs', *China Development Brief*. Available at: www.chinadevelopmentbrief.com/node/631 (Accessed 1 September 2007).

China Tuberculosis Control Collaboration. (2004) 'The Effect of Tuberculosis Control in China', *The Lancet*, 9432: 417–422.

Craddock, S. (2004) 'Beyond Epidemiology: Locating AIDS in Africa', in E. Kalopeni, S. Craddock, R.J. Oppong and J. Ghosh (eds.) *HIV/AIDS in Africa: Beyond Epidemiology*. Oxford: Blackwell Publishing.

Decosas, J. (2002) 'The Social Ecology of HIV/AIDS in Africa', UNRISD Draft Paper for HIV/AIDS Development Programme. Geneva: UNRISD.

Dolin, P.J., Raviglione, M.C. and Kochi, A. (1994) 'Global Tuberculosis Incidence and Mortality During 1990-2000', *Bulletin of the World Health Organization*, 72(2): 213–220.

Drain, P.K., Smith, J.S., Hughes, J.P., Halperin, D.T. and Holmes, K.K. (2004) 'Correlates of National HIV Seroprevalence. An Ecologic Analysis of 122 Developing Countries', *Journal of Acquired Immune Deficiency Syndromes*, 35(4): 407–420.

du Guerny, J., Hsu, L.N. and Hong, C. (2003) *Population Movement and HIV/AIDS: The Case of Ruili, Yunnan, China*. Bangkok: UNDP.

Edwards, M. (2007) 'Civil society', *The Encyclopedia of Informal Education*. Available at: http://www.infed.org/association/civil_society.htm (Accessed 10 August 2007).

Family Health International. (2011) 'STDs: The Burden and the Challenge', *AIDScaptions*. Available at: http://www.fhi.org/en/HIVAIDS/pub/Archive/articles/AIDScaptions/volume3no1/STDsBurdenAndChallenges.htm (Accessed 29 January 2011).

Fan, C.C. (2003) 'Rural-Urban Migration and Gender Division of Labor in Transitional China', *International Journal of Urban and Regional Research*, 27(1): 24–47.

Fan, C.C. (2004) 'On to the City and Back to the Village: The Experiences and Contributions of Rural Women Migrating from Sichuan to Anhui', in A.M. Gaetano and T. Jacka (eds.) *On the Move: Rural-to-Urban Migration in Contemporary China*, 177–206. NY: Columbia University Press.

Fang, J. and Kaufman, J. (2008) 'Reproductive Health in China: Improve the Means to the End', *The Lancet*, 372(9650): 1619–1620.

Fang, X., Li, X., Yang, H., Hong, Y., Stanton, B., Zhao, R., Dong, B., Liu, W., Zhou, Y. and Liang, S. (2008) 'Can Variation in HIV/STD-Related Risk be Explained by Individual SES? Findings from Female Sex Workers in Rural Chinese County', *Health Care for Women International*, 29(3): 316–335.

Farmer, P. (1999) *Infections and Inequalities: The Modern Plagues*. Berkeley, CA: University of California Press.

Fisman, D.N. (2007) 'Syphilis Resurgent in China', *The Lancet*, 369(9556): 84–85.

Gaetano, A.M. and Jacka, T. (eds.) (2004) *On the Move: Women in Rural-to-Urban Migration in Contemporary China*. New York: Columbia University Press.

Gandy, M. and Zumla, A. (2002) 'The Resurgence of Disease: Social and Historical Perspectives on the "New" Tuberculosis', *Social Science and Medicine*, 55(3): 385–396.

Gil, V., Wang, M.S., Anderson, A.F., Lin, G.M. and Wu, Z.O. (1996) 'Prostitutes, Prostitution, STD/HIV Transmission in Mainland China', *Social Science Medicine*, 42(1): 141–152.

Giles, J., Park, A. and Zhang, J. (2005) 'What Is China's True Unemployment Rate?' *China Economic Review*, 16(2): 149–170.

Gilfoyle, T. (1999) 'Prostitutes in History: From Parables of Pornography to Metaphors of Modernity', *The American Historical Review*, 104(1): 117–141.

Gill, B. (2002) 'China's HIV/AIDS Crisis: Implications for Human Rights, the Rule of Law and U.S.-China Relations', *Testimony before the Congressional-Executive Commission on China, Roundtable on HIV / AIDS*, 9 September. Washington, DC: Center for Strategic and International Studies.

Gill, B. (2006) *Assessing HIV/AIDS Initiatives in China: Persistent Challenges and Promising Way Forward*, A Report of the CSIS Task Force on HIV/AIDS. Washington, DC: Center for Strategic and International Studies

Gill, B., Chang, J. and Palmer, S. (2002) *'China's HIV Crisis'*, *Foreign Affairs*, 81(2): 96–110.

Gill, B., Huang, Y. and Lu, X. (2007) *Demography of HIV/AIDS in China*. Washington, DC: Center for Strategic and International Studies.

Grassly, N., Lowndes, M., Rhodes, T., Judd, A., Renton, A. and Garnett, P. (2003) 'Modelling Emerging HIV Epidemics: The Role of Injecting Drug Use and Sexual Transmission in the Russian Federation, China and India', *International Journal of Drug Policy*, 14(1):25–43.

Guan, J., Wu, Z., Li, L., Rotheram-Borus, M.J., Detels, R. and Hsieh, J. (2009) 'Self-Reported Sexually Transmitted Disease Symptoms and Treatment-Seeking Behaviors in China', *AIDS Patient Care and STDs*, 23(6): 443–448.

Halmshaw, C. and Hawkins, K. (2004) 'Capitalizing on Global HIV/AIDS Funding: The Challenge for Civil Society and Government', *Reproductive Health Matters*, 12(24): 35–41.

Halperin, D.T. and Bailey, R.C. (1999) 'Male Circumcision and HIV Infection: 10 years and Counting', *The Lancet*, 354(9192): 1813–1815.

Han, M, Chen, Q., Yang, H., Hu, Y., Wang, D., Gao, Y. and Bulterys, M. (2010) 'Design and Implementation of a China Comprehensive AIDS Response Programme (China CARES), 2003–08', *Journal of Epidemiology*, 39 (supp 2): ii47–ii55.

Hansen, P. and Li, M. (2002) *'Sexually Transmitted Infection Risk in Migrant Construction Worker Populations in Beijing, China'*, Paper presented at *Annual Meeting of the association of American Geographers*, March 22, Los Angeles.

Harris, J. and Todaro, M. (1970) 'Migration, Unemployment and Development: A Two-Sector Analysis', *American Economic Review*, 60(1): 126–142.

He, N., Detels, R., Zhu, J., Jiang, Q., Chen, Z., Fang, Y., Zhang, X., Wu, M. and Zhao, Q. (2005) 'Characteristics and Sexually Transmitted Diseases of Male Rural Migrants in Metropolitan Area of Eastern China', *Sexually Transmitted Disease*, 32(5): 286–292.

Hegel, G.W.F. (1991) *Elements of the Philosophy of Right*, ed. A.W. Wood, trans. H.B. Nisbet. Cambridge: Cambridge University Press.

Hesketh, T. and Lu, L. (2005) 'HIV and Syphilis in Chinese Internal Migrants', *AIDS*, 19(14): 1550.

Hesketh, T., Zhang, J. and Qiang, D.J. (2005) 'HIV Knowledge and Risk Behaviour of Female Sex Workers in Yunnan Province, China: Potential as Bridging Groups to the General Population', *AIDS Care*, 17(8): 958–966.

Hesketh, T., Li, L., Ye, X., Wang, H., Jiang, M. and Tomkins, A. (2006) 'HIV and Syphilis in Migrant Workers in Eastern China', *Sexually Transmitted Infections*, 82(1): 11–14.

Holtgrave, D.R. and Crosby, R.A. (2003) 'Social Capital, Poverty, and Income Inequality as Predictors of Gonorrhea, Syphilis, Chlamydia, and AIDS Case Rates in the United States?' *Sexually Transmitted Infections*, 79(1):62–64.

Hong, Y. and Li, X. (2008) 'Behavioral Studies of Female Sex Workers in China: A Literature Review and Recommendation for Future Research', *AIDS and Behavior*, 12(4): 623–636.

Hsu, L.N. (2004) *Building Dynamic Democratic Governance and HIV-Resilient Societies*. Bangkok, Thailand: UNAIDS and UNDP.

Hugo, G. (2003) 'Urbanisation in Asia: An Overview', Paper prepared for *Conference on African Migration in Comparative Perspective*, Johannesburg, South Africa, 4–7 June.

Hull, T.H., Sulistyaningsih, E. and Jones, G.W. (1998) *Prostitution in Indonesia: Its History and Evolution*. Jakarta: Pustaka Sinar Harapan.

Hunt, T. (2006) 'Lessons for Beijing from the Dickensian smog', *The Guardian*, July 28, 32.

IOM. (2005) *HIV/AIDS, Population Mobility and Migration in Southern Africa*. Geneva: IOM.

Kalipeni, E., Craddock, S., Oppong, R.J. and Ghosh, J. (eds.) (2004) *HIV/AIDS in Africa: Beyond Epidemiology*. Oxford: Blackwell Publishing.

Kaufman, J. (2005) 'China: The Intersections between Poverty, Health Inequity, Reproductive Health and HIV/AIDS', *Development*, 48(4): 113–119.

Kaufman, J. and Jing, J. (2002) 'China and AIDS: The Time to Act is Now', *Science*, 296(5577): 2339–2340.

Kaufman, J., Yan, L., Wang, T., and Faulkner, A. (1999) 'A Study of Field Based Methods for Diagnosing Reproductive Tract Infections in Rural Yunnan Province, China', *Studies in Family Planning*, 30(2):112–119.

Kaufman, J., Kleinman, A. and Saich, T. (eds.) (2006) *AIDS and Social Policy in China*. Cambridge, MA: Harvard University Asia Centre.

Kuznets, S. (1955) 'Economic Growth and Income Inequality', *American Economic Review* 45(1):1–28.

Landry, P. (2009) *Decentralized Authoritarianism in China: The Communist Party's Control of Local Elites in the Post-Mao Era*. Cambridge: Cambridge University Press.

Lau, J.T.F., Tsui, H.Y., Siah, P.C. and Zhang, K.L. (2002) 'A Study on Female Sex Workers in Southern China (Shenzhen): HIV-Related Knowledge, Condom Use and STD History', *AIDS Care*, 14(2): 219–233.

Levett, C. (December 27, 2006) 'Thais Battle for Affordable HIV Drugs', *The Sydney Morning Herald*. Available at: http://www.smh.com.au/news/world/thais-battle-for-affordable-hivdrugs/2006/12/26/1166895299831.html (Accessed 20 August 2010).

Li, L., Morrow, M. and Kermode, M. (2007) 'Vulnerable but Feeling Safe: HIV Risk Among Male Rural-to-Urban Migrant Workers in Chengdu, China', *AIDS Care*, 19(10): 1288–1295.

Li, L., Wu, Z., Rotheram-Borus, M.J., Guan, J., Yin, Y., Detels, R., Wu, S., Lee, S-J., Cao, H., Lin, C., Rou, K., Liu, Z. and The NIHM Collaborative HIV/STD Prevention Trial Group. (2009) 'Visiting Entertainment Venues and Sexual Health in China', *Archives of Sexual Behavior*, 38(5): 814–820.

Li, X., Lin, C., Gao, Z., Stanton, B., Fang, X., Yin, Q. and Wu, Y. (2004) 'HIV/AIDS Knowledge and the Implications for Health Promotion Programs Among Chinese College Students: Geographic, Gender and Age Differences', *Health Promotion International*, 19(3): 345–356.

Liang, Z. and Chen, Y.P. (2004) 'Migration and Gender in China: An Origin-destination Linked Approach', *Economic Development and Cultural Change*, 52(2): 423–443.

Lim, L.L. (1998) 'The Economic and Social Bases of Prostitution in Southeast Asia', in L.L. Lim (ed.) *The Sex Sector: The Economic and Social Bases of Prostitution in Southeast Asia*, 1–28. Geneva: International Labour Organization.

Lin, D., Li, X., Yang, H., Fang, X., Stanton, B., Chen, X., Abbey, A. and Liu, H. (2005) 'Alcohol Intoxication and Sexual Risk Behaviors Among Rural-to-Urban Migrants in China', *Drug and Alcohol Dependence*, 79(1): 103–112.

Liu, Y., Hsiao, W.C. and Eggleston, K. (1999) 'Equity in Health and Health Care: The Chinese Experience', *Social Science and Medicine*, 49(10): 1349–1356.

Lohmar, B., Rozelle, S. and Zhao, C. (2001) 'The Rise of Rural-to-Rural Labor Markets in China', *Asian Geographer*, 20(1–2): 101–123.

Lou, B., Zhou, Z., Connelly, Z. and Roberts, K.D. (2004) 'The Migration Experiences of Young Women from Four Counties in Sichuan and Anhui', in A.M. Gaetano and T. Jacka (eds.) *On the Move: Rural-to-Urban Migration in Contemporary China*, 207–242. NY: Columbia University Press.

Lu, F., Wang, N., Wu, Z., Sun, X., Rehnstrom, J., Poundstone, K., Yu, W. and Pisani, E. (2006) Estimating the Number of People at Risk for and Living with HIV in China in 2005: Methods and Results', *Sexually Transmitted. Infections*, 82(supp 3): 87–91.

Lu, L., Jia, M., Ma, Y., Yang, L., Chen, Z., Ho, D.D., Jiang, Y. and Zhang, L. (2008) 'The Changing Face of HIV in China', *Nature*, 455: 609–611.

Ma, Q., Ono-K, M., Cong, L., Xu, G., Zamani, S. and Ravari, S.M. (2006) 'Sexual Behavior and Awareness of Chinese University Students in Transition with Implied Risk of Sexually Transmitted Diseases and HIV Infection: A Cross-Sectional Study', *BMC Public Health*, 18(6): 232.

MAP. (2004) *AIDS in Asia: Face the Facts*, MAP Report. Washington, DC.

MAP. (2005) *Drug Injection and HIV/AIDS in Asia*. Washington DC: MAP.

Maurer-Fazio, M. Rawski, T. and Zhang, W. (1999) 'Inequality in the Rewards of Holding Up Half the Sky: Gender Wage Gaps in China's Urban Labour Market, 1988-1994', *China Journal*, 41: 55–88.

Meng, X., Anderson, A., Hou, X., Wang, Y., Sun, L., Zhang, X., Li, Z., Qui, B., Lang, Y. and Zhang, L. (2006) 'A Pilot Project for the Effective Delivery of HAART in Rural China', *AIDS Patient Care and STDs*, 20(3): 213–219.

MOH and UNAIDS. (2003) *A Joint Assessment of HIV/AIDS Prevention, Treatment and Care in China*. Beijing: China Ministry of Health and UNAIDS China Office.

MOH/UNAIDS/WHO. (2005) *Update on the HIV/AIDS Epidemic and Response in China*. Beijing: MOH/UNAIDS/WHO.

MOH and UN Theme Group on HIV/AIDS in China. (2004) *A Joint Assessment of HIV/ AIDS Prevention, Treatment and Care in China*. Beijing: State Council AIDS Working Committee Office.

Moon, S., van Leemput, L., Durier, N., Jambert, E., Dahmane, Jie, Y., Wu, G., Philips, M., Hu, Y. and Saranchuk, P. (2008) 'Out-of-Pocket Costs of AIDS Care in China: Are Free Antiretroviral Drugs Enough?' *AIDS Care*, 20(8): 984–994.

Moran, D. and Jordaan, J.A. (2007) 'HIV/AIDS in Russia: Determinants of Regional Prevalence', *International Journal of Health Geographics*, 6(22). Available at: http://www.ij-healthgeographics.com/content/6/1/22 (Accessed 29 January 2011).

Nagaraj, S. and Yahya, S.R. (1998) 'Prostitution in Malaysia', in L.L. Lim (ed.) *The Sex Sector: The Economic and Social Bases of Prostitution in Southeast Asia*, 67–99. Geneva: International Labour Organization.

Naughton, B. (2007) *The Chinese Economy: Transitions and Growth*. Cambridge. MA: MIT Press.

Nepal, B. (2007) 'Prosperity, Equity, Good Governance and Good Health: Focus on HIV/ AIDS Pandemic and its Feminization', *World Health and Population*, 9(3): 73–80.

Nguyen, V. and Stovel, K. (2004) 'The Social Science of HIV/AIDS: A Critical Review and Priorities for Action', Working draft prepared by the Social Science Research Council Working Group on HIV/AIDS. New York: SSRC.

Nolan, P. (2004) *China at the Crossroads*. Cambridge: Polity Press.

Oliveira-Cruz, V., Kowalski, J. and McPake, B. (2004) 'The Brazilian HIV/AIDS "Success Story" – Can Others Do It?' *Tropical Medicine and International Health*, 9(2): 292–297.

Oppong, R.J. and Ghosh, J. (2004) 'Beyond Epidemiology', in E. Kalopeni, S. Craddock, R.J. Oppong and J. Ghosh (eds.) *HIV/AIDS in Africa: Beyond Epidemiology*. Oxford: Blackwell Publishing.

Over, M. (1998) 'The Effects of Societal Variables on Urban Rates of HIV Infection in Developing Countries: An Exploratory Analysis', in M. Ainsworth, L. Fransen and

M. Over (eds.) *Confronting AIDS: Evidence from the Developing World*, 40–51. Brussels: European Commission.

Pan, S. (1999) *Three 'Red Light Districts' in China*. Beijing: Qunyan Publishing House.

Parish, W.L., Laumann, E.O., Cohen, M.S., Pan, S., Zheng, H., Hoffman, I., Wang, T. and Ng, K.W. (2003) 'Population-Base Study of Chlamydial Infection in China', *Journal of the American Medical Association*, 289(10): 1265–1273.

Parish, W.L., Laumann, E.O., and Mojola, S.A. (2007) 'Sexual Behavior in China: Trends and Comparisons', *Population and Development Review*, 33(4): 729–756.

Pei, X. and Rodriguez, E. (2006) 'Provincial Income Inequality and Self-Reported Health Status in China During 1991–7', *Journal of Epidemiology and Community Health*, 60(12):1065–1069.

Putnam, R. (2004) 'Bowling Together', *OECD Observer, No. 242*. Available at: http://www.oecdobserver.org/news/fullstory.php/aid/1215/Bowling_together.html (Accessed 30 January 2011).

Qian, Z.H., Vermund, S.H. and Wang, N. (2005) 'Risk of HIV/AIDS in China: Subpopulations of Special Importance', *Sexually Transmitted Infections*, 81(6): 442–447.

Ravallion, M. and Chen, S. (2004) 'Learning from Success: Understanding China's (Uneven) Progress Against Poverty', *Finance and Development*, 41(4): 16–19.

Remez, L. (2000) 'STD Rates Soar in China; Three in Four New Cases are Among the Unmarried', *International Family Planning Perspectives*, 26(3): 141–142.

Rozelle, S., Li, G., Shen, M., Hughart, A. and Giles, J. (1999) 'Leaving China's Farms: Survey Results of New Paths and Remaining Hurdles to Rural Migration', *China Quarterly*, 158: 367–393.

Ruxrungtham, K. Brown, T. and Phanuphak, P. (2004) 'HIV/AIDS in Asia', *The Lancet*, 364(9428): 69–82.

Schoepf, B.G. (2004) 'AIDS, History, and Struggles over Meaning', in E. Kalopeni, S. Craddock, R.J. Oppong and J. Ghosh (eds.) *HIV/AIDS in Africa: Beyond Epidemiology*. Oxford: Blackwell Publishing.

Schwartz, S., Susser, E. and Susser, M. (1999) 'A Future for Epidemiology?' *Annual Review Public Health*, 20: 15–33.

Shils, E. (1991) 'The Virtue of Civil Society', *Government and Opposition*, 26(1): 3–20.

Solinger, D. (1995) 'China's Urban Transients in the Transition from Socialism and the Collapse of the Communist "Urban Public Goods Regime"', *Comparative Politics*, 27(2): 127–146.

State Council AIDS Working Committee Office and the UN Theme Group on HIV/AIDS. (2004) *A Joint Assessment of HIV/AIDS Prevention, Treatment and Care in China*. Beijing, China: UNAIDS China Office.

State Statistical Bureau. (1990) *China Statistical Yearbook*. Beijing: China Statistical Publishing House.

State Statistical Bureau. (2004) *China Statistical Yearbook*. Beijing: China Statistical Publishing House.

Stillwaggon, E. (2006) *AIDS and the Ecology of Poverty*. New York: Oxford University Press.

Susser, M. and Susser, E. (1996) 'Choosing a Future for Epidemiology: I. Eras and Paradigms', *American Journal of Public Health*, 86(5): 668–673.

Talbott, J.R. (2007) 'Size Matters: The Number of Prostitutes and the Global HIV/AIDS Pandemic', *PLoS ONE*, 2(6): e543.

Tang, S., Meng, Q., Chen, L., Bekedam, H., Evans, T. and Whitehead, M. (2008) 'Tackling the Challenges to Health Equity in China', *The Lancet*, 373(9648): 1493–1501.

Thompson, D. (2005) *China Confronts HIV/AIDS*. Washington, DC: Population Reference Bureau.

Thompson, D. and Lu, X. (2006) 'China's Evolving Civil Society: From Environment to Health', *China Environment Series, Woodrow Wilson International Centre for Scholars*, 37: 27–39.

Tian, L, Li, J., Zhang, K. and Guest, P. (2007) 'Women's Status, Institutional Barriers and Reproductive Health Care: A Case Study in Yunnan, China', *Health Policy*, 84(2–3): 284–297.

Tismaneanu, V. (1992) *Reinventing Politics: Eastern Europe after Communism*. New York: Free Press.

Todaro, M. (1997) 'Urbanization, Unemployment and Migration in Africa: Theory and Policy', Population Council Policy Research Division Working Paper 104. New York.

Tucker, D., Henderson, G., Wang, T.F., Huang, Y., Parish, W., Pan, S.M., Xiang, S.C. and Cohen, M.S. (2005) 'Surplus Men, Sex Work, and the Spread of HIV in China', *AIDS*, 19(6): 539–547.

UNAIDS. (2002) *China's: Titanic Peril. Update of the AIDS Situation and Needs Assessment Report: UN Theme Group on HIV/AIDS in China*. Beijing: UNDP.

UNAIDS. (2004) *2004 Report on the Global AIDS Epidemic*. Geneva: UNAIDS.

UNAIDS. (2005) *A Scaled-up Response to AIDS in the Asia and the Pacific*. Bangkok: UNAIDS.

UNAIDS. (2006a) *2006 Report on the Global AIDS Epidemic*. Geneva: UNAIDS.

UNAIDS. (2006b) 'Statistics by Province of HIV/AIDS Epidemic (by the End of 2005)'. Available at: http://www.unaids.org.cn (Accessed 14 May 2007).

UNAIDS. (2007) *AIDS Epidemic Update*. Geneva: UNAIDS.

UNAIDS. (2008) *Redefining AIDS in Asia: Crafting an Effective Response*. New Delhi: Oxford University Press.

UNAIDS China. (2005) 'Sentinel Surveillance Data for the 1998-2000 Period, Including Seroprevalence and Behavioural Data'. Available at: http://www.unchina.org/unaids/ekey3right2.html (Accessed 1 November 2010).

UNAIDS/WHO. (2000) *Consultation on STD Interventions for Preventing HIV: What is the Evidence?* Geneva: UNAIDS.

UNAIDS/WHO. (2005a) *AIDS Epidemic Update: December 2005*. Geneva: UNAIDS.

UNAIDS/WHO. (2005b) 'UNAIDS/WHO Epidemiological Fact Sheet. 2004 China Update'. Available at: http://www.unchina.org/unaids/ (Accessed 10 June 2007).

UN Country Team China. (2004) *Common Country Assessment: Balancing Development to Achieve An All-Round Xiaokang and Harmonious Society in China*. Beijing: UN.

UN Country Team China. (2005) *Advancing Social Development in China: Contributing to the 11th Five Year Plan*. Beijing: UN.

UNDP. (2003) *Human Development Report 2003*. New York: UNDP.

UNDP. (2004a) *Thailand's Response to HIV/AIDS*. Bangkok: UNDP.

UNDP. (2004b) *Human Development Report 2004*. New York: UNDP.

UNDP. (2005) *Human Development Report 2005*. New York: UNDP.

UNDP. (2006) *Asia-Pacific Human Development Report 2006*. Colombo: Macmillan.

UNDP. (2007) *Human Development Report 2007*. New York: UNDP.

UNDP. (2009) *Human Development Report 2009*. Country Fact Sheets. New York: UNDP. Available at: http://hdrstats.undp.org/en/countries/country_fact_sheets/cty_fs_CHN.html (Accessed 3 April 2010).

UNDP. (various years) *Thailand Human Development Report*. Bangkok: UNDP.

UNDP/CDRF. (2005) *China Human Development Report*. Beijing: UNDP.

UNDP/UNOPS. (2001) *Assessing Population Mobility and HIV Vulnerability Guangxi, People's Republic of China*. Bangkok: UNDP.

UNESCAP. (2005) 'Gender and HIV/AIDS in the Asia and Pacific Region', Gender and Development Discussion Paper Series No. 18. Bangkok.

UNESCO. (2005) 'Review of Socio-cultural Research on HIV/AIDS in the Greater Mekong Subregion', Draft prepared by HIV/AIDS Coordination and School Health Unit. Bangkok, UNESCO.

Uretsky, E. (2008) 'Mobile men with money': The Socio-cultural and Politico-economic Context of High-risk Behavior among Wealthy Businessmen and Government Officials in Urban China', *Culture, Health, and Sexuality*, 10(8): 801–814.

van den Hoek, A., Yuliang, F., Dukers, N.H., Chen, Z.H., Feng, J.T., Zhang, L.N. and Zhang, X.X. (2001) 'High Prevalence of Syphilis and Other Sexually Transmitted Diseases Among Sex Workers in China: Potential for Fast Spread of HIV', *AIDS*, 15(6): 753–759.

van Doorslaer, E., O'Donnell, O., Ranna-Eliya, R., Somanathan, A., Adhikari, S.R., Garg, C.C., Harbianto, D., Herrin, A.N., Huq, M.N., Ibragimova, S., Karan, A., Ng, C.W., Pande, B.R., Racelis, R., Tao, S., Tin, K., Tisayaticom, K., Trisnantoro, L., Vasavid, C., Zhao, Y. (2006) 'Effects of Payments for Health Care on Poverty Estimates in 11 Countries in Asia: An Analysis of Household Survey Date', *The Lancet*, 368(9544): 1357–1364.

Wade, R.H. (2004) 'Is Globalization Reducing Poverty and Inequality?' *World Development*, 32(4): 567–589.

Wagstaff, A., Lindelow, M. and Wang, S. (2009) *Reforming China's Rural Health System*. Washington DC: World Bank Publications.

Wang, L., Wang, N., Wang, L., Li, D., Jia, M., Gao, X., Qu, S., Qin, Q., Wang, Y. and Smith, K. (2009) 'The 2007 Estimates for People at Risk for and Living With HIV in China: Progress and Challenges', *Journal of Acquired Immune Deficiency Syndromes*, 50(4): 414–418.

Watts, J. (2005) 'China's Shift in HIV/AIDS Policy Marks Turnaround on Health', *The Lancet*, 364(9418): 1370–1371.

Wilkinson, R.G. (2005) *The Impact of Inequality: How to Make Sick Societies Healthier*. London: Routledge.

Wilkinson, R.G. and Pickett, K.E. (2006) 'Income Inequality and Population Health: A Review and Explanation of the Evidence', *Social Science and Medicine*, 62(7): 1768–1784.

World Bank. (1997) *Sharing Rising Incomes: Disparities in China*. Washington DC: World Bank.

World Bank. (2004a) *World Development Indicators*. Washington, DC: World Bank.

World Bank. (2004b) *Addressing HIV/AIDS in East Asia and the Pacific*. Washington, DC: World Bank.

World Bank. (2006) *World Development Report 2006*. Washington, DC: World Bank.

World Bank. (2007) *Global Monitoring Report*. Washington, DC: World Bank.

World Bank. (2009) 'The World Bank and Civil Society in China'. Available at: http://go. worldbank.org/8IPDHI01D0 (Accessed 10 December 2010).

Wu, Z., Rou, K. and Detels, R. (2001) 'Prevalence of HIV Infection Among Former Commercial Plasma Donors in Rural Eastern China', *Health Policy and Planning*, 16(1): 41–46.

Wu, Z., Rou, K. and Cui, H. (2004) 'The HIV/AIDS Epidemic in China: History, Current Strategies and Future Challenges', *AIDS Education and Prevention*, 16(A): 7–17.

Xiang, B. (2004) 'Migration and Health in China: Problems, Obstacles and Solutions', Asian Metacentre for Population and Sustainable Development Analysis. Research Paper Series No. 17. Singapore: NUS.

Yang, D. (2004) 'Civil Society as Analytic Lens for Contemporary China', *China: An International Journal*, 2(1): 1–27.

Yang, X. and Xia, G. (2008) 'Temporary Migration and STD/HIV Risky Sexual Behavior: A Population-Based Analysis of Gender Differences in China', *Social Problems*, 55(3): 322–346.

Yang, X., Derlega, V.J. and Luo, H. (2007) 'Migration, Behaviour Change and HIV/STD Risks in China', *AIDS Care*, 19(2): 282–288.

Yang, X.S. (2004) 'Temporary Migration and the Spread of STDs/HIV in China: Is There a Link?' *International Migration Review*, 38(1): 212–235.

Zhang, H.X. (2004) 'The Gathering Storm: AIDS Policy in China'. *Journal of International Development*, 16(8): 1155–1168.

Zhang, K. and Ma, S. (2002) 'Epidemiology of HIV in China: Intravenous Drug Users, Sex Workers, and Large Mobile Populations are High Risk Groups', *British Medical Journal*, 324: 803–804.

Zhang, L., De Brauw, A. and Rozelle, S. (2004) 'China's Rural Labor Market Development and its Gender Implications', *China Economic Review*, 15(2): 230–247.

Zheng, T. (2004) 'From Peasant Women to Bar Hostess: Gender and Modernity in Dalian', in A.M. Gaetano and T. Jacka (eds.) *On the Move: Rural-to-Urban Migration in Contemporary China*, 80–108. NY: Columbia University Press.

Zhu, Y. (2003) 'The Floating Population's Household Strategies and the Role of Migration in China's Regional Development and Integration', *International Journal of Population Geography*, 9(6): 485–502.

Index

Note: page numbers in **bold** refer to illustrations.